The Government of France

Jean Blondel
and
E. Drexel Godfrey, Jr

Methuen and Co Ltd
11 New Fetter Lane London EC4

First published in the U.S.A. 1968
© 1968 by Thomas Y. Crowell Company
First published in this series 1968
Printed in Great Britain by
Fletcher & Son Ltd, Norwich
SBN (casebound) 416 28180 x
SBN (paperback) 416 28190 7

Editor's Foreword

In our time the study of comparative government constitutes one of many fields or specialities in political science. But it is worth recalling that the most distinguished political scientists of the ancient world would have had difficulty recognizing the present-day distinction between the study of comparative government and study in other subject areas of the discipline. Think of Plato, for example, whose works abound in references to the political systems of his own and earlier days. Or consider Aristotle, whose *Politics* and related writings were based on an examination of more than one hundred constitutions. Twenty centuries after Aristotle the comparative emphasis continued strong in the work of Montesquieu and Rousseau, among others. In the nineteenth century the comparative tradition entered upon a period of decline, but there are signs that the merits of comparative political analysis are once more gaining recognition. At many colleges and universities, the introductory course in political science is no longer focused exclusively on American government. The comparative approach—in politics, in law, in administration—is becoming increasingly important in the political science curriculum.

This book, one of a series, is designed to reflect that approach without, however, marking a sharp departure from the substance and method of most comparative government courses. Thus most of the books in the series deal with one national government. Several volumes, however, deal with more than one government, and the approach of the entire series is distinctly comparative in at least two senses. In the first place, almost all of the books include material descriptive of other political systems, especially that of the United States. In addition, the books follow a common outline, so far as possible, that is designed to promote comparative treatment. Of course, there is nothing to keep the instructor or student from treating a particular governmental system in isolation, if he chooses to do so. On the other hand, his lectures on political institutions and functions can be as comparative as he wishes.

A further advantage of this series is that each volume has been written by a distinguished scholar and authority in the field; each author is personally and professionally familiar with the political system he treats. Finally, the separate books make it possible for the instructor to design his course in accordance with his own interest or the interests of his students. One book may be substituted for another or any book put aside for one semester without affecting the others. The books, in short, unlike most one-volume texts, give the instructor maximum freedom in organizing his course. This freedom will be virtually unlimited as the forthcoming titles in this series complete a survey of representative governments of the world.

But to return to Aristotle once again, it remains true that the best judges of the feast are not the cooks but the guests. I have tried to indicate, why, in my view, the recipe for the series is a good one. Let all those who teach comparative government, and all those who take courses in that field, proceed to judge the books for themselves.

ARNOLD A. ROGOW

Preface

The Third Edition of *The Government of France* is entirely re-
vised and it takes into account the changes, both social and
political, which have occurred in France in the course of the
1960s. The rapid evolution of the French social structure, under
the impact of economic development, turned the Fifth Republic
into a much more stable regime than was forecast originally. This
is not to diminish the part played by General De Gaulle in the
reshaping of the institutions and, perhaps more importantly, in
the creation of a style of politics which has attracted almost universal attention, found numerous followers in the most varied
quarters, and been a source of anger or amusement for many both
in France and abroad. As in previous editions, the figure of the
General will be present on almost every page of this volume. But
the political forces are slowly changing, partly in reaction to De
Gaulle, partly under their own momentum, in response to the profound social changes which the previous regime, the Fourth Republic, had set in motion and from which the Fifth Republic, and
De Gaulle himself, have greatly benefited. This is perhaps why the
present French regime may not be a mere interlude; this is also
why it is so difficult to describe and to measure adequately. One
hopes only that this text will give readers a sense of the movements
which are taking place and of the choices which are being made,
even though the analysis of formal institutions may quickly be
overtaken by the rapid pace of political change.

J.B.

E.D.G., Jr.

Contents

1: The French Republican Tradition

INTRODUCTION

A perceptive son of France once remarked that throughout history his motherland has been obliged to live dangerously. This observer saw France's perilous history as the consequence of exposed geographic position. Others have claimed that the French people lived dangerously because their Celtic origins compelled them to combativeness; still others have ascribed France's adventurous life history to an inquiring and even aspiring national mentality, which some Frenchmen turned to individual genius in art, literature, and philosophy, while others were building both the most brilliant and the least exalted political traditions. Whatever the true causes, we are here concerned with a people whose relationship to life is as dramatic as their history has been, a people who have employed the same sense of daring in choosing their art forms, their fashions, and their cuisine as they have in building empires, in experimenting with almost every known form of political system, and in fighting innumerable wars and revolutions. It is no paradox, then, that some Frenchmen may have carried their disdain for the norms of middle class life, at any rate in the past, to a point of trembling danger.

France has often been described as a woman. The French people themselves have frequently chosen female figures to symbolize their country, suggesting in so doing the infinite variety they find in their homeland and the range of emotions which it induces in them. Indeed, the Frenchman sees in France all the qualities of feminity—the softness of her country side, the passion of her people, the pettiness of her national jealousies, the capacity to endure suffering under indignities, even the splendid mixture of beauty and ugliness of her older cities. They may love or scorn France, but because she is a woman they cannot ignore her. In fact, the absorption of the French people with France is the hallmark of their political life.

When a Frenchman speaks passionately of France he may be identifying himself with a moment in her history of which he particularly approves (or which he abhors) or he may be expressing admiration (or despair) at the whole kaleidoscope of French history, accomplishments, and failures. In his mind the motherland has lived not only dangerously but vividly; it has produced heroes and villains, though heroes and villains may not be the same for different men. Napoleon or Robespierre, Richelieu or

I

Clemenceau (to speak only of the dead) all belong in some way to the Parthenon of great political Frenchmen; they may at the same time be loved and hated, admired and rejected. The Frenchmen never quite relate themselves to one single current of political thought; indeed, they derive considerable satisfaction from sharing in the variety and richness of France's history. For some years, in the 1960s, it was fashionable to scoff at politics, but, as during previous phases of political "disengagement," antipolitical attitudes often were a sign of discontent with politics as they were, with the behavior of politicians, or with both. More profound changes in the relationship between Frenchmen and politics are, perhaps, in process: much of this book will be about these changes; but in the French political tradition apathy was often a form of protest and a disengaged person one who judged and measured those who were engaged.

Perhaps the cause for the Frenchman's fascination with the game of politics—even though he may be unwilling to cheer any of the players—is that French political history is a continuous current. There are almost no extinct species in French political zoology. Most of the present-day French parties claim multiple connections with the past. The Socialists, for example, claim the Jacobins of 1792 and the Communards of 1870 as their forebears (though the Communists make greater claims to have the latter as their ancestors). It is significant that as recently as the early 1960s, serious political commentators were speculating whether, if and when President De Gaulle left the political scene, he would not try to put forward as his successor the Count of Paris, the pretender to the Throne which has been empty since 1848. Political traditions and attitudes or beliefs associated with them rarely die in France, though they may be adapted to existing conditions. They may disappear for long periods, but somewhere they are being cherished to re-emerge when conditions are again favorable. Even French fascism, which took various forms before World War II (though none of these was really strong), and which certainly seemed to have been obliterated by the national revulsion against the collaborators during and after the German occupation of France between 1940 and 1944, reappeared in the 1950s, and indeed took new roots in Algeria because of the Algerian war.

For the most part, however, French political movements, although they may cling to the importance of their origins and to a few fundamental points of doctrine, go through a process of evolution as society changes around them, as their electorate shifts away from them, or, in some cases, as the goals which they originally set for themselves are attained. The most celebrated and caricatural example of such a mutation is given by the Radical Socialist party, which began life in the last quarter of the nineteenth century to preserve political and civil liberties as well as lay republicanism when neither was secure in the country. The party scarcely retains anything but its name from its glorious past; far from being radical and socialist, it tends to be conservative, though divisions among its leaders are such that one usually finds its representatives voting in all possible ways. It was, in many ways, the embodiment of prewar French politics: the great ancestors are being praised and honestly admired, but rarely followed; compromises and deals are the daily reality.

THE HISTORICAL PERSPECTIVE OF FRENCH POLITICS

French political history can be seen as a maze of threads beginning in various places, frequently crossing and tangling with one another, with new strands entering from time to time. To unravel this jumble for an understanding of its separate parts one must begin with the great rent in French history—the revolution of 1789. With great drama, and eventually with a missionary and military zeal which threatened *anciens régimes* throughout much of the rest of Europe, the French routed the monarchy, the aristocracy, and the privileged Roman Catholic Church in the name of liberty, equality, and the republican form of government. But the old order, though defeated, was not destroyed. Its defenders were able to revive the monarchy in the nineteenth century, and to delay for decades any definitive regulation of the Church's powers. Moreover, and more importantly, the anti-republican tradition resisted the passage of time; its supporters were to attempt to undermine all Republics from the First (1792) to the Fifth (1958), and are even today little reconciled to the processes of popular sovereignty.

The defenders of the Revolution and the Republic were not long in dividing over whether they should give priority to equality or liberty. In the early revolutionary period a great effort was made to destroy the unequal political privileges of the titled and aristocratic classes. In keeping with the notion that despotism and oppression were primarily products of the heavy hand of the State, the elimination of privileges was at first undertaken with a minimum use of government machinery, and attempts were made to portray the results as the product of the direct voice of the people manifested through popular meetings. The Declaration of the Rights of Man and the Citizen, adopted tumultuously in the Revolutionary Assembly of 1789, detailed the expectations of humble Frenchmen to be treated with equal justice before the law and to be regarded as equivalent to all other Frenchmen in the exercise of their rights and in the day-to-day conduct of their lives. The "Rights of Man" was primarily a political document; it represented the momentary ascendancy of the libertarians over the egalitarians; it did not consider the possibility that the economic advantages of a few might, even with a constitutional system, undermine the political liberties of the majority.

There were, however, strong undercurrents in the revolution which were bent on a leveling of all economic and social distinctions between men. The dictatorship of the Jacobins (1793–1794) was a move toward the use of the State as an instrument of vigorous social change. The efforts of the Jacobins did not prevail, and in fact were succeeded by the much more conservative (and stabilizing) regime which Napoleon installed after taking over power in 1799. However, the Jacobins added a new and powerful political strain to the matrix of French political development which was to assert itself several times in the nineteenth century, and most dynamically in the twentieth.

In the largest part of the nineteenth century the libertarians had only a shaky hold on France. This was a period of adaptation and experiment, as political strands became snarled by borrowing ideas from one another. The anti-revolutionaries returned in 1814–1815, though the legitimate monarchy which reappeared with Louis XVIII had to agree to a considerable dose of liberalism: the King proclaimed a Charter (though it was significantly dated from the "eighteenth year of his reign"—as if he had come to the throne when the son of the previous King was officially said to have died in prison); he acknowledged civil equality and political liberty. The reactionary attempts of his successor, his brother Charles X, ended in revolution in 1830; the French thought then that they were repeating English seventeenth-century history and put on the Throne a cousin of the last King, Louis-Philippe d'Orleans, who started as a liberal monarch believing in parliamentary government and ended ignominiously after having made too many efforts at manipulating Parliament instead of concentrating his attention on the new political aspirations of Frenchmen. The Revolution of 1848 (which swept all over Continental Europe as well) put an end in France to the liberal monarchy, and indeed to the monarchy altogether.

TABLE 1: FRENCH REGIMES

To 1789	*Ancien Régime:* Louis XIV, 1643–1715 Louis XV, 1715–1774 Louis XVI, 1774–1792
1789–1792	Constitutional Monarchy. Constituent Assembly. Constitution of 1791. First Legislative Assembly.
1792–1799	First Republic. Convention Constitution of 1793 (not applied). Directory Constitution of 1795.
1799–1804	Consulate. Napoleon First Consul. Constitutions of 1799 and 1802.
1804–1814 and 1815	First Empire. Napoleon I Emperor. Constitutions of 1804, 1814 (not applied), and 1815.
1814–1815 and	Restoration. Louis XVIII, 1814–1824. Charter of 1814.
1815–1830	Charles X, 1824–1830.
1830–1848	Orleans Monarchy. Louis Philippe I, 1830–1848. Charter of 1830.
1848–1851	Second Republic. Constitution of 1848. Napoleon Bonaparte (nephew of Napoleon I) elected President of the Republic.
1852–1870	Second Empire. Napoleon III Emperor. Constitutions of 1852 and 1870.
1870–1940	Third Republic. Constitution of 1875.
1940–1944	Vichy Régime. Pétain "Head of State."
1945–1958	Fourth Republic. Constitution of 1946. V. Auriol (1946–1953) and R. Coty (1953–1958) Presidents.
1958–	Fifth Republic. Constitution of 1958. Charles De Gaulle (1958–1965) and (1965–1972) President.

The most curious intermixture of political strands flowing from the Revolution was the imperial tradition into which Napoleon Bonaparte (1799–1814) stumbled, which his nephew perfected in the Second Empire (1852–1870) and which some modern commentators feel is being reincarnated in the Fifth Republic of General De Gaulle. The Napoleons cleverly exploited Rousseau's theory of the "general will," which in earlier days had been one of the cries of the revolutionary assemblies. Their apologists insisted that the Emperors' mandates to speak and act for France (unfettered by any powerful intermediate body) were legitimate because they served the popular will. To ratify imperial decisions, both Napoleons resorted to the use of the popular referendum (plebiscite was the name in their time, but the word came to have unpleasant connotations precisely because of the Bonapartes' use of the technique). According to their court theorists, the popular will was thereby expressed in the imperial person. Like the Jacobins, the Bonapartes appealed to the masses not only for political approval but for patriotic support (though the second Napoleon had to claim, in order to gain support, that "the Empire meant peace"—which was to be only partly true). The Jacobin "nation in arms" became the Napoleonic conscript armies. In fact, however, the imperial tradition was, despite some trappings borrowed from the Revolution, both anti-liberal politically, and socially rather conservative (though it was not reactionary, but aimed essentially at maintaining the rights of the newly enfranchised bourgeoisie). The apparatus of the State which Napoleon I devised became a large and often arbitrary instrument, which operated as a force of its own, deriving its powers from the personal strength of the Emperor, not from the French people as such. Indeed, in some ways, the Second Empire can be said to have been more progressive than the First: it was the period when France experienced her first and greatest industrial boom and really moved at last from a predominantly agricultural economy to that of a modern and developed society.

The division between the organ of political will—the Emperor—and the organs of State authority—the administration, the military establishment, the judiciary—represented an entirely new and unexpected arrangement after the Revolution had placed the stress on constitutional reform and on the problems of executive-legislative relations. The distinction between government and administration, never very clear until then, was established in part by accident, in part through the maintenance of the well-developed bureaucracy of the monarchy, and in part through the vigorous action of Napoleon I. Through him, France was given a well-functioning administration, codes of law, and a theory of the administrative process which were to be the envy of many countries for several generations. Not only is much of the State machinery created by Napoleon I still in existence in France, but, as under the Emperor, much of it remains outside the political arena. Since the last imperial period ended in 1870, many political battles have been fought, but they have largely been fought over governments and their policies, not over the administrative instruments of the governments.

The hardiest political tradition spawned in the Revolution was the republican. In a sense it was the truest revolutionary element; it survived all manner of assaults, distortions, and even the bitter mockery of those who from time to time momentarily

THE FRENCH REPUBLICAN TRADITION—7

eliminated it from the French political scene. As we have already noted, the revolutionaries who rose against the *ancien régime* tended to divide into those who sought political liberty and those who championed equality—although, of course, some pursued both goals. As the nineteenth century wore on and various political forms were tested, the libertarians were to give a meaningful and concrete definition to republicanism, but more and more the image of the Republic was employed by the egalitarians as a necessary beginning for the implantation of their own concepts of society.

The republicanism that emerged during the nineteenth century ultimately comprised only a few simple elements: insistence on the expression of the public will through a sovereign, a directly-elected assembly, a lay society, and distrust of executive authority as a threat to freedom, against which the people had an obligation to rise when and if tyranny appeared imminent. Several times the people did in fact take to the barricades, though this technique became much less common from the second half of the nineteenth century on, after having been rather successful in overthrowing regimes in the first. Under the Republic, this particular form of civic violence came to have a mythical value: it symbolized the revolt of the people against tyrants (and was to be used for the last time, more symbolically than effectively, against the Germans leaving Paris in 1944).

The egalitarians, at first socialists and later communists, have always employed the mystique of the barricades and have associated it with their own goals. Indeed, the evolution of French revolutionary regimes made this type of association possible. The Revolution of 1789, as we saw, quickly moved from "bourgeois liberalism" to egalitarian concepts. The Revolution of 1848, ostensibly fought to obtain an extension of the suffrage from the King, led to the end of the monarchy and, in a few months, to the temporary establishment of a semi-socialist society (return to normalcy did quickly take place, though, after the more extreme "Socialists" were defeated during four days of civil war in Paris in June, 1848). The Paris Commune that seized power in the capital following the collapse of the Second Empire in 1870 and the French defeat by the Germans in 1871 included various types of supporters of socialism, anarchism, and extreme forms of republicanism. It was in turn smashed by the more conservative republicans, and ended in one of the bloodiest episodes of repression in French history. Meanwhile, the French people had elected a National Assembly composed mainly of monarchists, primarily

to negotiate the peace settlement; but the Assembly started drafting constitutional laws, hoping that a monarchical restoration
could take place when the rival claimants (the "legitimists" and
the Orleanists—the supporters of the "branch" of 1815 and those
of the "branch" of 1830) would agree. But agreement was so
slow to come that the Republic triumphed by default, and almost
by accident, in 1875. The Third Republic was born, and the Constitution grudgingly put together by an Assembly in which a
majority of the members were not republican, and many were
strongly anti-republican, was to last until 1940. It was destroyed
by German arms after corrosive action by a series of attacks coming from both extremes and by the weakness and internal divisions
of its supporters, who proved increasingly incapable of solving
modern political problems.

Modern French history spans the Third, Fourth (1946–1958),
and Fifth Republics (since 1958); it was interrupted between 1940
and 1944 by the corporate state of Pétain, whose authority derived from German victory and not, despite the appearances of
a legal transfer, from the will of the French people. In many ways
the Vichy regime (so-called because the seat of government was
transferred to Vichy, in Central France, while Northern France
was occupied) symbolized all that was anti-republican in French
life, while the *Résistance*, which fought it incessantly, has often
been described as a pure revival of the republican spirit. Pétain
and his followers, composed of old-fashioned conservatives,
straight fascists, anti-Semites, disgruntled military officers, and
crass opportunists coming from all parties, set about to destroy all
vestiges of republican democracy. Political authority was vested
in the person of the Marshal; he was unencumbered by parliamentary organs, although he created a "national council" in which
the interests of vocational and social groups were theoretically
to be represented. In practice, employers spoke in the name of the
working class, and free trade unions were abolished; special stress
was put on the peasantry, which was supposed to embody all
the "true" traditions which had made France great; in fact, however, the "return to the land" was simply a means of satisfying
the German occupier and to limit the influence of an industrial
working class whose political attitudes were felt to be dangerous.
Most telling was the motto adopted by the new regime: "Work,
Family, and Fatherland" replaced "Liberty, Equality, and Fraternity." The traditionalist, conservative values of the *ancien
régime* were reimposed by fiat on a scornful people who, except

for a small minority, quickly came to reject the fumbling and posturing of a government which retained power at the point of Nazi bayonets.

The *Résistance* that began organizing about a year after the French defeat contained elements from all shades of French republicanism, ranging from conservative nationalists (De Gaulle was one of them) who despised the ignominy of German occupation and the pandering of the Pétainists to tough communist leaders who had been forced underground during the war and who turned ultra-patriotic after the German attack on Russia in 1941. Several distinct *Résistance* networks existed in metropolitan France; many retained particular political colorations, others were heterogeneous. As Allied victory became imminent the *Résistance* organizations expanded operations, and adopted military as well as political characteristics. Eventually, they came to dominate much of French life; in many parts of the country (and particularly in the mountains) *Résistance* elements were in control well before the arrival of Allied troops. When liberation was finally achieved, the *Résistance* was the main political force which counted in the country, though De Gaulle had created a government in exile long before, first in London, and later in Algiers. No wonder, then, that the new constitution which emerged in 1946 from the ruins of postwar France was a reaffirmation of republican principles with strong left-wing overtones adapted from the teachings of underground *maquisards*.

However, the strength of the Left was not sufficient to overcome some of the most awkward historical legacies of French political institutions. In fact the Fourth Republic was in many ways a streamlined version of the Third, emphasizing the purest republican traditions of a powerful, sovereign, popular Assembly, a weak executive, and an administrative apparatus which floated in an ambiguous limbo below the government. One degree remote from democratic responsibility, the bureaucratic administration did not only have permanency, however; it was to be the most powerful machine of change in modern French society; as we shall see, it was to use all the techniques at its disposal to give strength and energy to the new forces, gradually diminish the opposition of the traditional groups, and give to France, after little more than a decade, one of the most flourishing economic systems of the world. While the premiers and their cabinets were becoming targets of widespread criticism by the French public, and while criticism turned to disgust, the administration saw its influence increase. The end of the Fourth Republic coincided with the coming of age of a curious mixture of technocracy and democracy within the bureaucratic machinery itself.

De Gaulle's government is thus much more than just another step in French political history. In a sense it is a part of all of them. It borrows threads from innumerable political strands; it is limited by other traditions which, although not specifically represented in the regime, guide and channel the political attitudes and reflexes of the living Frenchmen who are its leaders. Conceived in adventure, the Fifth Republic is in the best tradition of French political history. It has already fashioned a mystique of its own, which will, if the lessons of the past are meaningful and if the transformations of the society come to full fruit, outlast the founder of the Fifth Republic and become embedded in the continuous flow of French political life.

2: The Background of the Social Order

In the 1950s and 1960s, France moved fast socially and economically; indeed, for many, the tragedy of modern France has been that politics did not keep pace with socio-economic change or has been very slow to respond to it. But while the transformations of French society gradually seem to bring about attitudes which were almost totally unknown to the French of previous generations or were only shared by a small minority, the traditional background remains strong and visible in many parts of the country and in many groups of the population. Among the long-standing characteristics of this social order, four, perhaps, have special prominence. First, the French population, long static at forty million, now reaching fifty million, has peasant origins, and the peasantry has been for centuries (we saw that Pétain tried to revive the "old spirit") the backbone of society and the basis of the political system. Second, and allied to it, France was a very divided nation, composed of several ethnic groups, with very different feelings, attitudes, and behavior, and often with little in common (not even, for a long time, the language). Third, the class system and particularly the division between "bourgeois" and "worker" (*ouvrier*) was of great importance: it was a question of status, of style of life, as well as of income. Fourth, France has always been, at least nominally, a Catholic nation: she was the "Eldest daughter of the Church," according to the traditional saying, and this led to religious wars and to the persecution of Protestants (mainly Calvinists) in the sixteenth, seventeenth, and eighteenth centuries. It was on such a social landscape that the Kings first and Napoleon later built a centralized administrative machine and that the Republic imposed a centralized political culture, both these characteristics being as important to the understanding of the strains and stresses of the traditional social order as the other long-standing forces in the community.

PEASANT ORIGINS

France was for a long time a peasant nation—indeed perhaps the only peasant nation in the world. This is not only because as many as 50 percent of Frenchmen were engaged agriculture in the middle part of the nineteenth century, and as many as a third before World War II. It is also because the vast majority of the persons

11

occupied on the land were owners of small plots, inherited from their parents, to which they were passionately attached. The Revolution of 1789 did not wholly, nor indeed even wholly deliberately, create the peasantry; but the dispossession of the Church and of many aristocrats led to the creation of a vast peasantry, which became attached to the Revolution inasmuch as it had given them the land (Napoleon stabilized the situation and made any return to the previous state of affairs impossible). But the peasantry was also, in a very modest way, part of the "capitalist" or "bourgeois" society, as the ownership of land created attitudes of individualism, of respect for property, and of fear of any social system which might lead to dispossession; these were to weigh strongly against any attempts made by various revolutionary movements to take over the government of the country.

TABLE 2: OCCUPATIONAL BREAKDOWN OF THE FRENCH POPULATION

	Active Population (in millions)	Percentage
Farmers	4.0	21.0
Agricultural Workers	1.2	6.3
Owners of Businesses	2.3	12.0
Professional Workers and Higher Management	0.6	3.1
Middle Management	1.1	5.7
White Collar Workers	2.1	11.0
Manual Workers	6.4	33.1
Service Workers	1.0	5.2
Other	0.5	2.6
	19.2	100.0

(Census of Population, 1954)

The traditional life of the peasant was difficult and even harsh. Plots of land were small; the problem of the smallness became compounded by the division of farmlands. Many peasants owned farms fragmented into odd-shaped and even non-contiguous parcels that resulted from generations of dividing and subdividing the family heritage, as the Civil Code of Napoleon decided that estates were to be divided equally between all the children. Fragmentation of land came to reach such proportions that productivity, even in rich areas, tended to be smaller in France than in

neighboring countries; incomes did not increase—and to counter-
act the fall in their living standards, French peasants took to limiting sharply the number of children (though many also left the
country for the towns) with the result that the birthrate became
lower in France than in all other developed nations. Psychologi-
cally, the effect was catastrophic: the toughness of rural life came
to be associated with a generally pessimistic view about the future.
Preserving what one had became a primary goal; change contained
potentially terrifying dangers. The outside world, whether the
city, the government, or the weather, came to be considered the
source of the gravest threats to the minimal stability of the present. Though peasants never ceased to respond when called to defend their country (in the European wars, and in the colonies),
their general relationship with the State was peculiarly unfriendly. They were organized democratically in their own communities (the *communes*), but they had few feelings of brotherhood and democratic association with the rest of the nation (and
indeed with their fellow peasants).

As we said, the flight from the land was one of the means by
which the lot of the remaining children of the family could be
in part alleviated (though in practice only in part, as the children
who stayed on the land had to repay in cash, over a number of
years, the estate of those who had left). Movements from village
to city were, all through the nineteenth century, characteristic
of Western Europe; they had in France less influence on the new
city-dweller than in other countries, however. Frenchmen who
had left the land kept the mark of their peasant origins for long
periods and often during the whole first generation. They had
become urbanized, in so far as they had no desire to return to
farming—but they did not shed their psychological heritage. Indeed, the reverse was even true: under the influence of the newly-
arrived peasants, residents of cities tended to take on attitudes
more characteristic of the land than of urban communities. Pre-
conceptions, fears, worries, and a rather negative and anarchistic
individualism came to dominate much of the middle and lower-
middle levels of French society—the shopkeepers, artisans, mechanics, workers in commerce and even in industry, as well as the
large numbers of French civil servants. While by tradition and
love of independence many arrivals wanted to set themselves up
in business, however small, unlucrative, and tiring, others longed
for security and looked for state posts, complete with holidays
and pensions, to be protected against the future. The peasant roots
of so many Frenchmen (often refurbished and revamped by

yearly returns to the family house for holidays, births, marriages, or funerals) tended to stamp indelibly some leaders, members, or sympathizers in all the political groups. They accounted for a strange understanding between people who found themselves otherwise on different sides of the ideological (or indeed even physical) barricade. They led to the development of a skeptical mind, suspicious of those in high places; they explain the love for the "small," "honest" man who is nonetheless prepared to bend the rules and the dislike for large combinations where vast sums are at stake and which Paris and Paris alone can be wicked enough to generate.

The peasant complex, as this orientation might be called, is thus a strong element in that much-discussed French characteristic, individualism. But it is also combined, in a strange association, with other elements, and this shows quickly its limits. It appears in the negative way in which Frenchmen react (or reacted, traditionally at least) to voluntary groupings; they did not believe in them, scarcely supported them, and thus could demonstrate, as through a self-fulfilling prophecy, that they received few benefits from them. But the respect for negative criticism, the fear of appearing "naive," the suspicion of all men and institutions were all forms of conformity, and indeed of conformism. These characteristics had considerable drawbacks for the French economy, made experiments an object of ridicule, and were indeed the very cause of the outside imposition of rules which the peasant community could not and would not establish. Society is always an equilibrium between various forces; in the French traditional social order, peasants and bureaucracy came to be opposites, the equilibrium being maintained by the contrasted action of both forces. But the society lost much strength by this perpetual warfare; curiously enough, the social democracy of the peasants was perhaps one of the main factors which slowed the development towards political democracy.

In the postwar period, however, these characteristics have come to change. The flight from the land has taken such proportions in the late 1950s and 1960s that new horizons are being perceived and hopes for a better future have come within the village. The action of the government and of the administration, as we shall see in Chapter Eight, transformed the economic conditions, and slowly the social conditions, in which peasants have to live. With less than one person out of five employed in agriculture, France has ceased to have, distinct from the rest of the nation, a body of citizens who alone can tilt the scales of the political system by strongly infiltrating all political parties. But political mores die hard; while social transformations affect the countryside and mold the attitudes of the coming generation, the present generation of politicians still thinks and acts in part like their older constituents. The political order on the land remains a product of the past, and the peasant origins of Frenchmen account, as we shall see later, for much of the behavior of political parties.

REGIONAL SECTIONALISM
AND THE INFLUENCE OF PARIS

The second characteristic of the traditional French social structure is its sectionalism. This was maintained partly by the size of the peasantry, but more general historical and geographical characteristics are also involved. Mountains or plateaus separate the country into natural regions and isolate certain areas from the main communication axes. Brittany in the West, the Southwest (sometimes known as Aquitaine), the Massif Central (a plateau which is in parts very rugged and desert-like), the Alpine area, Provence (named from the Latin *Provincia*—the southeastern tip along the Mediterranean has a very hilly interior though tourists tend mainly to think of it in terms of the *Côte d'Azur*) constitute sharply differentiated regions which remained, until fairly recently, culturally isolated from each other. They were isolated and different from the more accessible northern and Northeastern parts of the country, which have more plains, and thus an easier agriculture, more industry, and more natural lines of communication. History molded itself on these geographical constraints, and added a further dimension to them: local particularism was very widespread throughout the whole of the *Ancien Régime*, and many parts of the country, acquired as a result of marriages in the royal family or of wars between the King and nobles who established their authority over whole provinces in the Middle Ages, still kept many of their traditions and their legal customs, despite the centralizing efforts of the monarchy. The Revolution abolished provinces, created a uniform local government system, and began the process of unifying the law. But these efforts at centralization were the consequence of the weight of regional sectionalism, not a natural growth of the social system.

It is difficult to describe adequately the contours of French sectionalism. It manifests itself, as everywhere, through differences in accent, in turn often the product of the survival of local dialects, some of which, as in the South, have a Latin origin and are related to Italian (Provençal) or Spanish (Catalan), while others (Alsatian, Flemish) have Germanic roots and yet others (Breton or Basque) have little or nothing in common with the main European languages. But different forms of living are often also the consequences of the different climates, and these vary sharply if one moves from the humid but temperate Brittany to the cold Massif Central or Alsace and to the pleasant, almost Californian Mediterranean coast; the shape of traditional houses gives such a characteristic outlook to towns and villages in Alsace, Provence, or the Paris area that they seem to belong, in reality, to different countries. But these variations are the symbols of other and more profound variations in modes of living: the outdoor life in the clement South and Southeast contrasts with the indoor life of the much tougher North and East.

These differences have naturally led men to be very attached to their *petite patrie,* to their home area, and prevented them from feeling at ease when they move to another region. Conversely, the "stranger" who establishes himself in a new area finds real human relationships slow to develop, partly because he is not himself aware of traditions and customs. This, as we shall see, has important political consequences, as it effectively prevents (or used to prevent) people from attempting to stand as candidates in areas where they have no local roots. The effect is cumulatively increased in rural areas, admittedly; the general fear and dislike of strangers is simply accentuated (and rationalized) if the immigrant comes from far away. Doctors or lawyers often found it difficult to establish practice in a small town or village if they did not come from the neighboring district and did not have a feel for the local customs. Though recent changes, in particular the spread of the car and of television, have increased mobility and interpenetration, the sense of identity of the various regions, perceived in the wide sense, is far from dead. It may even be argued that the present trends in administrative regionalism will have the effect of maintaining some of the differences, although most of the bitterness and hostility will probably disappear.

The peculiar position of Paris has to be considered in connection with the sectionalism of the "provinces." The political, social, economic and cultural preeminence of Paris is beyond doubt, but it does generate resentment. Paris is much larger than any other French city or conurbation: while eight million people live in the Paris area (administratively the city has less than three million inhabitants) the next three conurbations, Marseilles, Lyons, and Lille, do not reach a million. None of the provincial capitals can even remotely be considered as alternatives or challenges to the metropolis: they are further down in an urban hierarchy in which the holder of the top position is undisputed. Unfortunately for the general health of the country, a kind of social hierarchy parallels this population hierarchy. Important things happen in Paris, whether in the theater or in the government, in university research or in business; things which happen in the large provincial towns are often derived from Parisian decisions, or are experiments conducted or controlled by men in the capital. Ambitious people, in all walks of life, either have always lived in Paris or aspire to live there; they may be "sent" to the provinces by the government or their firm, but such a posting in the "field" is not meant to last (people often keep their flats in Paris, or even continue to reside in Paris in order not to be out of touch). Anyone who has "arrived" has to be in Paris—and anyone who is not in Paris will sooner or later, in many subtle ways, feel that he has not arrived.

The rule, of course, is not general. Some Frenchmen are deeply attached to their provincial town; there are exceptions to the social law according to which people will eventually finish their working life in Paris if they are really good. But such exceptions tend to be noted, and they have to be explained. Most of those who stay in medium-sized or even large cities unquestionably feel the weight of the capital in many aspects of their daily life, and have some sense of deprivation which comes from not belonging to it. There is a general inferiority complex in French urban life which explains many political reactions from provincial representatives, anxious to assert the individual character of their towns. In recent years, problems in the social services and in particular in transport and housing have become so aggravated by the size of the metropolis that, under government influence, firms were urged to "decentralize" and to expand their business outside Paris. The move has not met with considerable success as the cost, economic and psychological, is often heavy. But some rejuvenation of provincial life is at present taking place, particularly as the factors which work against sectionalism, the car and television, also bring Paris nearer to an increasingly large number of Frenchmen. The move will probably gradually bear fruit; French participation in the wider economic context of the Common Market will also tend to decrease the social and cultural pre-eminence of Paris. But for perhaps another generation, Paris will remain an extraordinary pole of attraction to Frenchmen, as well as a drain on the better resources of the provinces, to an extent which is not comparable in any other European country. The pull and resentment which even London exercises is smaller, less dramatic, and altogether less prejudicial to Britain.

SOCIAL CLASS

The third influence affecting most Frenchmen, social consciousness, is a function of the cleavages which have torn the fabric
of modern society. To a certain extent it is an outgrowth of
the industrial revolution which started hitting France in the late
eighteenth century but only acquired its full momentum at the
end of the nineteenth. Social distinctions run sharp and deep,
particularly in the large cities. Although they began to diminish
from the mid-1950s, they are still very noticeable and sometimes
come to take a tone of profound bitterness, which accounts in
part for the permanence of a very large communist section of the
electorate. Class is mentioned less commonly in France than in
England; it is not an object of constant conversation; it is even
less the subject of jokes. This is probably because, in the last
resort, it is more profoundly felt as an unjust barrier. Though
Frenchmen rarely recognize it, class is as easily manifest as in
Britain, through accents, gestures, sometimes even dress; it is, of
course, linked to sectional characteristics and to the peasant origins
of the French, for someone who comes from the peasantry or
lives in a small provincial town experiences greater difficulties
in moving up the social ladder than someone who comes from
fairly humble origins but lives in Paris. But class is in itself a
means of distinguishing between Frenchmen irrespective of geography, and Frenchmen, in the depths of their hearts, know that the
distinction exists.

To talk about class is not to deny social mobility. Indeed,
movement from class to class takes place at about the same rate
in France as in other developed societies. These do not constitute
new developments, moreover; through education in particular,
large numbers of sons of peasants, of lower middle class employees, and even of manual workers have entered the middle
class. Some educational channels have indeed always been known
to make social promotion possible: a number of prestigious graduate schools, in particular the *École Polytechnique* and the *École
Normale Supérieure*, have been powerful instruments of social
mobility open to the very talented. Moreover, for these, problems of adaptation into the bourgeois milieu were somewhat eased
as it was readily recognized by all that social promotion did take
place through these graduate schools. At lower levels, numerous
other schools or examinations, particularly those leading to the
middle ranks of the civil service, the armed forces, the post office,

and the railways enabled the brighter sons and daughters of poorer families to enter the rather large French small bourgeoisie. Finally, thrifty working-class children often set up small businesses which they hoped slowly to expand—the owners of the business thereby acquiring a status (and a freedom) which their original jobs did not give them.

More perhaps than in other countries, social class is based primarily on occupation, partly on education, and only marginally on income. Though there is in France a tradition of respect for craftsmanship (governments often extol the skills of French crafts-men), the esteem for industrial manual work has always been very low, and this has an effect on the workers themselves: there is more pride among British workers, for instance, than there is among French *ouvriers*. This was perhaps because France only partially achieved its industrial revolution, and mainly in the northern and eastern part of the country (industrial workers never constituted more than a third of the working force). This was perhaps also because the traditions of independence and in-dividualism of the peasantry created a climate in which it was felt that those who worked for others, particularly if they sold only manual labor, were degrading human dignity. In some sense, they were showing themselves incapable of mastering their own fate; they were giving up and allowing their destiny to be controlled by someone else. Thus there arose both a contempt for the worker and a form of hatred directed at the man who was wicked enough to employ (and in some sense degrade) fellow human beings. As the welfare of the society required that some people should employ others, the psychological way out consisted in emphasizing how unintelligent workers were and how unable they were to improve their lot; meanwhile, social tensions were relaxed by a large-scale immigration of workers from parts of Southern and Eastern Europe where wages were lower. The mines, the building trades, certain sections of the engineering in-dustry were (and still are to a large extent) manned by men coming from Poland, Italy, or Spain (and, since the 1950s, North Africa, Portugal, and even Turkey). A subtle form of discrimina-tion usually enabled the French to move up rather quicker to supervisory functions, while the immigrant population, more tran-sient, sometimes illiterate, generally incapable of organizing itself in associations or trade unions, tended to contribute in large quantities to the supply of unskilled labor.

As in other aspects of the social order, considerable changes took place in the characteristics of class consciousness in the 1950s

and 1960s. It has been argued that France now has a "new working class," much more integrated in the fabric of society, much
less prepared to reject the whole of the social system and anxious
to share more widely in the affluence of the new capitalism. This
is undoubtedly true. Wages have increased substantially in the
postwar period (despite the communist claim that the proletariat
is constantly becoming poorer), and industrial organizations are
now bargaining with employers, as we shall see in Chapter Eight,
much more practically and much more successfully than they did
in the past. As everywhere in the Western world, differences between manual and white collar workers have decreased; as in the
United States, class distinctions tend gradually to be based more
on incomes than on occupation. As the peasant mystique becomes
less widespread, as middle-class gadgets and a middle-class style
of life (from the car to holidays abroad) are increasingly spreading and are spreading on the basis not of what people do, but of
what they earn, traditional class cleavages cease to be so sharp.
Vast new high-rise projects, financed largely from public funds,
house together people who work in widely different types of
jobs; they contribute to a social melting pot which contrasts with
the kind of separation, and almost of segregation, which used to
characterize working-class districts. By the late 1970s or 80s, the
characteristics of French social life will probably have been transformed to such an extent that most traditional differences will
cease to be appreciated, at least by the younger generations. The
break with the past will obviously take place more quickly in
Paris and the large cities than in the more community-minded
small towns, but the majority of the working class lives in the
large conurbations. Old French values may suffer from the change,
but a happier social order will emerge.

Here too, however, a cultural and political lag may outlive the
social transformation. As we shall note later, the rejuvenation of
the French economy since the late 1940s had little or no visible
effect on the behavior of the political leaders of the French working class and had only a slow and limited impact on the behavior
of the industrial leaders. These attitudes have been shaped by
generations of workers and have been reinforced by the stagnant
character of the economy in the interwar period. The pessimism
of the manual workers about their fate and that of their children
is eroded only in a limited and gradual fashion. An operation of
psychological conversion is in progress, which takes place perhaps
more slowly in the more collectively organized working class
than among the more individualistic peasants. The break is un-

likely to manifest itself in the form of dramatic changes on the political front, but the behavior of individuals will change, however permanent the institutions seem to be. This gradual movement is perhaps one of the most fascinating developments to watch in contemporary France in the social psychology of the working class.

THE CHURCH

France is essentially a Catholic nation: one million Protestants (Calvinists in the South, Lutherans in Alsace) and less than half a million Jews are the only other sizeable religious groups. But this Catholic nation is profoundly anti-clerical, in parts wholly de-christianized, and still very affected by the great political battles which led to the separation of Church and State in 1905. For the majority of Frenchmen, Roman Catholic practice is limited to baptism, marriage, and funeral. Weekly attendance at mass and general observance of religious prescriptions is limited to a minority, averaging at about a third, but it is not uniformly spread throughout the nation. Brittany and Alsace are areas of strong Catholic practice; the western part of the Massif Central and the Southeast are anti-religious, or at best unreligious. The historical origins of these variations are complex. Much seems to be due not to the priest but to the local gentry: where, as in Brittany, the mass of the peasants were kept deferent, the authority of the gentry managed to buttress that of the Church. Where, as in the Center-West, the local gentry was discredited and had to leave at the Revolution, the Church suffered irreparable damage.

Hence there is a traditional association, in France as in most predominantly Roman Catholic countries of Western Europe, between Church and social order, between religious practice and political conservatism. Throughout the nineteenth century, the Church hierarchy maintained close contacts with the leaders of the Right and this had considerable influence on the increasingly bitter attacks made by the Left, including the moderate Left, against the Church. In the last decades of the nineteenth century, the situation gradually became tense, as the Third Republic ceased to be led by Conservative monarchists hoping for a restoration and came into the hands of the Republicans. In the 1890s, the climax was reached with the Dreyfus case, in which a Jewish officer was accused and condemned for having betrayed secrets and which the military refused for a long time to re-open despite numerous signs that a judicial mistake had been committed. On the whole, the military, the Conservatives, and the Church appeared united in their opposition to the principles of the modern liberal state. Though separation between Church and State would probably have eventually taken place, "the Affair," as the Dreyfus case came to be known, precipitated the divorce. In 1905, by Act of Parliament, the privileges which the Church had were abolished, priests lost their status of civil servants and were no longer paid (with the side effect that Protestant ministers and rabbis also lost their State salary), and various religious orders were disbanded or had to leave the country (including the Jesuits who were not to be "tolerated" again before 1918 and not formally allowed in the country before World War II). The "Elder daughter of the Church" had completely broken with her past.

Most Roman Catholics became profoundly bitter and angry against the Republic. However, some started to realize that no amelioration could take place until and unless the Church ceased to be associated with "the Reaction" (to take the common political phrase used by the Left against the Right). In the eyes of the progressive Catholic minority, what was needed was an effort of adaptation based first on the acceptance of the Republic and of its liberal principles (which many Catholics were still not prepared to tolerate); second, on missionary work among the workers (who were quickly becoming wholly unchristian) and the peasants (many of whom lived in dechristianized areas); and third, on the development of a new social policy, based more on charity and compassion than on respect for authority. The changes had been helped in the 1890s by the pronouncements of Pope Leo XIII, though his successor, Pius X, seemed to return to more traditional views of the role of the Church in society: indeed, the first French progressive Catholic movement, created in 1894 by Marc Sangnier, le Sillon, was condemned by the Pope. But a new spirit had come and at least a fraction of the Church was henceforth to work for the reconciliation between Catholicism and the "living forces" of the nation.

Progress was slow in the interwar period: the main breakthrough occurred only in the 1940s and 1950s. A Christian Democratic party was formed and, as we shall see in Chapter Six, it was for a while to be one of the largest parties of postwar France. Workers and peasant organizations grew in strength, in particular among the young (the move was deliberate). The role of the workers' priests (condemned and disbanded in 1953 after the movement had appeared to the hierarchy to be dangerously secular in character) has been often mentioned, but, though less spectacular, the part played by the Catholic youth movements has been more profound and has given an entirely new image to French Roman Catholicism; indeed, these movements can even claim to have been instrumental in the general transformation of modern French society and to have quickened the pace of social modernization in many sections of the community.

Some antipathy against the Roman Catholic Church still exists, however; moreover, while the status of the Catholics and of the Church increased—enabling Church schools to obtain State subsidies, first in a limited way in 1951 and on a much broader scale in 1959—the main object of the change, the re-christianization of France, has probably not even begun to be achieved. Religious practice has not increased; indifference is probably as widespread; the weight of religion in the cultural patterns of society is not significantly higher than at the turn of the century. It is, of course, impossible to know whether, had progressive Roman Catholics not taken a new line, the fate of the Church would not have been worse. But the social consciousness of the Church has enabled Catholics to have a higher status in society, though it has not enabled the Church to play a greater part. There are few signs of change in the direction of greater practice. The political influence of the Church was probably more effectively destroyed by the 1905 separation than had been thought at the time.

THE ADMINISTRATIVE AND CULTURAL CENTRALIZATION OF MODERN FRANCE

Divisions run deep in France. Not all are due to the Revolution, as we saw; many date from a much earlier period. They cut across each other and lead to a fragmentation of the basic social attitudes which accounts for much of the ideological and political sectionalism of the country. There are oppositions between town and country, employer and worker, the provinces and Paris, Church and anti-Church. Admittedly, under the impact of modernization, many differences are being blurred; France is gradually becoming easier to understand and, as a result, simpler to govern. But the changes are slow and some political moves seem to reawaken oppositions which commentators had perhaps too quickly declared dead. On the surface, anti-clericalism does not appear to stir the population, for instance, yet in 1959, State subsidies to Church schools roused more opposition than any other issue and millions of Frenchmen signed a petition against the bill which Parliament was discussing. For a while, it seemed that Church schools would outstrip, in the minds of Frenchmen, the Algerian problem, unquestionably the most important issue of the day, particularly in view of the consequences which it had on the morale of the Army. Admittedly, the opposition to subsidies to private schools had more general political aims: opponents of the new Gaullist regime thought of rallying support by creating a major conflict over a traditionally contentious issue. But they did, significantly enough, rally massive support, and for a while France seemed more politically militant than she had been for years. The contrast between the almost total apathy at the death of the Fourth Republic and the interest shown over the Church schools issue seemed to demonstrate how deep traditional oppositions ran and how slowly the simplification process was taking place in contemporary French politics.

The very number and complexity of the social divisions accounts for State centralization, both administrative and cultural. If the French Kings, and later the Empire, had not given the country a strong and unified administrative system, it would probably not have survived. If the Republic had not attempted to give the country a uniform political culture running across geographical and social barriers, the Republic would probably not have survived. Administrative centralization was practiced by all regimes: it led, as we shall see in Chapter Seven, to the setting-up of an impressive network of State agencies throughout the whole country. The Republic inherited these agencies from the monarchy and Napoleon; it never really attempted to dismantle them (an early endeavor between 1789 and 1792 was soon to prove, or at least appear to the government, very damaging to the unity of the nation). The changes which took place when the Republic became more accepted at the end of the nineteenth century were piecemeal, remained somewhat limited, and still left the government with the right to intervene in the last resort if it so desired. Paradoxically enough, administrative centralization did not come seriously under attack before the second half of the twentieth century, precisely at the time when Western European countries were all becoming gradually as centralized as France under the impact of economic intervention and of social welfare legislation. In the nineteenth and even in the first half of the twentieth centuries centralization, however strong, was tacitly recognized by all as necessary for the State's survival; as a result, and almost by accident (though "enlightened despotism" characterized the French State for centuries), France came to have one of the best and most modern forms of State planning and one of the most enlightened higher civil service structures in the world. This may not have been in the past the main aim of centralization, but governments had quickly realized that a strong hand could be accepted only if it had a visible effect on the landscape, the cities, and the social benefits.

The real contribution of the Republic, mostly since the 1880s, was the new political culture; this spread almost uniformly, through the centralized educational system which was a by-product of the more general centralized structure of the State. For such men as Jules Ferry (1832–1893)—one of the most important Education ministers of the whole of the Republican period—the State education system was to give Frenchmen a political culture. This was to be liberal, lay, egalitarian; it was not to be imparted in a totalitarian fashion; it was to aim at developing the critical faculties of children. But it was, nonetheless, a culture imparted to all, particularly at the primary school level. It was based on the spirit and frame of mind which had characterized the writers of the French Enlightenment, and particularly Voltaire (1694–1778), who had waged for about half a century a war against the power of the Church and of the State, which not only robbed men of their liberty and reason, but obliterated the latter in the expectation of reducing thereby the number of competitors for power and for the satisfactions of society. From him comes the open mind, the persistent inquisitiveness, the rejection of authority which were to be (or are said to be) the characteristics of Frenchmen. The tradition was indeed modernized and applied to the Republic itself by Émile Chartier (1868–1951)—known under the penname of Alain—a professor of philosophy in one of the best known State secondary schools (the Lycée Henri-IV in Paris) who, during most of the Third Republic, embodied the purest tradition of libertarian individualism. He preached an unflagging resistance to authority in all its forms. Indeed, his teachings, though based on suspicion and defiance of tyranny of the highest order, clearly fostered the French negative attitudes towards government which were to prove damaging for the morale of the country at the time of the Second World War.

This critical frame of mind was probably instilled too quickly to too many, through the village schoolteacher, the *instituteur*, who was to become the "priest" of the Republic and whose opposition to the *curé* became the classic joke of French parochial politics before the two groups settled down in the second half of the twentieth century to a more stable and easy-going relationship. The republican ideology undermined the tradition of authority on which all states, even republican ones, have to be based; only the centralized administration could enable the State to maintain itself. But France probably needed to go through a period in which an ideology of criticism was paramount. At a time when most European countries were still governed by authoritarian governments and after the nation had gone through various regimes in the nineteenth century, authoritarianism seemed a permanent threat and the republican regime felt that it needed to instill among the masses a profound aversion to the "powers"; France might have been able to move gradually towards a liberal form of democracy even if the government had not tried to spread such an ideology, but it is understandable that politicians of the time should have thought it necessary to defend the regime in which they believed by extolling republican virtues and decrying non-republican ones. By emphasizing the right to criticize, by teaching others to use, and abuse, their critical minds, they created problems for their successors; the political system has been bedeviled in the twentieth century by the very success of the Republicans of the 1880s and 1890s who bequeathed their political culture to masses of their fellow citizens. But had the Republicans not been so successful, France might not have been a Republic for long. By and large, the mass of the population generally agrees after over a century of fights and oppositions to the tenets of republicanism. Many of the historical and geographical divisions of French society have thus been overcome, and the achievements of centralization, both administrative and cultural, surely constitute an interesting and, in the last analysis, tolerably successful experiment in social engineering.

The Constitution

As in most countries, a constitution is in France a means of legalizing a new social or political situation which is sufficiently different from past conditions to necessitate a redefinition of the political-legal base on which the authority of government and the rights of the people are anchored. Implicit in this definition is the existence of dissatisfaction with previous arrangements—dissatisfaction strong enough to justify defiance of the most basic legal contours of the State. In France, this defiance has often been expressed first by violence, with adjustment of constitutions following shortly afterwards. This is by no means a uniquely French phenomenon, but it has happened more often in France than in most Western nations. From 1791 to 1958, France has known sixteen constitutions, most of which were admittedly shortlived and two of which (those of 1793 and 1814) were not applied at all. Eight of the sixteen were born and dead in the quarter of the century which elapsed between 1789 and 1814; but, even if one considers the period after 1814, constitutional change has tended to take place every fifteen years or even sometimes less. The Revolution of 1830 brought about a new Charter for the monarchy. The Revolution of 1848 led to the Constitution of the Second Republic. The coup d'etat of Louis-Napoleon, who was to become Emperor under the title of Napoleon III (and not Napoleon II because the son of the Great Napoleon was deemed by the Bonapartists to have reigned, though he spent almost all of his short life in exile) brought about the Constitution of 1852. This authoritarian document was liberalized by stages in the 1860s and replaced by an altogether parliamentary text by the Emperor himself in 1870. The war, defeat, and Revolution of 1870 led in 1875 to the Constitution of the Third Republic, the only French constitution to date to have lasted over twenty years. Indeed it seemed for a while that abrupt constitutional change had become a thing of the past as the Third Republic appeared to have achieved a kind of equilibrium satisfactory to most Frenchmen. We shall have occasion to note that many features of the Third Republic still characterize French political practices of the Fifth. But the regime collapsed in the defeat of 1940: the last Parliament of the Third Republic voted "full powers" to Pétain, who, under the protection of the German invasion, sought to introduce, as we noted earlier, a "corporate State." The Third Republic (and much of its personnel) never recovered from giving in to Pétain and in some way agreeing to the demise of the

Republic. Hence, on his return to France, De Gaulle, who had led the *Résistance* first from London and later from Algiers, asked the people by referendum whether the Constitution of the Third Republic was to remain in force or a new document drafted. An overwhelming majority (96 percent) took the latter view, and with difficulty—two successive drafts had to be presented to the people, as the first was rejected in the popular referendum—the Fourth Republic Constitution came into force. It collapsed in May, 1958, effectively because a rebellion of French soldiers had taken place in Algiers, legally because the last National Assembly of the regime (in a way which was for many members of the Assembly rather reminiscent of what had happened eighteen years earlier) enabled the new Prime Minister, General De Gaulle, to draft a new Constitution and submit it to the people. A referendum thus took place in September, 1958, at which the Constitution of the Fifth Republic was adopted by 80 percent of the voters, in a record poll of 85 percent. The parallel which could be drawn between 1940 and 1958 ended with this overwhelming popular approval of the new regime.

It may seem legitimate to ask: What is the meaning of a constitution in the minds of the citizens of a country which has known so many? But, in fact, the answer is more simple than it would seem at first sight, at least for the French of the present generations. Since 1875, except for the Vichy period, France had three Republics, but has remained "The Republic"; with the expression of "The Republic" a number of concepts, of myths, even of emotions, are profoundly associated. What the Third, Fourth, and Fifth Republics have in common is a "certain vision" of the character of politics, based as we saw earlier on liberal, lay, democratic, and unitary principles. Differences between the three constitutions are, in the main, at the level of institutional arrangements; they are concerned with the types of changes which may be, could have been, and indeed sometimes are dealt with by amendments. In fact, perhaps the most momentous change which occurred since 1875 took place not through a wholesale constitutional upheaval, but through an amendment approved, admittedly, by referendum: the 1962 reform which led to the election of the President of the Republic by universal suffrage.

Yet, if "The Republic" and its principles are generally approved of by all, Frenchmen are well aware of the impermanence of constitutions. This does to some extent affect their behavior. The long spell of constitutional stability in the Third Republic has been superseded once more, since World War II, by a period in which French politicians are very unlikely to consider as "sacred" or even very significant the constitutional document under which they live. It does not follow that they are markedly more cynical about their Constitution than the citizens of other democratic countries; but more politicians in France than elsewhere are simply inclined to think of overall constitutional change as more than a remote possibility and to play down "mere" amendments when they can revamp the general frame. The events of 1958 clearly reinforced this feeling, simply because the Constitution changed once more. As a result, and very understandably, many had "waited for Godot," so to speak, ever since the beginning of the Fifth Republic and remained on the sidelines, as far as possible, with a new Constitution in mind.

It is a commonly held view that the Constitution of 1958 was tailor-made for General De Gaulle, who was to become in December, 1958 the first President of the Republic under the new regime. This is, in fact, only partly true; it would be truer to say that the Constitution is *becoming* more and more tailor-made for De Gaulle, partly as a result of constitutional amendment, partly as a result of customary change. We shall examine these somewhat more in detail in the next chapter. What has to be underlined, however, is the fact that the Constitution, as it was drafted in the summer of 1958, was very much the result of a compromise between the Gaullists and the other political forces which were deemed to be electorally much stronger than they in fact proved to be at the time of the referendum; this compromise was essentially an attempt at reconciling two very different views of the nature of the changes which were thought to be necessary. The Algiers rebellion and the inability of the last government of the Fourth Republic to deal with it had blatantly shown what was already clear in the previous decade, namely that a strengthening of the executive was imperative; we shall examine later the reasons for the weakness of the executive, most of which stem from the large number and loose character of the parties. Thus, many political leaders agreed on the desirability of stronger governments, and suggestions had been made for some time which devised various procedures by which this aim could be achieved. Meanwhile, De Gaulle wanted an entirely different type of executive, in which the President would have a much "higher" role and would be concerned with the "permanent" interests of the nation.

The compromise was difficult to arrange since the French "republican" tradition is opposed to and suspicious of the presidential system of government in which, as in the United States, the executive is legally separated from the legislature. This suspicion dates from the middle of the nineteenth century, in fact from the events which followed the implementation of the Constitution of 1848. The popularly elected President was then the second Bonaparte, who proceeded to overthrow the regime after only three years. Rightly or wrongly, supporters of the Republic thought that only a parliamentary system on the British model was suitable for France, if she was to keep liberal institutions, and this view seemed supported by the fact that the 1875 Constitution, the only one which lasted for a considerable period, was of a parliamentary kind: indeed, though the regime had been subjected to various internal threats, no one had been able to take over the government by force. Thus, perhaps naturally, the drafters of the Constitution of the Fourth Republic never conceived of any other system but the parliamentary model, though they introduced devices designed to increase the authority of the Prime Minister. These proved to be of no real value, but by 1958 the memories of 1848, kept alive by the experience of the Vichy regime under the German occupation and, very recently, by the military intervention in Algiers, made many political leaders wary of any change which would model the powers of the head of the executive too closely on those of the American President.

The Constitution of 1958 is therefore a compromise; it has potentialities in various directions. Some moves in one of the directions have already taken place. It is not at all inconceivable —indeed, it is very possible—that moves in another might take place in the future. At one level, the Constitution introduces a modified version of the traditional parliamentary system, strengthened by various devices, some of which had already been tried in the Fourth Republic, but many of which had been only conceived, and not turned into law, before 1958. This section is the "politicians'" Constitution. It has been described by its authors as a modernization of out-of-date practices. The assumptions underlying the Constitutions of the Third and Fourth Republics were not different from those on which the Revolution of 1789 had started: that the legislature existed to protect the people from the ambitious wielders of national executive power. By far the most effective way to achieve this aim was to parcel out small doses of power (which could be withdrawn at any time) to governments performing minimum essential tasks of day-to-day operations—governments which were not really dangerous because they were legally only committees of the all-powerful legislature. But the actual conditions of government under the Third and Fourth Republics were moving increasingly away from such a model. The weakness of the executive, its permanent subordination to the Assembly—or rather the insecure position which it held in relation to the Assembly, in great contrast to the secure position of the British executive in relation to the House of Commons—complicated the task of implementing an effective and consistent program of governmental action to the point where the system tended to defeat itself: premiers were forced to ask for emergency powers to carry out the programs of reform, particularly of a financial and economic kind, which the country needed. The complexities of industrial society in mid-twentieth century were beyond the capacities of governments without power, tenure, or freedom of action. Leaders who chose to defy the realities of legislative power in the Fourth Republic and displayed vigor and determination—men such as Pierre Mendès-France—tried to fortify their own authority by appealing to the public over the heads of the legislators. But in so doing they roused parliamentary hostility and, in the long run, risked falling in the political wilderness.

Moreover, a by-product of weak government had been the growth of administrative power: as we said, this trend had started before the Revolution under the *Ancien Régime* and had been continued by Napoleon. From the seventeenth century on, the Kings had sought to hold France together through the development of an efficient and centralized administrative machine, which practiced intervention in the economic field and thus tended to offset the weaknesses of French private enterprise. To a large extent, liberal institutions were superimposed on the administrative organization of the monarchy and the Empire; supporters of the Republic noted at the end of the nineteenth century that France "had the Republic on top, but the Empire underneath." Thus, the development of bureaucratic power in the twentieth century, which troubled all modern democratic states, tended to hit France rather earlier than any other Western nation. If premiers were weak by virtue of the strict surveillance imposed on them by suspicious legislatures, the administrators, entrusted with the day-to-day implementation of policies, often operated with much greater freedom; there was a degree of policy initiation by the bureaucracy which was much more extensive in France than elsewhere: throughout the twelve years of the Fourth Republic, perhaps the greatest experiment in social and economic intervention in the whole of the free world, the French Plan, was initiated, developed, and implemented with very little intervention on the part of the assembly and even of the government. But while the French technocracy was undoubtedly "enlightened," it was not really responsible. The weakness of the political structures, and in particular of the government, accounted for this failure.

Thus, demands for a strengthening of the executive grew in the course of the Fourth Republic on various technical grounds. But De Gaulle's conception of the role of the executive was a much more exalted one. His views were partly molded by his own past, which was that of a "nationalist" member of the military of the 1930s, but they were reinforced by the events of 1940, when the last President of the Third Republic, Albert Lebrun, gave in to the defeatist policies of Pétain and agreed to the combined collapse of the Republic and of independent France. De Gaulle was determined to modify the institutions in such a way as to make a repetition of such events impossible. Back from Algiers in 1944, he hoped that the newly-elected constituent Assembly would strengthen the executive, and in particular turn the President into a "guide" or "steward" of the nation. However, the Assembly, still motivated by the classic fears of Bonapartism which were discussed earlier, would not entrust the President with such a mission. De Gaulle thus decided to oppose the new regime and, in 1946, outlined his own views of what the Constitution should be in a famous speech at Bayeux, in Normandy. In particular, he asked for a strong President who would embody the legitimacy of the Nation, and could, in an emergency, prevent the disruption of the political system. He was keenly aware of the unconstitutional character of his own action in 1940, whereby he declared that the orders of the Pétain government were not binding on him and on the French people. He wanted provisions in the Constitution which would make it possible to avoid the kind of dilemma in which he had been at the time of the French defeat. The life and death of the Fourth Republic between 1946 and 1958 convinced him even more of the necessity of such provisions; as in 1940, De Gaulle's action in 1958 had a somewhat irregular character. Thus, once more, the dilemma between constitutional action and what De Gaulle calls "legitimate action" tended in his view to strengthen the case for a strong Presidency and in particular for the granting of emergency powers to the President in order to enable him to act if necessary beyond the "normal" arrangements of legal procedures.

Thus the Constitution of 1958 was born as a compromise between the "republicans" belonging to the political parties of the Fourth Republic, generally in agreement about the case for some measure of change which would increase the stability and effectiveness of the *executive*, and De Gaulle and his followers, who wanted essentially to enhance the role of the *President*. From the day De Gaulle came to power and committed Michel Debré to draft the new Constitution, the constraints stemming from tradition and the need for a compromise were evident. In delegating its constituent powers to De Gaulle on June 3, 1958, the National Assembly refused to let the new head of the government establish a Presidency on American lines: it was stated that the President had to be a different person from the Prime Minister (a key distinction of the "parliamentary" or "cabinet" system of government, as it makes it possible to have both a government which determines the policy and a President—or a King in monarchies—who "reigns but does not govern" thus ensuring the continuity of the State); it was also stated that the government was to be "responsible" politically to Parliament, and that it should remain in office only as long as it had the confidence of the majority of the National Assembly (this, too, being one of the key distinctions between the parliamentary and presidential systems of government). Perhaps somewhat surprisingly, De Gaulle did accept these limitations to his freedom to shape the Constitution; indeed, when presenting the new document later in the summer, Michel Debré argued very forcefully that the new system was parliamentary. But, as a result, De Gaulle was not at liberty to implement to the full his conception of the Presidency: Debré was to deem the President an "arbiter," not a "leader" or "guide." Admittedly, arbitration is an ambiguous concept; one could vary the interpretation from the idea of a more positive role (clearly De Gaulle's view) to that of a more neutral function (clearly the "correct" interpretation of the law of the Constitution).

With so many compromises having taken place at the beginning, it is not surprising that the Constitution should have been ambiguous in part and that efforts should have been made to modify both the letter and the spirit of the law. As De Gaulle remained the holder of real power in the first phase of the Fifth Republic, he has constantly made efforts to mold and remold the original text in the direction which he thought best, and he has been helped by circumstances. The Algerian war and the strain on the morale of the Army led to various covert and two overt attempts at overthrowing the government; this seemed at least to give substance to the claim that the President had to have emergency powers, though, as we shall see, the effectiveness of such powers is very much to be doubted. The evolution of the political system and the clashes between the opposition parties seemed to point to one and only one alternative to the confusion of the Third and Fourth Republics: namely the introduction of a full presidential system. At the same time, however, and possibly most importantly, De Gaulle benefited from the hitherto unprecedented fact of having in the National Assembly the support of a majority of deputies belonging to a party which was both disciplined and solidly behind him: the Gaullist party, the UNR, which was to be the instrument through which De Gaulle could obtain parliamentary approval for his policies, was the largest party at the first General Election of the Fifth Republic in 1958; it obtained almost an overall majority at the subsequent election on 1962 after De Gaulle had dissolved the Assembly when it overthrew the Government by a vote of censure. This characteristic sequence of most parliamentary democracies—censure, dissolution, return of a majority—had not taken place in France for over half a century, partly because of the number of parties and partly because of the subordination of the Government to the Assembly.

Thus it became possible for De Gaulle first, to intervene in a number of matters which were not clearly within the province of the President according to the Constitution; second, to show the weight of his stewardship at the time of the Algerian crisis; and third, to move for a change in the procedure of election of the President—though nothing was done to change the distribution of powers between President and Government and between executive and legislature. The first election of the President by universal suffrage, in December of 1965, seemed to vindicate De Gaulle's assertion that the popular election of the President would by itself increase the authority of the incumbent. The electoral campaign aroused considerable excitement (the turnout was greater than it had ever been, over 85 percent), and the opposition became much more united—since only two candidates could stand at the second ballot, a tendency to compromise appeared at the first. The popular election of the President may thus come to be a springboard in future moves towards presidential rule; it may equally be De Gaulle's last effort to bring the country round to his view of the political system. Only time will tell, but it is clear that the changes which have taken place between 1958 and

1965 have been at least as important (if not more important) for the shaping of the new regime as the text of the Constitution itself.

Five other arrangements need to be outlined before we consider in somewhat more detail the structure of the executive and of the legislature. First, in order to ensure the strengthening of the executive, which, as we noted, was desired both by De Gaulle and by the political leaders of the Fourth Republic, a number of limitations of a procedural kind, some of which were copied on procedural devices adopted by the British Parliament, were introduced into the Constitution. Restrictions are placed on the length of legislative sessions, on the freedom of deputies to initiate legislation (restrictions did exist before 1958, but they were not written in the Constitution), on parliamentary budgetary power, on the subjects which need to be regulated by law, on the number of parliamentary committees, on the length of debate when the Government wishes the discussion to be closed, and, perhaps most importantly, on the procedure by which the Assembly can censure the Government. The executive has a clear advantage in the distribution of power, a situation which did not obtain in the Third and Fourth Republics.

Second, the Constitution of the Fifth Republic increases somewhat the powers of the Upper Chamber, the Senate, which had very much suffered from the Constitution of 1946. In the Fourth Republic, the Senate, renamed the Council of the Republic in order to show its loss of status, had no overriding power to veto legislation; it could in practice only force the Assembly to discuss for the second time the bills which it had passed. Though a reform had taken place in 1954 which had slightly increased the powers of the Council, the main limitation was not substantially removed. In 1958, drafters of the Constitution attempted an imaginative rescue of the Senate, first by increasing its authority and magnifying its position of Upper Chamber, and second by deciding that the Senate could veto all bills, except if the Government wanted the Assembly to have the last word. Thus the Senate was no longer to be in the way of the Government (as it often had been in the Third Republic), but could prevent the National Assembly from embarking on rash and inconsiderate legislation which the Government felt no need for. In fact, while nobody had expected it at the time, the Senate proved much more "difficult" to the Government than the National Assembly, as Gaullists never managed to obtain more than a small minority of members in the Upper Chamber.

Third, great emphasis is placed in the Constitution of the Fifth Republic on the referendum, not only for constitutional amendments, but even for ordinary legislation. The Constitution of the Fourth Republic allowed for referendums in certain constitutional cases, but this was not mandatory if a substantial majority of Parliament adopted the amendment; in fact, no referendum took place between the adoption of the Constitution of 1946 and the adoption of the Constitution of 1958. But De Gaulle likes referendums (his ideal type of government could perhaps be defined as presidential rule tempered by an extensive usage of the referendum for important matters) and, between 1958 and 1962, the French people were asked for an opinion in no less than four cases. Two of these involved constitutional matters, but the other two, though dealing with the structure of the State (they concerned the future of Algeria) were designed to test the views of the people on policy. The referendum is clearly a device by which the power of the National Assembly is undermined (it was used in two cases as a substitute for a parliamentary debate and not merely to confirm a parliamentary decision) but it is also an indication of a new style of French political life. As it has not been used during the second legislature of the Fifth Republic, it may be that De Gaulle has come to see the advantages of Government through a majority in Parliament and is unlikely to use the weapon again, unless he wants to impose the "will" of the French people on a reluctant or lukewarm Assembly. But, whether as an interim or as an emergency procedure, the use of the referendum constitutes a break from the republican tradition which always asserted parliamentary supremacy. It is one of the ways in which the Gaullist Republic has been compared to the Empire. No other President besides De Gaulle is likely to have the moral authority to make the same extensive use of the new weapon.

Fourth, and potentially importantly, the Constitution of the Fifth Republic includes a provision for a Constitutional Council. Traditionally, in republican France, Parliament not only dominated the other institutions of government, but its decisions expressed in legislation were unchallengeable. There was thus no room for judicial review as practiced in the United States (though in this France did not differ from many European countries, including Britain). The establishment of the Constitutional Council points to a modest experiment in judicial review. A first and very limited move in this direction had already taken place in 1946; but as a result of the.restriction in the powers of the Assembly in the 1958 Constitution, the Council was made to function not only as an umpire between the two Chambers, as in 1946, but as an arbiter between the legislature and the Government. In a conflict or dispute over the distribution of powers between the two organs of the State—for example, in order to decide whether a matter should be dealt with by legislative action or by a regulation issued by the Government—the Council may be called to intervene. Like the United States Supreme Court, the French Constitutional Council is deemed to implement the Constitution, but, in so doing, it obviously has a wide scope for interpretation. Unlike the Supreme Court, however, it cannot be called by ordinary citizens to adjudicate in constitutional conflicts; only the President of the National Assembly, the President of the Senate, the President of the Republic and the Prime Minister can bring a dispute to the Council.

It is as yet too soon to state whether the Constitutional Council will remain a part of the "living" constitution. More than any other institution of the Fifth Republic, its existence implies a reversal of the traditional French constitutional theory of the supremacy of Parliament in statutory matters. Because it is independent of the legislature (though its members are appointed for nine years, one-third of them by the President of the National Assembly, another third by the President of the Senate, and the last third by the President of the Republic, and the terms are not renewable), it has served so far as a watchdog over a Parliament generally impatient with the limitations imposed by the Constitution. Indeed, it seemed often to be timid in relation to governmental intervention and particularly anxious to help the executive. Yet the Constitutional Council may survive the passing of De Gaulle, for its actions seem popular and the opposition parties, far from being opposed to this new experiment in judicial review, appear anxious to expand it; the progam of all the major noncommunist organizations for the 1967 General Election included a section aiming at creating a "real" Supreme Court. But such a change is unlikely to take place before the Gaullist phase of the Fifth Republic is over; meanwhile the Constitutional Council may eventually suffer a setback during the transition which will follow, particularly if a period of parliamentary supremacy replaces, as a reaction, the long spell of executive dominance which marked the early part of the Fifth Republic.

The fifth reform introduced by the Constitution of 1958 is mainly concerned with the past, though it may, in a rather different way, affect some political developments of the future. It is concerned with the abandonment, at first very partial and timid, and later full-fledged, of the principle of the unitary State which had dominated for generations the relations between France and its overseas territories. Up to and during most of the Fourth Republic, the principle of "assimilation," applied either conservatively or liberally, had remained practically unchallenged, at least among the French. Under this system, a French commissioner or governor-general took decisions, on behalf of the French Republic, in each of the colonies (renamed "overseas territories" in 1946), and local political leaders were admitted to the French Parliament on a full and equal footing (at least in theory, as, in practice, universal suffrage was slow to come, the principle of the common roll was accepted very late, and constituencies tended to be larger in population). French citizenship and participation in French political affairs were assumed to be the universal desire of the formerly dependent peoples. Only in the last two years of the Fourth Republic were provisions adopted which recognized the national character of overseas territories. Moreover, even then, the principle was maintained that these territories were being offered the opportunity to prepare only for autonomy within the framework of the French Republic and not for independence even in association with France.

The Constitution of the Fifth Republic went somewhat further, though in the first instance it did not provide for the possibility of independence. A French Community was established but in the 1958 version, at least, this organization was a far cry from the British Commonwealth. The constitutional articles describing the Community provided for a large number of powers to be exercised by the French Government and gave little scope for the "States of the Community" to exercise even a right of veto. The only organs created by the Constitution were an Executive Council presided over by the President of the Community (ex-officio the French President) and comprising the heads of the States of the Community and the ministers (all from the French Government) who dealt with Community matters; a Senate of the Community, whose powers were mainly consultative; and a Court of Arbitration, which was to deal with disputes between member-States. This was an important step, however, as a French Constitution had recognized for the first time that overseas territories should have the status of "states." Moreover, the political evolution was to overtake the provisions of the Constitution with great rapidity. Events in Algeria made it impossible for the French Government to entertain even remotely the possibility of colonial war with its possessions in West Africa. In 1960, the Constitution was amended so as to allow the States of the Community to become independent within the Community. (Article 86 of the Constitution had offered member-States of the Community the freedom to leave the Community, but not to become independent if they stayed within it.) With the granting of independence to Algeria in 1962, France ceased to have a major colonial problem, though there are still a number of smaller dependencies, all of which have much closer ties with France, since they have remained either "overseas departments" or "overseas territories." For these, too, the question of independence will arise. Indeed, and this is where the Constitution of the Fifth Republic may make future changes possible, ideas of self-government and regional autonomy have grown within metropolitan France itself. We shall see in later chapters how developments in the economic field may be leading to the creation of new *regions;* a new approach to political life may also increase local devolution of powers. While full-blown "federalism" within metropolitan France is clearly beyond current practical policies, the word is no longer "dirty" in political circles and it may provide the solution to some of the conflicts between the necessary movement toward large economic units and the demands for more self-government at the local level.

Frenchmen noticed very quickly that there was much "mixture" in the Constitution of 1958. For those who believe that the French are accustomed to seeking principles or systems of logic in their patterns of life and thought, this may seem surprising. The new Constitution does not, even after the most careful study, fit into any single philosophical mold. Its various parts do not mesh together and produce a system which could be neatly labeled "presidential" or "parliamentary." It includes elements of both; it was based on compromises between people whose political philosophies were widely different and who had opposed each other for the best part or even all of the twelve years of the Fourth Republic. No one had really obtained what he wanted, though, at first sight at least, De Gaulle seemed to expect rather less than what he could have hoped for and the political leaders managed to preserve the basic features of the "parliamentary" system.

The changes which have taken place since 1958 have all been to the benefit of De Gaulle, however. Practices and constitutional amendments have turned the Constitution more presidential— or at any rate more hybrid—than it was in its first phase. The Fifth Republic is more and more De Gaulle's Republic. Where the movement will stop is difficult to tell, not only because no one knows how long De Gaulle will remain head of the State, but also because no one knows either how far De Gaulle himself wishes to move towards presidential government. The present system enables him to exercise considerable powers; he runs the executive, as we shall shortly see in detail, but he can also control the legislature, thanks to the majority party which supports him and to the power of dissolution which he may, in case of necessity, use against the Chamber. But events may force De Gaulle to accept a clearer version of presidentialism. His views and subsequent policies have been modified in many fields, not only in the colonial field. Changes which have taken place in the nature and behavior of the political parties may indeed perhaps even lead him to recognize the value of a more precisely defined pattern of government which, by not being so closely dependent upon his authority, will be more likely to be maintained after his disappearance from the political scene.

: The Executive

Though we noticed earlier that the reality of the Constitution of 1958 was becoming more presidential, the theory remains largely based on the principles of parliamentary government. Indeed, according to Michel Debré, who was the chief engineer of the Constitution, "the parliamentary regime was the only one suitable for France." The system remains parliamentary, according to the letter of the law, because it has two basic features, which characterize all the parliamentary and cabinet systems of government throughout Western Europe and the old British Commonwealth: 1) the executive is divided into two organs: the Head of State, whose main function is to ensure the continuity of the nation, and the Government, which, led by the Prime Minister, is in charge of policy-making and policy implementation; 2) the Government is collectively responsible to the National Assembly, which can, by vote of censure, force its resignation.

The analysis of the working of the system is complicated, however, because during the formative period of the regime, the first President of the Republic, General De Gaulle, has taken over powers which were not constitutionally his, except in a purely formal sense. It is difficult to ascertain which of these powers will be retained in a substantive fashion by future Presidents, since De Gaulle's intervention was facilitated by the existence of the French equivalent of the "royal prerogative," which is mostly exercised by the Prime Minister in Britain and was indeed, before 1958, exercised mainly by the French Cabinet. Thus it is important that the position stemming from the letter and spirit of the Constitution should be made clear before one examines the extent to which De Gaulle has acted *ultra vires*, either formally, as was the case in some instances, or more commonly, informally.

THE PRESIDENCY OF THE REPUBLIC

The President of the Republic is meant to be the Head of State and, according to the letter and spirit of the Constitution, he should in normal circumstances be no more than that. De Gaulle's position has always been somewhat unclear on the theory of the office because of the combination of two reasons. First, he is simply not interested in many aspects of government; we shall see that there is a horizontal division of powers between De Gaulle and the rest of the administration, largely because, in the last resort, De Gaulle cares much more for certain "exalted" aspects of politics than for others (when writing his memoirs on the period immediately following the end of World War II, he noted that he pitied Germany at the time because the only things which its government could be involved in were housing and reconstruction). Second, De Gaulle appears to be concerned mainly with periods of emergency in his analysis of the "ideal type" power of the President. He wanted, as we saw in the previous chapter, to avoid a repetition of the 1940 situation in which the last President of the Third Republic had no power to intervene while the Government was conceding defeat. Thus it is not possible to argue that even De Gaulle himself would want the President to have the kind of power which is bestowed upon an American Chief Executive; he probably wants the President to be in a position to intervene if and when the latter thinks that the "long-term" interests of France are at stake.

Thus the President of the Republic has only a limited set of powers in normal times. The bulk of these existed in the Third and Fourth Republics, and at best, the Constitution of the Fifth Republic simply marked a return to the situation of the Third Republic on a number of points where the Constitution of 1946 had trimmed the powers of the President to the benefit of the Prime Minister. There is therefore nothing unusual, by French "republican" standards, in the following eight powers being granted to the President: 1) Appointment of the Prime Minister and of the ministers on the proposal of the Prime Minister (but the President does not have the power to dismiss the Premier); 2) Promulgation of laws voted by Parliament; the President may ask Parliament to reconsider a law within two weeks of its having been voted, but he has no power of veto; 3) Signature of decrees, including those appointing some higher civil servants and officers of the armed forces (but the decrees must be approved by the Council of Ministers); 4) Chairmanship of the Council of Ministers; 5) Chairmanship of the High Councils of the armed forces; 6) Right to send messages to the National Assembly; 7) Ratification of treaties, which are negotiated in his name; 8) Power of pardon.

All these powers existed in the Third Republic, a regime which was not conspicuous for the authority of its Presidents; practically all of them existed in the Fourth. The President of the Fourth Republic had lost the power of formal appointment of the Prime Minister (but he had a power of "designation" of the candidate who was to be formally appointed by the National Assembly; the substance and practice were not modified) and the power to sign decrees (which had been given to the Prime Minister in order to increase his status, not so much vis-à-vis the President as vis-à-vis the rest of the Government). Moreover, it must be noted that in all three Republics, decisions of the President are not valid unless countersigned by the Prime Minister and, where appropriate, by some of the ministers. The technique of the countersignature is basic to the operation of the parliamentary system; the "seal of authority" of the State, so to speak, is given to a decision in the form of the presidential signature, but the only persons who are deemed to be responsible are the members of the Government and not the Head of State. No particular significance must therefore be attributed to the fact that the President of the Fifth Republic signs decrees or ratifies treaties; this is deemed simply to mean—in the tradition of French constitutional practice—that the President gives State authority to measures decided by others who have countersigned them.

There are four powers which are new to the Fifth Republic and which are the prerogative of the President alone, however. But, by their very nature, and by the restrictions to which they are subjected, they are powers which can be exercised only at rare intervals or in emergencies. In these cases, the President does not require the countersignature of the Prime Minister; they are truly and substantively presidential acts. First, the President can dissolve the National Assembly. In most parliamentary systems, and in particular in Britain, the right of dissolution is entirely open to the executive, and thus deadlocks in the governmental machinery can be solved by an appeal to the people. This was not the case in France, and it had indeed always been argued, wrongly as the analysis of political parties in Chapter Six will show, that one of the main problems of the French Republic was the fact that the executive could dissolve the Assembly only in special circumstances or with certain guarantees. In the Third Republic, the right of dissolution could be exercised, but only after approval of the Senate; in fact, the prerogative was used only once, in 1877, in order to maintain a conservative government in power, and the result was the return of a radical majority, the eventual resignation of the President of the Republic, and a customary *modus vivendi* whereby the right of dissolution was no longer used. In the Fourth Republic, the right of dissolution was, rather as it is in the Federal Republic of Germany, limited by rigorous conditions and linked to two cabinet crises occurring under certain conditions within eighteen months of each other. It was used once, in 1955, but had little effect on the nature of the political game. Since 1958, the Constitution has allowed the President to dissolve, not more than once a year, after having consulted the Prime Minister and the Presidents of the two Chambers of Parliament. Thus the President can, if he so wishes, try to solve a deadlock between Cabinet and Parliament by asking the people to adjudicate, but he cannot repeat the process nor can he use the procedure in order to force a Government on a reluctant Parliament. Unless he wishes to resort to a *coup d'état,* the President must accept the verdict of the people or resign— as was the case in the 1877–1879 episode: his choice is between "submission or resignation" (*"se soumettre ou se démettre"*). When, in 1962, De Gaulle dissolved the first Parliament of the Fifth Republic (after four of the five years of the Assembly had elapsed), he acted in a perfectly constitutional manner; the Government had been defeated by a vote of censure (over the procedure adopted by the Government to change the method of election of the President of the Republic, a procedure which clearly was not constitutional, as we shall see), and the President decided not to accept the resignation of the Government, which had been forwarded to him by the Premier, but to dissolve the Assembly instead. The General Election of November, 1962 sizeably increased the Gaullist representation in the House; thus the people had vindicated De Gaulle's decision to dissolve.

The second and third new powers give two opposite opportunities to the President in relation to the submission of bills to the people. On the one hand, the President may decide that a constitutional amendment proposed by the Government to Parliament need not be approved by referendum after it has been adopted by Parliament (which is the normal procedure). In this event, the proposal is sent to a joint meeting of the two Chambers instead of going through the two Chambers separately. This provision is probably designed to accelerate the procedure in cases of rather technical amendments; it has been used in 1960, in order to make it possible for the Community to be transformed into a loose confederation of independent states, and in 1963, to change the timing of the sessions of Parliament.

On the other hand, the President is entitled, on the basis of Article 11 of the Constitution, to refer certain Government bills to the electorate: bills "dealing with the organization of public authorities, carrying approval of a Community agreement, or proposing to authorize the ratification of a treaty which, without being contrary to the Constitution, would affect the functioning of institutions." This Article has led to the clearest cases of unconstitutional action on the part of the President, both in spirit and in letter. Controversies arose at three levels. First, the Article states that the President "may, on the proposal of the Government during parliamentary sessions or on the joint proposal of the two assemblies": in the three cases in which the Article has been used, twice over Algeria and on the last occasion over the method of election of the President, the initiative clearly came from De Gaulle himself; the *form* of a "proposal" by the Government was respected, admittedly, but no one doubted who the real originator of the proposal was. A power which was meant to be one of "arbitration" (to take a favorite Gaullist expression) had been transformed into one of positive action. Second, the Article certainly intended, though it did not expressly state, that the bill be discussed and adopted first by Parliament. Never had there been before, in French practice, any suggestions that a bill might be adopted *either* by Parliament *or* by the people; clearly, the latter procedure has the effect of leaving no opportunity for amendment of the governmental proposal at any stage of the public discussion. Yet in all three cases, the bill was submitted to a referendum and was not discussed by Parliament. Third, and this time without any shadow of doubt, a bill presented in this way to the people cannot be a constitutional amendment. Though Article 11 says that "the President of the Republic may . . . submit to a referendum any bill dealing with the organization of governmental authorities . . ." this is unquestionably to the exclusion of the Constitution itself, since Article 89 provides for a special procedure which includes a referendum (except in the case mentioned above). Yet De Gaulle used Article 11 to introduce the proposal that the President be elected by universal suffrage—which entailed a modification of Article 6 of the Constitution. This proposal, which led to the referendum of October, 1962 and created considerable stir (including, as we saw, the fall of the Government and the dissolution of the National Assembly) was possibly the one case of unconstitutional action by the President which can in no way be "cleared" (the Council of State, asked about the procedure, declared that the use of Article 11 was improper; the Constitutional Council, in one of the several cases in which it appeared to be "subservient" to the executive, declared itself incompetent). The people did approve of the change, however, and the discussion about the unconstitutional character of the action has thus become somewhat academic.

The fourth new power of the President is the one which created most controversy at the time of the drafting of the Constitution (unlike Article 11 which passed almost unnoticed). Article 16 allows the President to assume full powers in certain emergencies:

When the institutions of the Republic, the independence of the nation, the integrity of its territory, or the fulfillment of its international commitments are threatened in a grave and immediate manner, and when the regular functioning of the constitutional governmental authorities is interrupted, the President of the Republic shall take the measures commanded by these circumstances, after official consultation with the Premier, the Presidents of the Assemblies and the Constitutional Council.

He shall inform the nation of these measures in a message.

These measures must be prompted by the desire to ensure to the constitutional governmental authorities, in the shortest possible time, the means of fulfilling their assigned functions. The Constitutional Council shall be consulted with regard to such measures.

Parliament shall meet by right.

The National Assembly may not be dissolved during the exercise of emergency powers.

Article 16 was hailed by De Gaulle's supporters as the means by which constitutional catastrophes such as that of 1940 could be avoided; opponents saw in it the means by which a legal dictatorship could be established. In fact, neither seems to be the case. The Article bears the stamp of De Gaulle's initiative, but it is handicapped in two ways: first, the guarantee given to Parliament is somewhat ludicrous, if one really thinks in terms of emergencies of the kind mentioned in the first part of the Article; second, powers of this type are no substitute for authority; the fact that the President is mandated to act in this way ("The President shall take the measures . . .") does not in reality give him the power to command the armed forces, the civil service, or any other body. Indeed, one wonders whether De Gaulle did not in fact come to have second thoughts about the Article, after he had the experience of its use in 1961, following the "putsch" of four generals in Algiers. Article 16 was set in motion; a number of measures were passed (including one setting up a Court of Justice). Very quickly, however, various problems arose. Was Parliament entitled to discuss the measures, and only the measures? Or could it discuss anything *but* the measures? If so, what is the value in having it meet? What is the responsibility of the Government in connection with these measures (which are presidential)? When Article 16 ceases to be invoked, do the measures taken lapse *ipso facto*? Must one distinguish between temporary and permanent ones (e.g., the creation of a court)? The operation of the Article proved so cumbersome that it was a great relief for the Government (more than for Parliament!) when at the end of the summer of 1961, Article 16 ceased to be operative. The ones who seemed to have benefited most from the emergency were the farmers, whose lobby was able to make itself more felt, thanks to the Chamber's being in permanent session.

Such are the powers of the President. The new ones clearly point to the main preoccupation which De Gaulle had in overseeing some of the provisions, namely that the President should have "authority" to act as an arbiter. This is probably why, after having accepted, in the first instance as a matter of compromise, that the President of the Republic be elected by a limited electoral college, De Gaulle insisted on seeing through the amendment of 1962 aiming at the election of the President by universal suffrage (with a two-ballot or "run-off" system, the second ballot taking place two weeks after the first between the top two candidates). Opposition to a popular election of the President (the President was elected by the members of the two Houses in the Third and Fourth Republics) was largely due to the fear of "Bonapartism"; as we noted, the only popularly elected President, Louis-Napoleon, turned himself into an Emperor after a *coup d'état* in 1851. In 1958, the political leaders insisted that the President should not be elected by the whole people. A compromise was found, which led to the creation of an electoral college of about 80,000 delegates, mainly representatives of local authority, but this had the defect of over-representing the rural areas. De Gaulle was elected under this arrangement in December, 1958 (he obtained 80 percent of the votes). But the system was unsatisfactory; the size and composition of the electoral college were difficult to justify, and more important, De Gaulle probably feared that after his disappearance Parliament might want to return to the old system which, in his view, did not give enough authority to the President and led to the election of parliamentary manipulators rather than "guides," "stewards," or even "arbiters." He cunningly thought that if popular election was established, it would probably be more difficult for Parliament to come back on the reform, particularly if it had proved successful. It was indeed successful; not only did the people approve of the reform (though unconstitutionally presented) by a majority of over three to two (61.7 percent voted yes), but the first election of the President, in December, 1965, was, as noted earlier, a great occasion for the French people. De Gaulle's reelection was somewhat difficult (he received only 44 percent of the votes cast at the first ballot and 55 percent at the second ballot, with only two candidates left in the field), but the difficulty itself indicated the popularity of the contest. Right and Left became more committed to the popular election of the President than they had ever been; the procedure did work. It may be that, as a result, the Presidency will acquire some of the authority which De Gaulle certainly wished it had had in the past, though the President clearly does not have the powers which he would certainly be granted in a presidential system.

THE GOVERNMENT

While the role of the President is to ensure a "guardianship" of the nation, the role of the Government is to govern. Article 20 of the Constitution states plainly:

The Government shall determine and direct the policy of the nation.
It shall have at its disposal the administration and the armed forces.

And Article 21 continues:

The Premier shall direct the operation of the Government. He shall be responsible for national defense. He shall ensure the execution of the laws. . . .

It is difficult to be less ambiguous. Though the President of the Republic, according to customs dating from the Third Republic, chairs the Council of Ministers, it is the Government as a whole, and in particular its leader, the Prime Minister, who is responsible for the policy of the nation.

As in many other countries, the position of the Prime Minister grew gradually in the course of the last hundred years. The Constitution of 1875 did not formally recognize the Premier, but in practice all governments had a head, who was known then, rather illogically since the President of the Republic chaired the meetings of ministers, as the "President of the Council of Ministers." However, because French governments tended to be uneasy coalitions of prima donnas and representatives of weak parties, the Premier was more often a compromiser and a manipulator than a leader. The Constitution of 1946 sought to increase the authority of the "President of the Council" by an increase of powers (hence the trimming of some of those of the President of the Republic) and by the introduction of certain provisions designed to give the Premier more influence over the Government: the Premier alone was to be designated by the Chamber, and he was to appoint freely the rest of the Cabinet. But these measures were of no avail, as the traditions of compromise and weak coalitions remained the rule. There was little difference between a Premier of the 1930s and a Premier of the 1950s.

The Constitution of 1958 did keep, nonetheless, some of the provisions of the Constitution of 1946 which aimed at buttressing the power of the Premier (now named Prime Minister for the first time). Hence, the statements of Article 21 (leadership of the Government, responsibility for national defense, exercise of the *"pouvoir règlementaire"*—i.e., the power to implement the laws— authority to make appointments to the posts which the President of the Republic is not specifically designated to appoint). Moreover, throughout the Constitution (and we have noted some examples already) the Premier is called for advice; this happens in cases of dissolution, in cases of use of emergency powers (Article 16), and for constitutional amendments. The Constitution stresses the leadership role of the Premier as much as is compatible with the position of the President of the Republic (which the Constitution wishes to establish firmly) and with the collective character of the government (which was maintained from the previous two regimes).

As in most parliamentary democracies (though not in all, Germany being an example of the opposite practice), the French Government was and remains legally a collective organ. This means that decisions of the French Government are deemed to be decisions of all of its members. Collective decision-making is shown by the fact that the important measures of the Government are taken in the Council of Ministers (we noted earlier, for instance, that decrees are signed by the President of the Republic after they have been approved by the Council of Ministers); while the Premier can and does give advice to the President on some matters, it is the Government which is empowered to "determine and direct the policy of the nation." Collective decision-making is also associated with collective responsibility; this operates through the mechanisms of the vote of censure, which entails, if adopted, the resignation of all the ministers. As in other parliamentary democracies, the conflict between the Prime Minister's leadership and collective decision-making is a difficult one to solve. Clearly, there has been less collective decision-making since 1958 than before, but this is much more due to De Gaulle's intervention than to the strong leadership of the Prime Minister, as we shall see in the next section.

Moreover, constitutional provisions and formal arrangements have not modified very markedly the internal structure of the French Government in the Fifth Republic. Names of ministries change from time to time, but the only major reconstruction concerned the armed services (the three separate service departments have been abolished) and it followed an evolution which began in the Fourth Republic. Typically, a Government would have about twenty ministers (slightly fewer than in the last years of the Fourth Republic—partly because the number of "Ministers of State" or "Vice-Presidents of the Council" has been reduced, as these corresponded essentially to the necessity of maintaining in office some political leaders whose support was needed); it would also include a number of Secretaries of State (about a half-dozen —again somewhat fewer than in the Fourth Republic, particularly towards the end).

Behind generally similar formal arrangements, however, some important differences affect the decision-making processes and the whole nature of the Cabinet. At least three of these need to be mentioned. First, ministerial instability has sharply decreased. In the first seven years of the Fifth Republic, France had only two Prime Ministers, Michel Debré and Georges Pompidou; only two Premiers of the Fourth Republic lasted for over a year and no Prime Minister since 1875 lasted continuously in office as long as Pompidou. But stability is not in danger of becoming immobility, as indeed was shown by the change from Michel Debré to Georges Pompidou, even though rumors of change which circulate are unlikely to prove correct. Ministers, on the other hand, move fairly frequently. Before 1958, it was very often noted that Prime Ministers changed much more often than ministers, as if the chairmanship of the Cabinet rotated while the membership remained fairly stable. The rate of change has thus not been markedly modified. While Maurice Couve de Murville remained in charge of Foreign Affairs for over eight years, other departments had a fairly rapid turnover: four different persons held the post of Minister of Finance between 1958 and 1966.

Secondly, attempts have been made, though with rather mixed results, to effect a "depoliticization" of the Government. De Gaulle was very anxious to bring about a change, partly on the grounds that the Government should in some sense be (like himself!) above the daily turmoil of political life; the Government should run the State, and De Gaulle still seems to conceive of politics as an activity which somehow can be divorced from State policy-making, a view which probably stems from the part played by the civil service in the running of modern France. The Fifth Republic has thus been characterized by various attempts at introducing into the Government more administrative practices and more administrators. On coming back to power, in May, 1958, and before the new Constitution was drafted, De Gaulle appointed to his Cabinet members of the civil, foreign, and colonial services, a practice which had been abandoned, except in time of war, for over half a century, and placed these men in some of the key positions. The Minister of Foreign Affairs, for instance, was from the career foreign service. Overall, Fifth Republic cabinets have been between a third and a quarter composed of ministers coming from the administrative corps. The second Prime Minister of the regime, Georges Pompidou, was a teacher and a banker, but never participated in politics before 1962, except as a personal adviser to De Gaulle in the early postwar period.

Another attempt was made in a different way to reduce the temperature of politics: Article 23 of the Constitution, introduced at the specific request of General De Gaulle, forbids ministers to remain members of Parliament after they have been appointed to the Government. This provision, though not unknown in some other parliamentary democracies (Holland, Norway), is nonetheless somewhat peculiar; it does not fit with the idea that the Government emanates from the majority of the Assembly and has to defend its program in Parliament. Indeed, in the French system, ministers do come and speak (though they do not vote) in Parliament. Clearly, De Gaulle hoped that this arrangement would force ministers to abandon their "politician's" outlook and take a "ministerial," i.e., presumably "statesmanlike," air when becoming members of the Government, but it is not clear that the arrangement has had much success. Quite apart from having had a number of rather clumsy effects (such as the appointment of a "substitute" to all members of Parliament in order to avoid a cascade of by-elections at each ministerial reshuffle), the procedure does not appear to have led to considerable variations in the attitudes of the ministers (M. Pompidou has been hailed as a great parliamentarian) except in so far as the system as a whole is dependent on the authority and style of the General, and does not rely so much on compromises, deals, and coalitions.

THE WORKING OF THE EXECUTIVE IN THE FIFTH REPUBLIC

The third institutional change is so closely linked to the practice of the work of the executive during the Gaullist period of the Fifth Republic that structure and behavior need to be considered together. Though, as we saw, the official constitutional arrangements call for a collective executive, it can be doubted whether the Debré and Pompidou cabinets, particularly in certain fields, operated as cabinets in the usual sense. As we noted, the President of the Republic is not constitutionally entitled to determine policies, except in emergencies. Yet, from the very start, De Gaulle intervened in a number of "privileged" sectors to a degree which could in no way be justified either by the texts or even by a liberal interpretation of what constituted emergencies. Admittedly, the Algerian war created an emergency, *de facto* throughout all the period during which it lasted (it ended in 1962 by the granting of Algerian independence) and *de jure* during the six months following the Algiers *coup* which prompted the assumption of powers under Article 16. But De Gaulle did not only intervene in Algerian matters. He showed his desire to lead the country's policies in practically all aspects of foreign, Community, and military affairs. In practice, the President seemed to act according to a division of functions which led to a distinction made by the President of the National Assembly, J. Chaban-Delmas, at the UNR Congress of 1959: on the one hand, there was to be a sector in which the President would initiate and indeed make policy; this was said to be composed essentially of foreign and defense matters, and to include certain key institutional problems, such as the method of election of the President. The second sector was said to comprise all other matters, whether political, social, or economic, in which leadership is generally (but not always, if the situation appears critical) left to the Government. "The presidential sector covers Algeria, not forgetting the Sahara, the Community, foreign affairs and defense. The second sector covers the rest. . . ." In fact, there has been even further interference from the Presidency, as De Gaulle himself admitted in 1964: "Clearly, it is the President alone who holds and delegates the authority of the State. But the very nature, the extent, the duration of his task imply that he is not absorbed without remission or limit by political, parliamentary, economic and administrative contingencies." It is the Prime Minister who deals with these "contingencies," which are his "lot, as complex and meritorious as it is essential." Thus, when De Gaulle is tired of certain policies, he intervenes, as at the end of the bitter coal strike of the winter of 1963 or in order to make sure that France possesses a computer industry, and not merely in such exalted matters as the recognition of China or the stopping of British entry into the Common Market.

Presidential intervention had a double effect on the workings of the government. First, it meant that collective decision-making by the Cabinet, meeting in the Council of Ministers, became something of a myth. Ministers have sometimes been *told* of decisions at meetings of the Cabinet which was supposed to make them. In one case, a speech made by De Gaulle led to ministerial resignations—while the decision should have been collectively taken. Rarely has a consensus emerged during the Council of Ministers which was not the product of presidential "guidance." Moreover, in order to ensure that this "guidance" should be effective, De Gaulle no longer lets the Cabinet meet outside his presence, a practice which was still common in the early period of the Fifth Republic and had become established in the middle period of the Third (meetings of the ministers outside the presence of the President were known as *Conseils de Cabinet*, to distinguish them from the *Conseil des Ministres*, where the decisions were formally and constitutionally taken). Second, the Cabinet was in a sense broken by the practice of hierarchical decision-making, more reminiscent of American executive decision-making than of parliamentary modes of behavior. The President either sees one of the ministers alone and (with or without the Prime Minister) decides on a line of policy, or he organizes committees, allegedly of the Cabinet but in practice chaired and led by the President himself, to deal with a particular problem. This technique of Cabinet dismantlement through the establishment of presidential committees was so common around 1960 that it seemed for one moment that the Cabinet might purely and simply disappear. Since the end of the Algerian war, however, these presidential committees have become less prominent (partly because the Community ceased to have much importance roughly at the same period). But they are still influential in military matters. Moreover the existence of a large presidential staff, overflowing the Elysée Palace, shows the extent to which De Gaulle is determined to keep abreast of developments. The numerous *chargés de mission* and *conseillers techniques* of the President keep the Head of State informed, enable him to intervene at "official level" when the matter is of no great concern, and give material for his actions at ministerial level if the question is more important. While this "parallel" organization might have been crucial for the survival of the regime in the early period when defenders of French Algeria appeared willing to destroy the Republic from inside, this political justification has long ceased to exist. The presidential secretariat is clearly an instrument without which it would be impossible for the Head of State to retain sources of information independent from those of the Prime Minister and thus to influence directly the course of events.

CONCLUSION

Developments such as these are clearly wholly dependent on the authority and constant will of General De Gaulle. Very little of what has happened is likely to be permanent unless the regime, after De Gaulle's departure, moves firmly towards presidential rule. Only De Gaulle can expect to have at his devotion a Prime Minister who, like the British Prime Minister in the early years of George III, is essentially concerned with "political, parliamentary, economic and administrative contingencies." For such a relationship to be maintained, President and Prime Minister must come to the fore from two entirely different planes of politics; indeed they must—as King and Prime Minister in the British eighteenth-century example—represent two different forms of legitimacy. It is because De Gaulle is right, in fact though not legally, in saying that he has embodied legitimacy in France ever since 1940, that he can afford a system which places him on a totally different plane from the rest of his Government. In America, Government and President are indeed on two different planes; but this is, after all, because the President alone is elected by the people, while the members of the executive are, in the strict sense of the word, the President's creations. Popular election could give the French President a similarly exalted status, but on condition that the ministers owed all their political authority to the Chief Executive; as long as the parliamentary system exists, and whatever arrangements are in force to oblige ministers to resign their seats, a large proportion of the members of the Government will come from the political "class," and will hope to trade their allegiance and support for certain specific demands. Even in the Gaullist phase of the Fifth Republic, the President cannot avoid the appearance of such personalities: there was a political risk even for De Gaulle in getting rid in 1960 of the old Conservative leader of the early 1950s, Antoine Pinay. But the risk was even greater in getting rid of another Minister of Finance, and another Conservative, Valery Giscard d'Estaing, early in 1966, because the latter is much younger and threatens to constitute an alternative pole of attraction to the Gaullist party.

Thus the executive of the Gaullist phase of the Fifth Republic is bound to have many transitional features. On the length of De Gaulle's stay in power depends the direction of the profound and permanent moves. The longer the system is maintained, the more likely it is that other party leaders, including those of the Left, will be attracted to quasi-presidential rule. If this were to happen, the President might retain most of his present powers (though these will probably be formalized), but the Prime Minister will disappear from the scene and collective Cabinet decision-making will also be abandoned. If De Gaulle does not remain long, there will be a return, though perhaps slow and checkered, to previous practices. The President will retain for a while some of the aura which De Gaulle gave to the office, but real power will gradually move back to the Prime Minister and his colleagues. It is because the future does not seem fixed and the two possibilities almost equally possible that any move taking place under De Gaulle may have important consequences for the future of French politics. The final verdict will have to be suspended, though, until long after De Gaulle has left the scene. Post-Gaullist France will take time to settle. Only after some years have passed will it be possible to state whether, in the end, Gaullism was a mere episode and a parenthesis in the evolution of the French executive, or an interesting, complex, and sometimes unconscious move in political engineering.

c

5: The Legislature

The stepchild of the Fifth Republic is the legislature. In the past, French political life swirled around the lobbies and paneled chamber of the Palais Bourbon, seat of the National Assembly stolidly situated on the left bank by the Pont de La Concorde. Not only was the greatest share of political business of the Third and Fourth Republics conducted in the lower house of Parliament (called the Chamber of Deputies during the Third Republic, but renamed the National Assembly in 1946), but on more than one occasion political battles were fought in the streets surrounding the Palais, as Frenchmen sought by direct action either to influence the legislature or to destroy it. The Chamber came to symbolize the Republic and all its works; it finally became the focus of all criticisms aimed at the shortcomings of French politics. Careers were often fashioned on the basis of learning and perfecting the intricacies of political behavior as traditionally practiced in the Assembly; those who did not learn to practice these techniques well were often frustrated at having to remain on the sidelines, with little more to do than to play Cassandra or attack the "system." Sometimes, however, the Chamber experienced dramatic moments in the competition between great orators, immersed in critical issues and exercising almost total freedom of debate.

Perhaps because it was the arena where the "Rights of Man" were first enunciated and defended, the Assembly became in time the repository of republican legitimacy—in theory the cockpit where the representatives of the people jousted for public recognition of their views. In the nineteenth century, the highest duty of the deputy was to preserve the rights and liberties of his constituents against the encroachments of potentially tyrannical State officers; we noted earlier the complaint that the administration of the Empire was still there despite the Republic. Inevitably, however, confusion over rights and privileges developed; the deputies became more and more parochial and tended to regard their function as the defense of advantages which had accrued to their district by circumstance, natural good fortune, or government action. From protectors of civil liberties, the deputies were slowly transformed into the champions of vested and often purely local interests, a development which is not uncommon in many legislatures, particularly the United States Congress, whose mores resemble in many ways those of the French Parliament before 1958. The relationship between the legislators and the Premier and his ministers, however, remained essentially the same. The ministers were constantly called on by indignant legislators to justify or explain actions of the Government or its servants which threatened the individual dignity or the economic privileges of the Frenchman.

In these circumstances, the mark of a promising Premier was his ability to deflect or postpone the demands which poured in on the Government for the extension of special privileges, or to blunt the biting criticism of legislators who regarded the Government as the plunderer of local treasure, if not the epitome of "reactionary" obscurantism. At the same time, the Premier who wished to survive was constantly forced to nurse along the coalition that constituted his majority, pleading with his own ministers (or their friends) not to lead the attack against him, while compromising the integrity of his legislative program in order to maintain the cohesion of his cabinet. To compound his difficulties, the Premier had to submit the various plans of his legislative program to the committees of the house, often hostile, whose chairmen were usually more anxious to further their own careers (perhaps by replacing the relevant minister) with brilliant critiques of the legislation under discussion than to contribute to the forward progress of public business. Here, too, parallels can be drawn with the committees of the United States Congress, though the French Parliament never resorted to the kind of public grilling through hearings which have characterized its American counterpart. Perhaps and most important, though—and this time in contrast with the United States, where the Administration remains in office whatever happens, for four years—the Chamber could, virtually without notice and always without fear of reprisal, since the right of dissolution had been customarily abolished after 1877, yank the rug from under any government by defeating legislation on which the Premier counted, or, by using the procedure of "interpellation," discuss any problem which was deemed to be important, but could sometimes be trivial or parochial and thus force the resignation of the Premier and his ministers.

In all this there was a supporting philosophy to which the parliamentarians of the Third and Fourth Republics clung doggedly. Since the Revolution the enemies of republicanism were believed to be lodged in havens where they could exercise influence disproportionate to their numbers. These havens included the Church, the bureaucracy, and the armed forces. A kind of rampant anarchism ("*le citoyen contre les pouvoirs*"—"the citizen against the powers," all the powers, whatever they were, to take the expression of the philosopher and essayist of the Third

Republic, Alain) prevailed among the French people in general and among their elected representatives in particular. Thus harassment of Government operations could be justified as a republican virtue. There were also some more personal reasons for the anti-ministerial attitudes of many deputies: the faster the pace of Government change, of the rise and fall of cabinets, the greater the opportunities for numerous deputies to win the coveted title of minister, and if the actual chance was not greater, at least the expectations were great; periods of cabinet crises were intense, as deputies expected to be called, were disappointed if they were not, and felt even more bitter if some of their enemies were. The main skill which was required to win appointment to a cabinet post was a large number of parliamentary colleagues whom the candidate could bring with him to support the coalition which a new Premier was trying to build, a small number of enemies, a reputation—often based on little hard evidence—for an ability to compromise, good will, and no trace of arrogance. One way of winning good will was to avoid clinging to power when the Government was about to fall; one had to have the grace to desist, because one knew that one might very well belong to the next coalition if one showed that one was prepared to go. Thus cardinal sins against the Assembly were committed by those who tried to "appeal" to a higher court (in this case the people) against the Assembly. Because Pierre Mendès-France talked to the people in 1954 in a language which was convincing, deputies felt that he was not playing the game; because Edgar Faure used a miscalculation of some of the deputies which gave him the opportunity to dissolve the Assembly at the end of 1955, he was never forgiven by the old guard of the Fourth Republic and ceased to be of "minister material" because he could not be trusted to keep to the rules of the game.

The system had many obvious faults, but it existed for a long time: only defeat led to its downfall in 1940; only a succession of colonial retreats led to its downfall in 1958. It did give France its one long real period of liberal government; it accustomed ministers and presidents to coming and going. It was thus far from wholly "disfunctional," particularly before the time when government intervention in economic and social matters made swift executive action more and more necessary. The system was helped, too, by the very administration which the Kings and Napoleon had given France and which the Republic modified, wisely enough, only slowly and piecemeal. Transfer of legislative responsibility to the executive also took the form of "decree-laws," enabling the Government to act on behalf of Parliament. Criticized and even attacked as unconstitutional under the Third Republic, indeed made unconstitutional under the Fourth, "decree-laws," renamed "outline laws" in the 1950s, helped the Government to bypass the legislature and helped the legislature to find a comfortable way out of its own political deadlocks. To that extent, the regime showed resilience and a sense of adaptation. It did not, however, go further: though numerous schemes were proposed to increase the stability of the Government (through automatic dissolution of Parliament at each Government crisis, for instance), none was ever adopted. The personal stakes were too high; the life of a parliamentarian was too often punctured by the ritual of the governmental crisis; reform could not come from inside. Only because the framers of the Constitution of the Fifth Republic operated outside the atmosphere of Parliament could some drastic measures be taken to curtail parliamentary privileges. But only because De Gaulle was there would the rights be curtailed in fact as well.

GENERAL PRINCIPLES OF ORGANIZATION OF PARLIAMENT IN THE FIFTH REPUBLIC

In order to bring about a change in the behavior of parliamentarians, the framers of the Constitution of 1958 decided to introduce a number of technical devices generally designed to enhance the position of the Government and to give the Chambers the possibility of controlling, but not of blocking, executive action. These devices can be analyzed under five sets of headings. First, there are general provisions aimed at reducing the length of the harassments and at diminishing the opportunities of conflict in the general organization of Parliament. Second, the scope of legislation is reduced and that of the governmental prerogative correspondingly increased. Third, opportunities for guerrilla and open warfare during the debates over legislation are reduced by the introduction of a number of restrictions. Fourth, the operation of censure motions is severely restricted and the classic procedure of the "interpellation" abolished. Fifth, an overall control of parliamentary activity is provided by the possible intervention of the Constitutional Council. To these five types of devices, one should add the extended power of dissolution given to the President of the Republic, since, provided it remains effective as it clearly was in 1962, the members of the National Assembly are likely to feel less disposed to show vindictiveness against the government if they know that they might rock their own boat by trying to sink the executive ship.

As we noted in Chapter Three, Parliament is composed of two Chambers, the National Assembly and the Senate, the Upper House having regained the title, but not all the powers, which it had under the Third Republic, while the Lower House kept the name which the Constitution of 1946 had given it. The National Assembly is elected for five years (if it is not dissolved before), by direct universal suffrage; the electoral system is known as the *scrutin d'arrondissement à deux tours*, that is, a two-ballot (or run-off) system within single-member constituencies (taking place on two successive Sundays). This type of electoral system was used during most of the Third Republic, but it had been replaced in 1945 by proportional representation, which was kept during the whole of the Fourth Republic, though with considerable modifications in the direction of the majority system. Proportional representation was advocated by the Left (and to some extent by the right-wing and Christian parties) as the two-ballot system traditionally favored center parties. At the first ballot, only candidates receiving 50 percent or more of the votes cast in the constituency are elected. In a country which has numerous parties and splinter groups, the number of candidates elected at the first ballot is small: at the General Election of 1936, the last before World War II, only 185 deputies out of 618 were elected at the first ballot; at the General Election of 1958, the first of the Fifth Republic, only thirty-nine deputies out of 465 for metropolitan France were elected at the first ballot (ninety-six out of 480 in 1962). Between the first and the second ballot (at which the candidate who gets the most votes is elected irrespective of his percentage, but at which only candidates who obtained more than 10 percent of the votes at the first ballot can stand), deals take place and candidates withdraw voluntarily, sometimes without further ado, sometimes "in favor" of other candidates better placed in the race. In general, this kind of arrangement tends to be to the advantage of the center candidates, who can receive votes from the right in left-wing constituencies, and the left in right-wing areas.

Despite the fact that the two-ballot system is thus more "unfair" than proportional representation, it is more popular in the nation, partly because it is simpler, partly because the deputy is more likely to be known to his constituents, since districts are smaller than with PR; moreover, modifications of PR had taken place in 1951 as a result of the fear of a deadlock which might have been provoked by a combination of communists and right-wing deputies: parties were allowed to agree in advance to alliances (*apparentements*) which enabled them to obtain all the seats in a constituency if they had the majority of the votes; these arrangements were designed to favor mainly candidates from the center parties and had therefore created a widespread feeling of unjust "cooking" of the electoral system. The single-member system had the advantage of being no fairer to the communists (in view of the mechanics of the second ballot) but not appearing to be deliberately aimed at limiting the representation of the extreme Left by legislative fiat. In fact, however, the system did not operate in 1958 and in 1962 quite as had been forecast: the Gaullist Party did very well, and increasingly well, at the two successive ballots of the two General Elections. It obtained almost an absolute majority of seats in 1962 (jumping from 189 to 229 seats for metropolitan France) and with a small group of "independent" deputies elected under the Gaullist banner, the President could count on the support of the Chamber. This unprecedented development had much to do with De Gaulle, the transformation of the electorate, and the "nationalization" of political attitudes which will be analyzed in the next chapter. A polarization between Right and Left had taken place which made the election more "British" in character than it had been for a generation and perhaps more.

The Senate, sometimes nicknamed the "Grand Council of the French Communes," is elected for a much longer period (nine years, as in the Third Republic, with one third of its members retiring every three years), by representatives of local authorities. The electoral college is complex in detail; it does not include all the municipal councilors of all the local authorities (of which there are 38,000—with some very small, as we shall see in Chapter Seven), but only some of them, depending on the size of the commune. Overall, however, the electoral college is biased in favor of the small villages, as even the tiniest local authority has one delegate, with the resulting effect that the third of the population which lives in places under 1,500 inhabitants have slightly over half of all the delegates. Senators are themselves elected on the basis of the *département* (equivalent to an English county), and the number of senators per *département* varies according to the population; there are also two ballots, with the delegates coming to cast their vote at the county town and the two ballots taking place in succession on the same Sunday. Rural over-representation led to an entirely different complexion of the Senate from the National Assembly. The big winners in the Senate are the center-right parties, mostly Conservatives or traditional Liberals ("Radical-Socialists" as they are known in France—see Chapter Six) while the Gaullist Party, which swept the towns and big cities, did not succeed in having more than a very small minority of senators at each successive election to the Senate since 1958. Hence a considerable tension between the two Chambers and between the Government and the Senate; hence the fact that the Senate did not in fact see its status enhanced as a result of the new regime, in contrast with what had been expected. Indeed, in several instances, leakages inspired by the Government or the presidential office suggested that constitutional reforms might be under way in order to abolish the upper house or at least to modify drastically its composition.

The change in the electoral system of the National Assembly was designed to decrease the size of the opposition in Parliament, since it was hoped that the center, rather than the extremes, would benefit from the new arrangements. But several other devices written into the Constitution (the electoral law is not part of the Constitution, which simply states that the deputies "shall be elected by direct suffrage" and that "the Senate shall be elected by indirect suffrage"—Article 24) tend to create a better general climate to give the Government more breathing space. First, both houses of Parliament sit for only about six months in the year, in the autumn and the spring, unless the Government decides to call for a special session or unless Article 16 is invoked. Article 29 also says that "Parliament shall be convened in extraordinary session at the request . . . of the majority of the members comprising the National Assembly. . . ." but President De Gaulle interpreted this negatively when the question arose for the first time in 1960, as if the Article had stated that only when a majority of the members requested such an extraordinary session might Parliament be recalled; he also argued that it was up to him to grant the request—and he refused to do so in the circumstance (on the grounds that Article 30 says that extraordinary sessions, unlike ordinary sessions, are opened and closed by a decree of the President of the Republic).

Second, the President of the National Assembly is elected for the whole duration of the legislature, instead of once a year, as was the case before 1958; this had led to tensions and conflicts before the Assembly had started its business, thus creating climates of ill-feeling (the President of the Senate is elected after each partial reelection of the Senate, every three years). The President of each House is assisted by what is known as a *"bureau,"* which is composed of several Vice-Presidents and Secretaries drawn from the various parties with some regard to their strength in the House; they continue to be elected every year, but, as there is quasi-proportional representation, troubles are less common and arrangements usually take place beforehand. The President of the Assembly (since 1959 Jacques Chaban-Delmas, of the Gaullist Party) and the President of the Senate (Gaston Monnerville, a member of the "Radical" Party who has been at loggerheads with General De Gaulle for a considerable period and is indeed totally "ostracized" at ceremonial events because he bitterly opposed the way in which the 1962 reform of the election of the President of the Republic took place) are among the first personalities of the State and they are, as we saw, constitutionally consulted by the President in various circumstances (such as dissolution or the use of Article 16). They conceive of their role more as Speakers of the United States House of Representatives than as British Speakers of the House of Commons: though of necessity impartial in the actual conduct of debate, they do attempt to influence, by informally talking to members, the conduct of business. Before 1958, these offices were stepping stones to the Presidency of the Republic, where indeed the same qualities of informal advice and backstairs influence were necessary (Vincent Auriol was President of the National Assembly when he was elected President of the Republic); hence the fact that contests sometimes tended to take place when the time came to appoint the President of one or the other house.

Finally, a third arrangement—which brings us nearer to the actual process of lawmaking—also tends to increase the role of the Government in the organization of Parliament: this comes indirectly from the fact that the Constitution decreases the powers of the *Conférence des Présidents*, a body which plays a similar part to the Rules Committee of the House of Representatives (and indeed resembled it in its behavior before 1958). It is known as *Conférence des Présidents* because it includes the Presidents of the committees and the Presidents of the "parliamentary groups" (which is how parties are known in the chambers). It is chaired and called to meeting every week by the President of the House and its function is to decide the business of the House for the coming sittings. Before 1958, the Government had obtained the right to send a delegate to the *Conférence*, and this delegate could state which bills or questions it would like to see debated, and in what order, but the governmental "delegate" could not vote, and the decisions taken by the *Conférence* were often at considerable variance from those which the Government had hoped for. The tactics consisted in trying to avoid debate on measures which the Government wanted but deputies disliked and thus create embarrassment through inaction. Since 1958, however, this kind of negative filibustering is no longer possible, through the combined operation of the apparently innocuous Article 43, which states that "Government and Private Members' bills shall, *at the request of the Government* (our italics) or of the Assembly concerned, be sent for study to committees especially designated for this purpose," and of the more sinister-looking Article 48, which states that "the discussion of the bills filed or agreed to by the Government shall have priority on the agenda of the Assemblies in the order set by the Government." Thus the Government can disregard whatever feelings there may be against bringing the bill forward in the *Conférence des Présidents* and make sure that the bill is first sent to a committee and then extracted from the committee and presented to the floor of the House.

SCOPE OF LEGISLATION

Traditionally, as is logical in a country which adopts a parliamentary system, the French Parliament could legislate on any matter. The Constitution merely regulated the principles of organization of the public powers; there was no Supreme Court, as we saw, to rule laws "unconstitutional" or to prevent Parliament from interfering in certain fields. The Constitutional Council established in 1958 now has some powers (which we shall examine more closely later in this chapter), but these are based to a large extent on an entirely new conception of the law which has been brought forward by the new Constitution. In the past laws (*lois*) were defined merely as texts adopted by Parliament, by contrast with decrees (being texts adopted by the whole government) and *arrêtés* (being texts adopted by a minister or a local authority). These documents derived their legal power from each other; the Government could not make decrees, and ministers and local authorities could not make *arrêtés* unless a law (and if necessary a decree as well) had authorized the authority to do so, in most cases specifically (for instance by stating that "the Minister of ———— shall adopt by *arrêté* the rules implementing the present Article"), but sometimes generally (it had always been recognized that the Government had general powers to issue decrees to implement legislation, this being known as the *pouvoir règle-mentaire*). This hierarchy meant that, in practice, decrees and *arrêtés* tended to deal with less important matters than laws. But, formally, at least, the distinction between the three types of documents simply came from the type of public body which was empowered to issue the text.

This situation was felt to be doubly disadvantageous. On the one hand, it meant that Parliament was always free to invade, if it so desired, the field which had been previously dealt with by *arrêté* or decree; nothing prevented Parliament from legislating on trivial matters and such instances did occur if there was some powerful electoral reason which compelled the deputies to do so, but once some matter had been regulated by a law, it was difficult to go back, as only a law can amend another law. Thus parliamentary interference increased indefinitely, time could be wasted on small matters, and occasions for action by private lobbies were multiplied. On the other hand, this expansion of legislative action had in fact the effect of diminishing the real role of Parliament in important matters, as if Parliament had been weaving around itself a spider's web which could no longer be cut to size but had to be destroyed; it became common for Governments to ask for a wide delegation of the power to modify laws by decree (hence the expression *decree-laws*, or *outline laws*). In a country where the authority of the Government is sufficient to prevent the chamber from overstepping its rights, as in Britain, the legislative supremacy of Parliament has fewer disadvantages; in a country such as France, where the Executive is traditionally weak, many felt, understandably enough, that a restriction of the scope of legislation would have beneficial effects.

Hence the complex Article 34 of the Constitution which purports to prevent undue parliamentary interference by defining the scope of legislation in detail. A detailed definition is indeed necessary if the limitation is to be effective, but the problems which are raised by this limitation are difficult to solve and the interpretation of the clause has proved tricky on various points. After having stated that "all laws shall be passed by Parliament" (which also means that laws are passed by Parliament only), the Article proceeds to elaborate what laws are by stating that "laws determine the rules" (*règles*) relating to a number of listed matters: civil rights, the fundamental guarantees of public liberties, the obligations of the citizen for purposes of national defense, nationality, personal status, property in marriage, inheritance, the definition of crimes and penalties attached to them, criminal procedure, the organization of the judiciary, taxation, the electoral system, the fundamental guarantees of civil servants and of members of the armed forces, the creation of categories of public corporations, the nationalization of private property. The Article then adds that "laws shall determine the fundamental principles" relating to certain other matters: the organization of national defense and of local government, education, social security, the law of property and commercial law, labor and trade union laws. Finally, the Article states that its provisions "may be elaborated and completed by an organic law."

The list is fair; it includes all the important matters which one would expect a Parliament to be concerned with. But three difficulties have to be faced. First, what is meant by "rules" (*règles*) in the first part of the Article is not entirely clear; the word "*règle*" has no precise meaning in French law. If one argued *a contrario* from the second part of the Article which talks about "principles," one would be led to conclude that Parliament decides *all* the rules relating to the matters listed; if so, there would be no decree-making power of the Government on these questions, which would indeed be going back on the previous situation. This is not what the drafters of the Constitution intended to do, but the problem may arise. Second, and a potentially more worrying source of trouble, there is no way of being sure of what a "principle" is, and yet the Article argues that only the "principles" of education law, for instance, have to be defined by law; conflicts have already arisen, as was to be expected. The arbiter, on this point, is the Constitutional Council, but the matter has clear political undertones: if Parliament were to gradually delve into the "details" of legislation, the Government would have to conduct a difficult series of battles in the Constitutional Council which would undermine its authority, perhaps as much as previous battles aimed at preventing Parliament from legislating on trivia. Third, the last provision, which mentioned the possibility of "elaboration and completion" by an organic law, can also be quite ominous for the Goverment. If, after De Gaulle, the French Executive loses some of its newly-acquired authority vis-à-vis the Chamber, it might well be faced with threats of "elaboration and completion" of Article 34 which would in fact undermine it.

The drafters of the Constitution tried to buttress the system by introducing yet another distinction, this time not between laws and other types of texts, but among the laws themselves. Before

1958, there were only two types of laws: "ordinary" laws and the Constitution. The latter had a higher status than "ordinary" laws, though, there being no Supreme Court, the practical effect was small; the main one was that the procedure of constitutional amendment was longer and more difficult. But we noted that the Constitution dealt mainly with the organization, in its broad lines, of the governmental system; rights were not mentioned in 1875 and, though stated in 1946, were merely "declared." In order to strengthen the Government in relation to Parliament, in order also to bring some realism to the question of delegation of legislative power to the Government, the Constitution of 1958 introduced two new types of "documents," named "organic laws" and "ordinances." "Organic laws" (of which we mentioned one example in relation to Article 34) are laws which are passed by Parliament with a somewhat more stringent procedure than that of the ordinary law: a delay of fifteen days must elapse between the moment it is submitted and the moment it is passed by the Chamber to which it was first presented; opposition by the Senate entails another vote by an absolute majority of the members of the National Assembly (except if the organic law concerns the Senate, in which case both houses must pass identical texts); finally, and most importantly, organic laws must be deemed constitutional by the Constitutional Council before they can be promulgated. Thus it is hoped, for instance on Article 34 (as well as on matters concerning the organization of Parliament and various other constitutional bodies, which are regulated by "organic laws"), that the Constitutional Council will prevent Parliament from overstepping its powers. On the other hand, if Parliament wants to delegate its legislative powers (or if the Government asks for and obtains powers of delegation from Parliament), any amendment of legislation made by the Government in this way takes the form not of a "decree-law" as before 1940, but of an ordinance, which has to be ratified by Parliament at the end of the delegation period. Thus Governments cannot go too far and be granted too many powers by a Parliament overburdened or frightened by a sudden crisis, as was often the case in the 1930s, and the Government hopes to have the Constitutional Council on its side in cases of parliamentary encroachments.

The machinery is therefore complex; it needed to be if it was to meet the problems at all satisfactorily. As it stands, it is not even certain that it does. In the Gaullist phase of the Fifth Republic, clashes centered on Article 34 have not been very numerous, though the Government has referred matters to the Constitutional

Council from time to time (it has sometimes done so in advance, in order to obtain advice before legislation is presented to Parliament); decisions of the Constitutional Council on this point appear to be fair, and they have not always favored the Government. What the position will be in due course seems to depend on how much time the procedure will have had to "settle." As long as the National Assembly is reasonably happy with the Government and does not aim at resorting once more to guerrilla tactics, some *modus vivendi* may be maintained, but the difficulties inherent in Article 34 are sufficiently numerous to enable experienced and skillful parliamentarians to take advantage of them to undermine the authority of the executive and gradually reestablish the legislative supremacy of the Assembly.

THE LEGISLATIVE STRUGGLE

In a "parliamentary" system the two main activities of a Parliament consist in voting laws and in controlling the Government. But the two are intertwined, as previous analyses have already shown. Before 1958, it was indeed through the development of the legislative struggle that the patience, wits, and skills of ministers were being tested, since, in the last resort, a Government needs laws to implement its program and needs particularly one law, the financial law, merely to survive. Thus, though we shall see that the question of the control of the executive leads to certain specific problems and certain particular arrangements, it was naturally on the legislative process that the drafters of the Constitution of 1958 concentrated a large part of their "engineering" talent. In order to understand the purpose of the reforms, the best way is to follow the sequence of legislation, note the traps which deputies used to set for the Government, and see how the Constitution of 1958 intervenes on the side of the executive.

A bill debated in the French Parliament goes through the following sequence—not very different from that which bills go through in the United States Congress. After having been laid on the table of either Chamber, by a member of that Chamber (or by the Government—but finance bills must be presented first to the National Assembly), the bill is sent to a committee, which discusses it and can dismiss, amend, or adopt it; the committee then reports (each bill has a *rapporteur* from the committee which reports on the bill as amended) to the House, which discusses the bill first in general, then article by article (and if necessary paragraph by paragraph), and votes on each article; there is then a final vote on the bill as amended. It goes at this point to the other House, which follows the same procedure. If both Houses agree on the same text, the bill is sent to the President for promulgation (we saw that he could ask for a second deliberation, and has fifteen days to do so, but has no veto power; requests for second deliberations are very rare, and are normally aimed at correcting technical errors which had been overlooked). If the Houses disagree the bill goes again to each House; if there is still a disagreement, a joint committee comprising an equal number of members of each House is set up, with a view to coming to a common text. Only if the Government intervenes, as we shall see, is there a possibility of preventing deadlock if the two Chambers still disagree (in the Fourth Republic, the National Assembly could override the opposition of the Upper Chamber).

We have already noted that the Constitution of 1958 eliminated two sources of potential anti-Government action, one at the very first stage, when the bill is sent to a committee, and the other at the report stage, when the bill is due to be debated in the Chamber. But there were many other possible sources of friction. As can be expected, committees constituted very powerful hurdles. Organized, as in the United States but not in Britain, on the basis of specialist subjects (finance, foreign affairs, interior, etc.), the twenty or so committees of the pre-1958 Parliaments had great opportunities to give trouble to the Government. They comprised the members of the "parliamentary groups" (elected on the basis of proportional representation) who were most interested in the problems concerned, or had electoral reasons from their constituency's point of view to appear interested. Their chairmen, elected every year together with vice-chairmen (the seniority system never took roots in France, though some Chairmen did remain for long periods at the head of their committee), were naturally men of influence within their sphere of competence; they were natural leaders of any opposition in this field; they were the real "shadow ministers," and indeed behaved like shadow ministers, often hoping to acquire the minister's job at the next governmental crisis (and thus were unlikely to be very keen to prevent the occurrence of such crises); they were recognized as shadow ministers by all, both by the Government who always took care to appear to listen to what they said and by the Chamber which always gave committee chairmen the right to speak in reply to ministerial points.

Committees made life difficult for the Government because they were built as if oppositions were to be maximized, but they also made life difficult because the procedure of the Chambers gave the committee full responsibility in relation to bills. When a bill, whether coming from the Government or from a private member, went to a committee, it became in effect the committee's bill. The committee could so alter its substance that it could emerge unrecognizable. But whether this happened or not, the committee's bill, not the original document, was reported to the House, and any return to the original text technically had to take the form of amendments to the committee's bill. This procedure, which might be acceptable in relation to private members' bills, many of which were drafted very quickly and without much technical help, was disastrous for the Government; the Government constantly had to make sure that the economy of the bill was not upset by a whole series of changes which had taken place in committee and which might have to be opposed, one by one—without always knowing what the outcome was to be, particularly if, as a result of a protracted discussion, the debate on the floor went far into the night.

The Constitution of 1958 sought to reduce drastically the power of committees from one of complete control of the legislative process to one of advice given to the House on the line to take on the bill in general and on the various clauses. Hence two sets of provisions were adopted, one of which was perhaps too clever to be really successful. On the one hand and at first sight rather cunningly, Article 43 limited to six the number of permanent committees in each House. It was perhaps hoped that, like the House of Commons committees, they might not be specialized; it was certainly hoped that they would become so large that they would include more than merely experts aiming at fighting private battles with ministers (they are from sixty to 120 strong). But, despite various rulings from the Constitutional Council, the Government could not avoid the setting up of informal subcommittees, which tend to correspond to some extent to the old committees and are better able to discuss legislation in detail; the effect of Article 43 seems therefore to be small. On the other hand, and more successfully, committees are no longer empowered to substitute their bills for those of the Government, as Article 42 states that the discussion on the floor has to take place on the Government's text; changes suggested or approved by the committee are submitted to the House, but as amendments.

During the discussion on the floor of the House, harassment of governmental legislation often took place in many other ways. A very common one, which consisted of withholding amendments until the bill came to the floor (so as either to embarrass the Government and its supporters at the last moment, or lead to delay by forcing a reference back to the committee) is now forbidden. Only amendments which have been discussed in committee need to be discussed on the floor, unless the Government is prepared to see them discussed. But the most drastic arrangement, which was attacked from the start for being potentially dangerous and which provoked anger from time to time as it was being used, is the procedure of closure. Article 44 allows the Government to request each Chamber to vote by a single vote on the text under discussion (this has been known as *vote bloqué*.) As the Article stands, it is clearly liable to abuse; there is no restriction on the moment at which the Government can use the procedure, or indeed any safeguards at all. It is difficult to see, however, what safeguards could be written into the Constitution which would not at the same time so limit the operation of the Article as to make it of little use. Safeguards have to come from the Chamber itself, which should not tolerate abusive requests for closure and is in a position to rebel (by rejecting the bill) if the Government insists on very quickly bringing the debate to a close. In fact, neither the Debré nor the Pompidou Government used the procedure of closure too often or too early, perhaps partly because the Assembly also showed the limits of its patience, even in an overall situation of strong majority government. The National Assembly would not bear a constant use of the closure system any more than the British Parliament would be prepared to tolerate a Government which constantly introduced the guillotine.

The Constitution gives the Government two other sets of powers relating to the legislative procedure. Finance bills have to be treated differently from other laws, since they have to be passed by a given time. Before 1958, French Parliaments were notorious for their delaying action in respect to the budget; indeed, the budget was customarily one of the hurdles which few Governments passed safely, and this in turn increased delays, as a new Government had to be formed and re-think the budget before the finance bill could be approved. In order to redress this situation, the Constitution of 1958 limits to seventy the number of days during which Parliament can discuss and decide on the budget; if it has not settled matters by the end of the period, the Government becomes entitled to promulgate the finance bill by Ordinance. In fact, this stringent weapon has not had to be used, and budgetary procedure has taken a much more normal turn than before in the Fifth Republic; debate over specific items is often long and sometimes tough, but budgets are now voted on time and the techniques of either holding the clock at midnight on 31st December (the end of the financial year in France) or of voting "provisional twelfths" (the granting of money for a month while the debate went on) have now wholly disappeared.

Finally, the Government, and the Government alone, can end a deadlock between the two Houses by asking for yet another reading by each House of the text adopted by the National Assembly; if there is still disagreement between the two Houses, the National Assembly is called to vote again, and this decision is final. Thus the Senate is not in a position to do what it was criticized for having done before 1940, namely blocking governmental legislation, particularly of a progressive kind. But the Government can benefit from the Senate's legislative veto if it finds it convenient; only if both Houses agree is the Government forced to accept legislation of which it does not approve.

The legislative struggle thus goes on with wholly different weapons in the hands of the protagonists. The Government is not permanently on the defensive. Some have said—indeed, many have done so—that the 1958 Constitution went too far in tilting the balance in favor of the Government. This is, in the light of past experience, very arguable. If it is recognized that something had to be done to strengthen an executive which was traditionally weak and against which all means of procedure were used with great skill, very strong procedural checks had to be built to prevent the game from following its "normal" rules. In reality, the danger does not perhaps so much arise from the fact that the measures might be too strong, as that they might be ineffective, if the authority of the Government once more diminishes. The political "engineering" of the Constitution of 1958 is a brave effort; if it proves unsuccessful, one can perhaps legitimately ask whether constitutional measures aiming at redressing structural ills and weaknesses are ever to prevail under adverse circumstances.

THE VOTE OF CENSURE

Only in a relatively recent period has the question of the vote of censure, in France and in other parliamentary democracies, appeared to constitute a major problem. Traditionally, as can be seen by the British practice, Parliaments were entitled to censure Governments at will; this was assumed to be a funda-

mental right of Parliament, though censure might immediately
be followed by dissolution. But in France and in some other
countries, ministerial instability led to a questioning of this "in-
alienable" right. If the parliamentary system was to die because
Governments fell too often, it appeared reasonable to limit the
right of censure so as to preserve the parliamentary system as
well.

Assuming a desire to limit the right of the Assembly to censure the Government, one is immediately confronted with serious
difficulties. The first concerns legislation. If the Government cannot be censured easily by the Assembly, but if the Assembly can
easily reject legislation proposed by the Government, and in particular reject or delay financial legislation, the Assembly might
well obtain, indirectly, what it would have wanted to obtain
directly through a vote of censure, namely the fall of the Government. Thus, if governmental stability is to be achieved, procedures have to be devised which limit not only the conditions
under which the motion of censure can be operative, but also the
conditions under which legislation can be rejected without a vote
of censure. The solution seems to be receding as soon as one
tackles the problem; in the last resort, one is trying to prevent
Governments from resigning of their own free will, yet, if the
Government is not given the means which it feels necessary to
achieve its ends, it can always be tempted to resign, whether or
not it has been subjected to a motion of censure.

Procedures limiting the right of the Assembly to censure the
Government must therefore be made broad enough to cover the
case of legislation. It is because they had not done so that the
framers of the Constitution of 1946 had made so little progress.
French Governments continued to fall during the Fourth Republic simply because they were not given the laws they wanted,
and not because they were technically refused the confidence of
the Assembly. Various schemes were put forward, usually linking
the fall of Cabinets with an automatic dissolution. But, as these
would have punished the Assembly for playing at a game which
deputies were both expert at and very fond of, it would have
been surprising if the reform had been adopted.

The technique invented by the framers of the Constitution of
1958 in Article 49 is therefore, not surprisingly, both drastic and
clumsy. First, the seriousness of the censure motion is brought
home in two ways: the motion has to be signed by one tenth of
the deputies and forty-eight hours must elapse before the debate
takes place. If the censure is rejected, the same members cannot

sign another motion during the same session (there are two sessions each year). Second, as the Constitution of 1946 had done,
the Constitution of 1958 gives the Government the benefit of
the abstainers; the Government is defeated only if there is an absolute majority of the Assembly against it. However, as it could
look strange if a Government were maintained in office though
the number of deputies supporting it were positively smaller than
the number of those opposing it, the Constitution decides by a
clumsy arrangement for a face-saving device that only the opponents of the Ministry will record their votes. As a result, one
cannot know how many supporters, and indeed if any at all, the
Government has on a given vote of censure. Third, if the Government wishes to see a bill through, encounters difficulties, and is
prepared to resign if it does not obtain the law it wants, it can
"stake its responsibility on the vote of (the) text." In this case,
the text becomes law *without a vote*, unless a motion of censure
is tabled; if the censure is not adopted, the Government is safe
and the bill adopted.

It can be argued that only with a procedure of this kind
could the system be foolproof. Under the arrangements of the
Constitution of 1958, it is not possible for the Assembly to use the
technique of "interpellation" and suddenly overthrow the Government. When the deputies want to control the executive, they can
do only one of two things: they can use the procedure of the
question, which was introduced by the Constitution, allegedly
on the British model, but in fact came to be transformed into a
series of small debates without votes, all taking place on the same
day of the week; or they can table a motion of censure. The
Government may initiate a debate on its program or on a declaration of general policy and, if it so wishes, stake its responsibility
and set the procedure of censure in motion itself. But outside
these cases, the Assembly is confined to the discussion of laws.
Thus, control and even discussion of policy is very limited indeed.
Here, almost certainly, the Constitution went too far. The excesses of the Third and Fourth Republics may have led to the
introduction of a stringent procedure, which also had to be
clumsy and even bizarre. But the weapon is too heavy; it is difficult to handle because, somehow, it seems unfair. Under the Gaullist phase of the system, the technique has been used, indeed in a
number of cases; in September, 1962, as we noted in Chapter
Four, the censure was indeed voted by the Assembly. But it is
doubtful whether Governments will be able to insist for very long
on this technique of negative or even silent confidence. Already

under both Michel Debré and Georges Pompidou, the use has been moderate and the Government has been surprisingly ready to agree to legislative proposals coming from the Assembly and to important amendments to governmental bills (including finance bills). However disciplined, the majority was not prepared to vote the original text and the weapon of the censure motion was perhaps felt to be too heavy to be used more than exceptionally; it had to be reserved for the very broadest questions.

This might be unavoidable, as the loopholes would be numerous if the procedure was simple. But perhaps the real solution is a different one. The practice of the Fifth Republic has shown that even a strong Government, backed by a strong President, could not use Article 49 more than in a few crucial instances. It had often been argued before 1958 that Governments were prone to fall, not only because the Assembly laid traps at the executive, but also because the executive was overanxious to see its legislation adopted intact by Parliament. This does happen now in Britain, but the British Government, relying on a tightly disciplined party, can afford this luxury; yet this was not British practice in the middle part of the nineteenth century; it is clearly not the practice in the United States, where the veto power and various means of pressure do not give the President more than a limited influence over legislation. If French Governments were prepared to let Parliament make many changes in the details of bills, the Government may not have so often to use all its power and authority; and by not dissipating its power over too many matters, the Government may be more effective in the really crucial cases. Thus the clumsy procedure of Article 49 may have some indirect value: it may oblige both Government and Parliament to adopt more realistic practices in their relationship, though another, less caricatural technique might have had some similar effects. The procedure of Article 49 may well be one of the first to go after the end of the Gaullist phase of the Fifth Republic, although it may have had some value in helping to define more clearly the scope of parliamentary and governmental action.

THE CONSTITUTIONAL COUNCIL AND EXECUTIVE-LEGISLATIVE RELATIONS

We mentioned the Constitutional Council and its general role in many instances. It played an important part in the transformation of executive-legislative relations in France, though with De Gaulle at the helm, one does not know whether the Council buttresses the Constitution or De Gaulle the Council. One of its powers—not its most important—relates to referendums and national elections, both presidential and parliamentary, which it must officially "declare" and settle in cases of disputes. There have indeed been disputes after each election, particularly in very close contests (before 1958 disputes were settled by each House), and the Council seems to have been somewhat overprone to quash elections and impose by-elections, while showing perhaps some slight prejudice against the opposition parties. Its second set of powers relates to the Standing Orders of both Houses which, though not "organic" laws, have to be submitted to the Council before coming into force. This provision led almost immediately to a sharp conflict between Parliament and Council, as various clauses had been re-introduced in the Standing Orders along lines of pre-1958 arrangements, which the Council rightly felt contrary to the new Constitution and quickly proceeded to quash; one of these had allowed for the possibility of a vote following debates on questions and thus would have indirectly brought back, though in a limited way, the practice of interpellation. This was wiped away, not surprisingly, by the Constitutional Council. Third, the Council has periodically had to intervene in order to interpret and implement the difficult Article 34. Though its decisions have usually been in favor of the Government, the Council also on occasion did side with the legislature, particularly in the latter part of the Gaullist regime, as if either the Council felt that the political situation might be about to change or if the pressures (moral and probably somewhat unconscious) had tended to diminish.

CONCLUSION

France has thus experienced a new form of parliamentarism, which has been labeled "true parliamentarism" by its supporters and condemned as the end of Parliament by its opponents. Clearly, the legislature has lost many of its old rights. The "game of politics" is no longer practiced according to the rules which prevailed for three quarters of a century and had therefore become the norm for both members who reveled in the system and outsiders who criticized democratic government, on the grounds that it was synonymous with irresponsible parliamentary behavior. Many of the attacks against the new arrangements are, perhaps not surprisingly, based on an old system which seems to have acquired virtues since it disappeared. In fact, the French National

Assembly is not particularly sheepish; and the moderation of its attacks against the Government does not come only—indeed, far from it—from the constitutional changes.

Whether one considers the first legislature (1958–1962) or the second (1962–1967), one finds numerous instances of restiveness, rebellion, and executive retreat. As we noted earlier, the Government succeeded in surviving because, in many occasions, it was prepared to give in. It gave in on the details of many budgets; it gave in on substantial sections of many bills, the most recent example being that of the reform of the turnover tax, where opposition coming from all quarters, and based on purely electoral considerations, resembled very closely the behavior of pre-1958 Parliaments. And if the Government did not give in as much on certain other arrangements, as for instance on amnesty, it was only after using all the possible resources of the procedure and applying the "whip" as strongly as it could to its own supporters (and over thirty Gaullist deputies and nearly forty other supporters of the administration did not vote for the Government at the very last division). Admittedly, as it has often been noted, the Government has tended to give in on matters concerned with the "second" or governmental sector and the Assembly could do very little in matters pertaining to the "first" sector, in which presidential action was almost wholly free: there have been debates on foreign affairs and on nuclear defense, but rather infrequently; they tended to end by the use of the censure procedure, and they did not appear to deflect the President at all from the course which he had chosen. This is, indeed, the case, but the French Parliament is not the only legislature which finds itself unable to have much influence in foreign affairs. The United States Congress is somewhat hampered by the fact of the separation of powers; the British Parliament, though more accustomed to debate foreign affairs, is surely as impotent (and indeed perhaps more impotent as far as home legislation is concerned) as the present French Parliament. The pendulum did swing, but it did not swing as far, nor as violently, as might have been the case. And observers usually forget practices in other countries in the second half of the twentieth century when they look at the French Assembly.

Yet the Constitution is not responsible for the whole change. The real change came from the accession to power of a President who, probably alone, could impose a Government on a Parliament which otherwise would quickly have returned to past practices; particularly in the critical early years, when Algeria was a source of profound conflict, irresponsible behavior almost overwhelmed the Assembly and was thwarted only by the determination of the President. But, more importantly in the long run, changes in behavior came from changes in the party structure. While the first Parliament came closer to resembling some of its predecessors, the second looked more like a German or British Parliament, because, for the first time, a majority party—and a disciplined majority party—could deliver the relevant votes at the end of each debate. The Government did not cease to make deals; it had, as we saw, to make many openly; but it also had to make an entirely different type of deal, more akin to those which the British Government makes with its parliamentary party. These result from meetings, normally held in private, at which members of the executive come to explain their policy, agree to give way on some points, and state where they cannot give in. Parliament thus becomes less important as an open arena; the unexpected seldom takes place there.

It is thus natural that we should go to the parties, and to their possible future, after having considered the structure in which the Fifth Republic has attempted to mold French politics. Parties appear monolithic; Parliament loses some of its life. But if parties are more disciplined, and if Parliament is not to provide exciting moves, another development—and perhaps the most critical one—has yet to take place. When it ceases to be a place where events happen, the legislature must become a place through which people are informed, where the fights between Government and Opposition are made clear to the mass of the politicized public; in short, Parliament must become a forum for what comes to be a permanent election campaign between the main parties. This the French Parliament has not yet become; the mutation from the old to the new role is difficult and slow, and it is made even more difficult by the climate of "transition" in which French deputies and senators have remained, as have all Frenchmen, since De Gaulle came back to power. Furthermore, the change has to come from the opposition, which, not being united, finds it difficult to operate on the basis of concerted action. But only if and when the change comes will it be possible to say that practices of the Third and Fourth Republic Parliaments are definitely over. Yet, in this difficult process the Gaullist interlude may well have helped the French legislature to move more quickly in the direction of "responsible" parliamentary behavior than any other regime since the turn of the century.

6: Political Parties

The French party system is unique in the Western world, and probably in the world as well. Even though, as we have already indicated, and as we shall see in more detail in this chapter, present transformations seem to show a tendency toward simplification, the process is slow, and by no means irreversible. France is not unique in having a large number of parties; various Continental European countries, and Scandinavian countries as well, have many parties. She is not unique in having loosely-organized parties; American parties are also loose federations. She is already somewhat original in having a combination of both. But the French party system has two other characteristics which, added to the others, tend to produce a situation which defies characterization: first, France has both loosely-organized and very disciplined parties, as if all the possible geological layers, long buried elsewhere, had remained at the surface there. Second, these parties are both extremely volatile and extremely resilient; they split and break with considerable ease and eagerness, but the political bent—not the ideology, as this would suggest schools of thought and programs—which characterizes each of them is sufficiently permanent to lead eventually to reunions, rearrangement, or simply brotherly coexistence (though brotherhood should not necessarily be taken here as synonymous with friendship). The only party system in the whole of Western Europe which comes in any way close to the French in complexity is the Italian, but any student of Italy will already have recognized from this presentation how simple Italian party structures are in comparison to French ones.

In order to attempt to analyze this strange mixture of organizations of all kinds, history and geography, sociology and psychology all have to be used. Not that any of these disciplines, or even all of them together, have been able up to now to "explain" why France has the parties which it has, and in what proportions. But these disciplines all give some clues, most of which have some explanatory strength. The complex political history of France may explain why there is—or was up to recently—a section of the population which did not accept the Revolution, while others were extreme revolutionaries. But history and geography have to be linked if one is to account for the permanence of certain traditions in some areas more than in others. Right and Left, the anti-revolutionary right and the revolutionary left as well as other forms of right and left, are written in the countryside, as are geographically located the areas of deep religious prac-

tice and the areas of "dechristianization." Broadly speaking, the
northern half is more right-wing than the southern half, the West
and East are particularly Christian, traditional, and inclined to
vote conservative, while the Center and Southeast are both "progressive" and dechristianized. But matters have to be taken further,
as social cleavages between workers and employers, rural and
urban dwellers, and probably as psychological traits as well—the
individualism of many Frenchmen is probably not just a myth—
have to be taken into account. The analysis of French political
parties is a rich subject of study, which has not ceased to fascinate
the French; but the entry into the study is difficult and can be
painful.

GENERAL CHARACTERISTICS OF THE FRENCH PARTY SYSTEM

Let us proceed historically, and try to bring in geography, sociology, and psychology as we go along. With the Revolution, a
number of "factions," "tendencies," and even schools of thought
developed. They led broadly to four main currents. As the Revolution had had two stages, a liberal and an egalitarian, one finds,
through the nineteenth century, "moderates" and "progressives"
among the "republicans." Indeed, these often changed names,
almost from one generation to the next. When, in the 1880s, a
moderate was a mere "republican," the progressives called themselves "radicals." But "radicals" grew in numbers and expanded
into the center, and progressives, dissatisfied with the more timid
of the "radicals," moved towards "radical-socialism," and indeed
"socialism." For many progressives inside the Socialist Party, at
the end of World War I, socialism, which had condemned the
war in principle but joined it in practice, appeared a weak form of
"progressivism": communism came into being, under the impact
of the Russian revolution, of course, but naturally embedded in
what appeared to be a perpetual leftward movement of the current of French politics. But the movement stopped there: Trotsky-
ism never managed to grow to a point where it could challenge
the official Communist Party; the nature of the Communist Party,
the fact that it is very different from the "progressives" of the
past, has clearly much to do with what might be termed the end
of the law of the leftward movement.

We thus encountered, at the same time, two "currents,"
three "parties" (Radical, Socialist, and Communist), a law that
the left is constantly overtaken and the refutation of this law,

and the fact that the structures of moderate and progressive parties have tended to vary. But two other currents, as we said, were born from the Revolution. They could be deemed to divide the Right, in a first approximation, but they are more complex than just a division between "moderate" and "extreme," "reactionaries" and "conservatives." They come from the "royalists" and the "bonapartists," as one could have expected, but they were to be profoundly modified as no King was made to come back and as Napoleons ceased to be in sight. They created two trends, two brands, which, according to the nature of the problem, were alternatively to the right of each other. Royalists became "traditional conservatives," anxious to maintain the status of those who had status, of the notables, of the Church, of the Army. Bonapartists were more aggressive in their outlook: their nationalism was often violent, but their social policies more "left-wing"; they were "fascist" before the day, but with a stress on authoritarian rather than dictatorial government; and, with their minds turned toward past greatness, they were less determined to embark on new adventures. They provided those Frenchmen who were both disgruntled and petty-bourgeois with an outlet and an example. All, or nearly all, authoritarian or semi-authoritarian movements of modern France come from them, whether directly, as with Boulanger in the 1880s or the "Leagues" in the 1930s, or less directly, as with Gaullism in the 1950s and 1960s; even Poujadism, the "radical right" of the small shopkeepers of the mid-1950s, became nationalistic—over Algeria and the other overseas possessions—in a way which was reminiscent of Bonapartism, because it was linked, or at least linked itself, to traditions of "authoritarian republicanism," which is what Bonapartism has been for generations of Frenchmen.

It is time, however, to mention two further points, which though distinct, have been linked in the panorama of French political life: the religious question and the peasant problem. As we noted in Chapter Two, nearly all Frenchmen are Catholic, at least nominally, but some Frenchmen are more Catholic than others. The Catholic hierarchy, which had been critical of the Revolution and heavily attacked by the revolutionaries, was naturally allied to the royalists, and later to the traditional conservatives who descended from them (but not to the "bonapartists," most of whom were anti-religious); a syndrome was created, which associated Church with right, and "republicanism" with anti-Church attitudes. Vainly, in the early part of the century, some efforts were made to dissociate some elements of the Church from the stigma of "reaction." Even as late as the 1930s, cleavages between Right and Left had profound religious origins, at least ostensibly, and even in the 1950s and 1960s, the syndrome dies hard. Meanwhile, however, the "progressive Catholics" (if the expression is not a contradiction, which it would have clearly seemed to be to "republicans" of the turn of the century) had the good fortune of benefiting from the stigma attached to the traditional conservatives by the support which many of them gave to the Vichy regime; after the Liberation the "progressive Catholics" could almost have taken over, for lack of competition, the allegiance of the traditional conservatives, but this was not to be for long, since the traditional conservatives either preferred to throw their lot with the new "bonapartists" which Gaullists quickly came to be, or indeed to try, slowly but successfully, to recover the lost ground. But a new force, that of "progressive" or at least "republican" and "acceptable" Catholicism, had been born. Added to the traditional conservatives and the "bonapartists," it constitutes the third of the three main elements opposed to the three movements which, as we saw, emerged from the revolutionary groups, the "radicals," the socialists, and the communists.

But the importance of the peasantry has to be considered if we are to analyze realistically these six forces—the ones which we shall examine in more detail in the course of this chapter. France is, as we saw in Chapter Two, probably unique in having had, since the Revolution, a very large peasantry, composed mainly of small holders deeply attached to their land. This, coupled with a slow birthrate in a relatively static society—at least up to the 1950s —had the effect of stabilizing and "fixing" political attitudes in the shape which they had in the latter part of the nineteenth century. The peasantry created around itself a civilization of small towns and villages, populated with shopkeepers, artisans, and small professionals. Together, these various groups tended to live in a restricted, self-contained horizon: political traditions were not likely to change—whether these traditions were of the Right or of the Left, whether they were associated with "republicanism" or conservatism. This is why one finds both a persistence of attitudes in many areas, and very sharp "borders" between types of political attitudes. One such border exists in the Center of France, along a North-East-South-West axis (which divides the *Départements* of Creuse, Corrèze, and Lot from those of Puy-de-Dôme, Cantal, and Aveyron); other borders run *within* the *Départements*: in 1913, André Siegfried noted the existence of a "pocket" of left-wing attitudes in the *Département* of the Côtes-du-Nord in Brittany, and the *Département* of Lozère in the Massif Central is likewise divided between a northern half which is right-wing and a southern half which is left-wing. These attitudes are all longstanding, and they are often associated with religious feelings, though this is not always the case, as some dechristianized regions are left-wing while others are right-wing (as for instance Burgundy, two hundred miles southeast of Paris).

The peasantry does not only "fix" political behavior in many regions. It tends to create modes of political allegiance which have accounted to a large extent for the characteristics of parties in the National Assembly. Since the horizons of the rural communities are rather limited (though less so than in the past) the political allegiance tends to be rather personal. Within the framework of the broad political "trends" (Right or Left, conservatism or republicanism), electors vote for candidates whom they know, or have heard of. This accounts, in the first place, for the persistence of a strong though unwritten "locality rule": candidates who come from elsewhere (*parachutés* is the French expression) have little chance of success in the countryside. Typically, on the contrary, men with political aspirations start by being municipal councilors in their village or town, then district councilors, and, if fate is on their side, they try for the National Assembly. Thus, also, the fact that national party behavior is of little concern to the small town and village voter. This is what is meant by electoral "sectionalism": voters do not vote for a candidate because he has a certain party label; they vote for the candidate because he is a local man and the party label is something which he negotiates with headquarters when he has been nominated, or, sometimes, after he has been elected. Hence the lack of any party discipline of men elected in this way; hence the not surprising fact that many, particularly on the Right, called themselves "Independent," to the extent that the traditional conservatives have come to be known as the "Center of Independents and Peasants." If cross-pressured between party and local demands, traditional conservatives opt for local demands; if their position is secure locally, no amount of party pressure is likely to influence them.

This analysis applies to the peasantry, to villages and small towns. It does not apply to industrial areas and to large cities. There, as in other countries, party allegiance is based on "class feelings," on national party identification, and on interest-group behavior. Industrial workers vote mainly for the parties of the left, employers and white-collar workers, for the center and right-wing parties. But the importance and the permanence of the peasantry and of the small towns had three effects. First, it enabled "undisciplined" and sectional behavior to survive much longer in France than it did in other countries. Second, it forced almost all parties, whether consciously or not, to have a "peasant" and "small town" wing as well as a city wing. From the Communists to the extreme Right, all political groups had to accept that they were a coalition, either of workers and peasants, or of employers and peasants, luckily often separated by geography; this remained a source of permanent tension, constant misunderstandings, and ideological gymnastics. Third, the internal conflicts and the characteristics in discipline stemming from the small town basis of the party worked to the advantage of the undisciplined against the disciplined, the small town men against the city representatives, the professionals against everybody. With so many parties and groups, members of disciplined parties were counted in advance one way or the other. This left the members of the undisciplined fringe, who mostly represented the small towns and were normally composed of professionals (doctors, lawyers, sometimes schoolteachers) with vast possibilities of maximizing the price of their support. Thus, in the parties as in Parliament, demands for a streamlining or "nationalization" of political attitudes were not likely to be adopted.

Change has started to come, however, and the developments of the Fifth Republic have tended to precipitate it. With the modernization of France in the 1950s, the peasantry has diminished in size; small villages have come to be depleted, while large towns have increased in strength. The base of the undisciplined parties or of the undisciplined factions tends gradually to shrink. Moreover, in the villages and small towns, the car and television have brought new attitudes: "sectionalism" disappears and national attitudes prevail. Thus, as we saw in Chapter Two, a new national consciousness has come into being: one based on relative affluence, the desire to consume more, and gradual urbanization. Thus, also, the relative decline of old stereotypes, whether of a religious or a political kind. This made possible the truly great event in French party life, if not of the century perhaps, at least of the postwar period: the invasion of the Gaullist party, first in 1958, but more so in 1962, in places where the traditional Right used to be strong. For the first time, national feelings replaced sectional behavior: men voted for candidates whom they did not know, simply because they were Gaullists; and the "notables" of the countryside suffered astounding defeats where they had been assumed to be, up to then, almost unchallengeable.

The 1962 Gaullist victory is thus a great political event in the history of modern French politics. But it is also seriously limited in two ways. First, it may well be shortlived, for it could be followed, after De Gaulle's departure, by divisions, splits, and a return to lack of discipline. As we shall see, the Gaullists do not form a very structured party; the *Union pour la Nouvelle République* is still more united by the common allegiance to the leader than by other characteristics, though a common approach to problems is gradually emerging. As we indicated earlier, the Christian Democratic Party did also make great inroads in the right-wing vote just after World War II, but the traditional conservatives soon took many of their electors back. The UNR has lasted longer, and it did not split, but it still has to survive the succession period, and few would be prepared to predict that this will easily take place. Second, the Left, the heirs of the "republicans," is divided, and necessarily so, as long as a quarter to a fifth of Frenchmen will continue to vote Communist and the danger of dictatorial takeover will therefore appear real to most other Frenchmen. Thus the Left is weak, and the weaker it remains, the less voters and politicians of the Center will find it necessary to choose between the two. There is truth in the feeling that, as long as there are Communists, divisions and impotence will both affect the Left, maintain the undisciplined Center in being, and make it somewhat unnecessary for the Right to unite in order to remain in power.

Thus, though France seems in a transitional stage in respect to its parties as well as to its Constitution, the detailed study of the parties needs to be conducted, as in the past, on the basis of the six main groupings. Even the 1962 election, which brought about a great change, still left enough strength to the other groups to enable them to return to the front of the political scene. As one can see from Table 3, the ebb and flow of parties from 1946 to 1962 has been very small on the Left, marked at the Center, and very strong on the Right. The chances of total disappearance of any of these parties, at least in the next decade (unless major fusions take place, some of which are in process as we shall see), are very remote indeed. A slow simplification is occurring, however, as the traditional movement to the extreme left is stopped, which benefits to parties of the Center-Left, and as a new kind of Right is taking the place of the traditional conservatives.

TABLE 3: ELECTIONS TO THE NATIONAL ASSEMBLY SINCE WORLD WAR II

a) Percentage of votes cast for each party (Metropolitan France only)

	Total votes (millions)	Comm.	Soc.	Rad. & Ass.	MRP	Ind. Cons.	Gaull.	Other
1945 June	19.2	26.5	24	11	25	13	—	0.5
1946	19.9	26	21	11.5	28	13	—	0.5
November	19.2	28	18	11	26	16	—	1
1951	18.9	26	14.5	10.5	13	12	22.5	1.5
1956	21.5	26	15	15.5	11	15	4	13.5 (mainly Poujadists)
1958 1st ballot	20.5	19	15.5	11.5	11.5	23	17.5	2
1958 2nd ballot	18.0	20.5	14	8	7.5	23.5	26.5	—
1962 1st ballot	18.3	22	15	8	9	15	32	—
1962 2nd ballot	15.2	21.5	16.5	7	5	9.5	40.5	—
			Federation and Other Left		Democratic Center	Gaullists and Independent Gaullists		
1967 1st ballot	22.9	22.4	21.0		12.8	37.8		6.0
1967 2nd ballot	18.8	21.4	25.0		7.1	42.6		3.9

b) Seats (France and overseas)

	Total seats	Comm.	Soc.	Rad. & Ass.	MRP	Ind Cons.	Gaull.	Other
1945	586	161	150	57	150	64	—	4
1946 June	586	153	129	53	169	67	—	15
1946 November	618	183	105	70	167	71	—	22
1951	627	101	107	95	96	98	120	10
1956	596	150	99	94	84	97	22	50 (mainly Poujadists)
1958	578	10	47	40	64	129	206	81 (mainly from Algeria)
1962	480	41	67	45	38	51	234	4
1967	486	73	Federation and Other Left 121		Democratic Center 30	Gaullists and Independent Gaullists 244		18

THE COMMUNIST PARTY

France is one of the five countries of Western Europe which has a large Communist Party, the others being Italy, Finland, Greece (although the CP is now banned, the left-wing EDA has clear Communist support), and tiny Iceland. This situation has always puzzled observers, both French and foreign, and it is becoming daily more puzzling. Simple "economic" explanations are obviously not sufficient; the standard of living is as high in France as in other Western European countries, development is as fast, and expectations should be similar. Those who hoped, in the late forties, that an improvement of living conditions would be accompanied by a substantial Communist decrease have been disappointed. The Communist vote was somewhat reduced, but not at the time and not for economic reasons. While countries which had medium-sized Communist parties after the war (such as Belgium or Sweden, where the electoral strength of the Communists was in the region of 10 percent) saw this support dwindle, the countries where the Communist Party received between a fifth and a quarter of the votes, mainly Italy, France, and Finland, experienced great stability on the extreme Left. In France, the only inroads made in the Communist electorate were due to De Gaulle: the Constitution of 1958 was adopted by 80 percent of the voters, among whom were perhaps a fifth of the Communists; at the General Election of November 1958, the Communist vote slumped from 5.5 to 3.9 million, but it remained stable in 1962, the party having received then just over four million votes. Indeed, as abstention was higher, the percentage of votes cast for the CP rose from 19 percent in 1958 to 22 percent in 1962 and 1967. The Fourth Republic started in 1946 with 28 percent of the votes cast for the Communists; after twenty years of opposition and after considerable changes had taken place in the social and economic structure of the country, the party had lost only a quarter of its vote and there were no signs of a further fall.

As we noted already, one reason for the strength of the Communist Party is historical: the party benefited from the "law of the leftward movement of parties." The Socialist Party was somewhat discredited in the eyes of left-wingers at the end of World War I; discontent was widespread among deputies and rank and file. The break took place in 1920, at a Congress at Tours, over the question of joining the Communist International. A majority of members of the Socialist Party, anarchists as well as communists, followed the minority of deputies who created the "French Section of the Communist International." But the beginnings were difficult: numbers slumped by the late 1920s and results at the polls were discouraging. As explained in Chapter Four, the electoral system benefited the center parties, and electors preferred to vote Socialist or Radical at the second ballot—disregarding tactics of isolation put forward by the Communists. By 1932—a good election year for the Left—the Communists had little to be complacent about. They had ten seats in Parliament; they were in a splendid and impotent political isolation, and had found little support among the organized workers.

Recovery came from a change of tactics—and from the fact that the Socialists agreed too easily on these new tactics. From 1934 onward, the Communists began a campaign in favor of "working class unity." They disbanded their trade union and advised their members to join the large working class organizations, which were Socialist. They brandished the "Fascist" menace and succeeded in convincing Socialists and Radicals to agree to a Popular Front alliance for the General Election of 1936. This was to be the real Communist starting point. Gaining 15 percent of the vote, over eighty deputies, an almost entire hold on the Red Belt of Paris, some successes in the countryside, as well as a foothold in the trade unions and the opportunity to hold the newly-created Socialist Government to ransom (by "supporting" it though refusing to participate in it), the Communist Party suddenly became a power in the land, which it never had been before, but which it has not ceased to be up to the present day.

The *Résistance* provided a second boost to the extreme Left. Up to 1941, when the war was labeled "bourgeois" and "imperialist" by Russia, the French Communists refused to participate in the defense of the country (their deputies were banned from Parliament in 1939) and even supported the Germans in the early period. But after the Nazi invasion of the Soviet Union, the Communist Party took a leading part in the *Résistance*. They gained considerable prestige as a result (they nicknamed themselves the *parti des fusillés*—the Party of the Shot), successfully infiltrated the underground trade union organizations, and made inroads in parts of the countryside (particularly in those regions which the *Résistance* had freed from the Germans and had controlled long before the Liberation). De Gaulle had no alternative but to offer them posts in the Government which he created in the summer of 1944 on his return to France. At that time, however, the Communists appear to have genuinely believed that they could take over power by legal means, and their Secretary-General and leader, Maurice Thorez, who became Vice-President of the Council, made unceasing efforts to boost production and reconstruction. By the end of 1945, however, troubles arose over De Gaulle's refusal to give them one of the key ministries (it was said that they tended to place men of their own in the ministries which they ran); a year and a half later, in May, 1947, they left the Government, never to return. With the intensification of the cold war, they used their trade union strength to harass the Government (the strikes of November, 1947 were among the most difficult episodes of postwar French politics). But the Government won, and the Communist challenge became less and less effective, as political strikes proved ineffective and more and more unpopular in the working class. By the end of the Fourth Republic, the Communist Party was a nuisance, not a menace; it could help anyone, Gaullists, Conservatives, even Poujadists, as much as Socialists, to overthrow governments—but it could do little to achieve its aims.

By then, the French Communist Party had come to be criticized for its complacency, its total lack of life, as much as for its own internal dictatorial methods. Purges had taken place from time to time; these had enabled Maurice Thorez to remain at the helm of a large machine (potential successors were successively "shown" to be wrong or traitors to the Party). But vitality seemed to be lacking. While the Italian Communist Party under Togliatti's leadership gave signs of independence and vigor, the French counterpart remained "Stalinist" for years after the death of Stalin, felt no official worries over Hungary, urged no liberalization; it simply repeated the theory of the impoverishment of the proletariat in capitalist regimes—a classic, though by then wholly inaccurate, part of the Marxist-Leninist doctrine. This enabled the CP to weather its defeat of 1958 without much trouble, but it did not make for a very rosy future. In the early 1960s, however, signs of "liberalization" became more numerous, though they have remained limited and lukewarm and have always been followed by a return to doctrinal rigidity. Ideological troubles arose among communist students, particularly in Paris. The strength of left-wing groups fighting against De Gaulle or against the Algerian war, the loosening of the grip of Maurice Thorez (who died in 1964) and his replacement by Waldeck-Rochet, a leader endowed with the qualities of the fox, not those of the lion, accounted for this slow unfreezing. Above all, perhaps, the appearance of a majority government of the Right brought home more clearly than before the fact that the Communists were condemning both themselves and the whole of the Left to remaining perpetually in the wilderness, if they maintained a rigid doctrinal purity. At the presidential election of 1965, the dilemma was clear, and Waldeck-Rochet gave in; faced with having to choose between launching a Communist candidate who would gain only Communist votes and show the isolation of the Party and supporting a Center Left candidate, the Communist leader finally and reluctantly took a momentous decision: no Communist candidate was to be placed in the field. It was the first time since 1932 that a major contest was to take place in France without being profoundly bedeviled by the problem of the Communist vote. The event may forecast more important changes, since Communists are clearly on the defensive; yet it seems unlikely that the electoral strength of the Party will cease to embarrass, divide, and hamper the Left, even if the Gaullist phase of the regime lasts.

Why, thus, is the French Communist Party so strong electorally, and what do Communist electors think they do when they vote for the Party? Tradition plays a large part, of course, but one of the most potent political factors has been the fact that the Communist leadership has succeeded in draining to its advantage the anarchistic tendencies of the disgruntled working class and the anti-government ("anti-them") attitudes of sections of the peasantry and the petty-bourgeoisie. On the one hand, manual workers have long felt that the CP was the only party which was irrevocably prepared to stand for them; whatever the palinodes of the Soviet Union (the Soviet Union is "the land of the working class," in any case, and it has to be defended, though the same apparently does not apply to China!) the manual workers felt that only by voting Communist could they protest against the government, the employers, the bourgeois system in general. These feelings, on the other hand, are linked to the anti-"establishment" and egalitarian tendencies of other sections of the community. They are naturally more marked in the parts of the country which are more individualistic, less prepared to accept organization, such as the Center and the Southeast (all along the Mediterranean coastline), than in the East and West. They do account for the paradox that the most anarchistic or individualistic of Frenchmen can conceive of the Communist vote as a natural mode of expression.

It is often said that the Communist vote is a "protest" vote, and that it is only that. It is clearly a protest vote, but it is an exaggeration to see in the Communist voters just "Socialist" electors who vote in another way. Surveys by the French Institute of Public Opinion have shown conclusively that there was a "Communist conscience," to take the expression of the author who analyzed them, Pierre Fougeyrollas. All other groups in society (including workers) believe that it is not possible to increase wages and salaries without affecting the price levels, but Communist voters do not. All other voters have supported European integration for a long time; as early as 1950, electors of all social groups (including workers) were favorable, but Communist voters were strongly opposed. Very few (5 percent) of the Communist voters felt any indignation at the Hungarian repression, while 22 percent were happy and 28 percent relieved. In 1952, 58 percent of the Communists felt that the United States was preparing an aggressive war, while the maximum percentage of voters of other parties who condemned the United States on this score was 3 percent. This is not to say that Communist voters disagree on all matters with the rest of French electors and that there is no consensus on any problem; there is consensus on a "neutral" policy, among all parties, as there was consensus against the governmental instability of the Fourth Republic and on some other, rather negative, attitudes. But the cleavages between Communist voters and the rest of the population are sharp on many important and positive issues, and these are far from being concerned only with foreign affairs.

The existence of such a self-contained group having attitudes which conflict, in many ways, with those of the rest of the members of the community, must be accounted for. It seems that the fact that the Communist Party has been both a large and tightly-knit organization for over a generation has much to do with it. The Communist Party is the only French party which can be deemed to have created a "society," and a very disciplined and hierarchical one at that. Not that the membership is exceptionally large, at least by world standards (though by French standards it is considerable): there are about 300,000 Frenchmen (or about 8 percent of the voters of the CP) who are paid-up members. But these members have been, for long periods in the case of many, tied to the Party through the network of cells (of a few members, mostly on the basis of residence, despite the somewhat unsuccessful efforts of the Party to create large numbers of factory cells), of sections, departmental (county) and national organizations. Decisions are taken on the basis of "democratic centralism"—the classic communist expression which is alleged to mean that proposals are discussed but that no criticism is allowed once the measure has been adopted; in fact, the system makes for little democracy and considerable centralization, since most members have no opportunity to know how decisions have been taken, reports being always fragmentary and designed to *explain* decisions taken rather than inform (a "bourgeois" notion) on debates and viewpoints. The Party Congress meets in principle every two years (with a smaller Conference called in the years in which the Congress does not meet); it is not a forum for discussion but a place where the members of the two inner bodies, the Central Committee (a body of about one hundred which meets every month) and the Executive (a body of twenty which meets every week), expound the problems, trounce deviationists, and rally support to the cause. Most important of all, as in the other CPs, is the Secretariat, headed by the Secretary General, who is the leader of the party. Never has there been many major rank and file revolt, nor indeed any trouble from the parliamentary party.

Nor, indeed, would a revolt be possible. This is not only because the heads of federations and sections, as well as of cells, are devoted to (and controlled by) the leadership, and aim at "explaining" problems to the mass of followers. It is also because the Communist society is such that any one who leaves the Party, after having spent years within the fold, finds himself an outcast, without friends and leisure activities. This, of course, is not the case for very top people who, after leaving the CP, may write about their experiences, be sought by other politicians, or indeed create another party. But ordinary faithful are not so well placed. Indeed, in most cases, the idea of leaving does not even enter their minds, whatever disagreements they may have with the party line. The Communist society, with its newspapers (*L'Humanité* is one of the seven morning Paris papers, and, though the Communist press has declined since the end of World War II, it is still larger than that of any other party), its young people and women's organizations, its hold on many trade unions, its grip on a tenant association, its network of specialized periodicals for various groups (in particular peasants), its sporting and recreational activities (the *Fête de l'Humanité* is a big event in the Bois de Vincennes in Paris) can take the whole of the life of the faithful and isolate them from the rest of the community. Thus it can be understood why the Hungarian repression was not seen *as such* by French Communists; thus it can also be understood why supporters of smaller Communist parties, in other Western countries, have been more exposed to non-Communist ("bourgeois") views than the voters of the French or Italian CP.

Indeed, this environmental influence of the Communist Party can be noted within France itself, since areas of CP strength, whether in the cities or in the countryside, are proportionately more Communist, among all social classes, than the percentage of workers would warrant on the basis of the national average. There are clusters of Communist influence: as we saw, peasants of the Center or the Southeast are often Communist; but Communist manual or white-collar workers are also clustered, for instance in the Paris Red Belt, in some mining areas of the North, and in the Marseilles and the Le Havre areas. Over-all, the Communist Party does not obtain much more than half its votes from manual workers (but somewhat less than half of the manual workers' vote for the party), one-eighth of its voters are white-collar workers, about 6 percent peasants, and 4 percent small shop-keepers. But fluctuations can be very large: the socialization into the Communist Party is a lengthy process, which for many, starts from family and childhood. It tends to be almost indelible.

The Communist Party is thus the epitome of the successful organization, particularly in relation to other French political organizations—but of an organization which exists for its own sake. One cannot say with certainty how much the Communist Party has helped the French working class, by leading employers and governments to agree to concessions for fear of the CP's increasing its strength. But the debit side of the balance sheet is perhaps more apparent. The French Left has been torn; it has devoted much energy to discussing problems of ideology, of "line" in relation to the Communists, and thus has been consequently unable to work out the problems of opposition to the Right. Left-wing governments have been paralyzed, as in 1936, or even prevented from coming into being as often after World War II by the presence of the Communist Party. The question is not to decide who is to be blamed, though on this difficult and complex problem the blame is probably shared by all. But the question is surely, for the future of French politics, whether, and if so when, the Communist Party will either markedly decrease in strength, or transform its character so much that it will become indistinguishable from the Left of the Socialists. With the changes of the 1960s, this prospect is no longer, as it was a decade earlier, wholly unrealistic. Only if it happens, however, will the difficulties of the Left be overcome permanently.

THE SOCIALIST PARTY

The French Socialist Party looks like a poorer brother of the CP. Born as a united party in 1905, and named "the French section of the second working class international" (SFIO), it originated from two socialist groups created in the 1890s, one led by Jean Jaurès, which was humanitarian and liberal, and the other by Jules Guesde, which was Marxist. Up to 1914, the party practiced "noncollaboration" with bourgeois governments, and it looked as if it was gradually going to win a commanding position. After the 1914 General Election the party had about one hundred deputies—or one sixth of the Chamber. Jaurès, the great humanitarian leader, tried with all his strength to rally all the anti-war forces, but he was assassinated just before the conflict started and French Socialists, like their German colleagues, were gradually made to accept the *"Union Sacrée":* even Guesde entered the Cabinet.

The Communist split of 1920 had little effect, in the first few years, on Socialist strength, but the war was more instrumental in bringing about changes in attitudes. Noncollaboration with the "bourgeois" State ceased to be the rule. Socialists did not participate in cabinets, but they supported them more often. The trade unions, led by Socialists, were called more often to advise and participate in decisions; old-fashioned capitalism was being replaced by a mixed economy. Socialists became more "bourgeois," noting perhaps that socialist parties abroad were coming to power or participating in governments, but seeing also that in many other countries, and in France as well, other enemies of the Republic might be more dangerous than capitalism. By the 1930s, however, the economic depression, the threat of fascism, and the change in the Communist tactics led to a return to a more "purist" left-wing attitude; after the 1936 General Election, at which the Socialists did reasonably though not outstandingly well (they obtained 147 seats—or about a fourth of the total, a small increase compared to 1914), the Party appeared as the great winner, having led to victory the Popular Front coalition which included the Radicals on their Right and the Communists on their Left, as well as various splinter socialist groups around the SFIO. For the first time a Socialist, Léon Blum, was called to head the Government: for a few tense spring days, the dream seemed to have become reality.

But the victory was hollow. Expectations of manual workers had been increased so markedly by the election result that sit-down strikes soon became the norm in large factories; the Communists pushed for takeovers while the Radicals were already soft-pedaling. Blum, a follower of Jaurès, a *grand bourgeois* who strongly believed in both equality and liberty, made a number of important reforms (the forty-hour week, paid holidays, collective bargaining), but he did not succeed in retaining the confidence of the workers or in acquiring—of course—that of the employers. Financial difficulties grew and the Government, in trouble with the Senate, resigned after a year. The Socialist Party was never to have such an hour of glory, though Blum did again head two cabinets, both short, in 1938 and 1946 (the latter having been somewhat successful in stabilizing prices at a difficult juncture) and though Guy Mollet, the Secretary General of the Party since 1946, was to head the longest Government of the Fourth Republic. Divided over Pétain in 1940, the Socialist Party did nonetheless take an important part in the *Résistance*. It became central to the first coalitions of the Fourth Republic, but having soon to fight on two fronts, and particularly against the Communist threat, it found itself obliged to acquiesce to measures and policies with which many of its voters disagreed and which even its ministers hardly condoned. Support in the country dwindled: from about 25 percent in 1945, the Party fell to about 15 at the end of the Fourth Republic; it had 145 deputies in 1945—as in 1936—but only 100 ten years later; there were to be only forty Socialist deputies after the 1958 General Election (and sixty-five in 1962).

The Socialist Party had ceased to appeal to the new and expanding sections of the community; its electorate was still mainly based on manual workers, white-collar employees, and peasants (respectively, about a third, a fifth, and an eighth), but its share of the younger generations was smaller than that of any party except the Radicals, and of the residents of large towns it had the smallest share of all parties. Its membership had declined drastically, from over 300,000 in the first few years after the Liberation to probably not more than 50,000 in the early 1960s. It had suffered from splits and expulsions, the major one having taken place in 1958, when, after years of opposition to the Algerian policy of the Party (Guy Mollet had promised autonomy at the 1956 General Election but found on becoming Premier that the only line he could or dared follow was that of stepping up the military buildup against the insurgents), a section of the Party, including some deputies, withdrew, on the occasion of De Gaulle's coming to power. The Autonomous Socialist Party, later renamed

United Socialist Party when it joined with other small socialist splinter groups (it enlisted the support of Pierre Mendès-France), took only a fraction of the Socialist electorate with it (2 or 3 percent of the popular vote), but for a declining party the blow was serious, and for a while appeared mortal.

Yet, despite its failings, and though its postwar Secretary General and leader, Guy Mollet, has been branded as a dictator of the Party, the Socialist Party is perhaps the only large French political group which could be deemed to be moderately democratic. Members, organized in sections (many of which are largely sleepy bodies meeting somewhat irregularly) and in *fédérations départementales* (at the county level), are represented, through an elaborate system of proportional representation, at the Congress, which meets once a year; at the National Council, which meets when an emergency arises; and even at the Executive Committee (*Comité Directeur*), which runs the Party on behalf of the Congress. Debates at the Congress and National Committees are open and frank (sometimes perhaps too frank). Votes are taken often, indeed on all major issues. Admittedly, with such a small membership, the Secretary General can exercise his patronage more effectively than he would be able to if the Party were much larger; some federations are strongly rumored to be "his"—not only his own, in the Pas-de-Calais, in the North of France, but others in various parts of the country. But opponents, too, have their "fortresses," as, for instance, Gaston Defferre, for years the *de facto* contender to the leadership and for some months a candidate for the Presidency of the Republic, who is mayor of Marseilles and can be said to run the federation of his *départment*. Discussion is never suppressed, though techniques of persuasion may include advantages and favors which go beyond ideological argument. Guy Mollet can justly and proudly note that, if the members wanted to, they could overthrow him— which did not happen for twenty years because of the political skill of the Secretary General and not through the use of the big stick, the silencing of opponents, or the purges of dissenters.

By the mid-1960s, however, the Socialist Party had begun to show more resilience. Its support of the Gaullist Government lasted only a few months and ended when a stabilization program of a conservative character was launched in the early part of 1959. The Party seemed to want to use the opportunity which arose to slowly build itself into the mainstay of the opposition; for the first time for decades, and thanks to the electoral system, it had more deputies than the Communists (forty-five against ten in 1958, sixty-five against forty-one in 1962). It could thus be the main opposition group in the Chamber; at the 1962 General Election, Guy Mollet developed both a subtle policy of arrangements with the Communists whereby in some cases, but not in all, there was alternative support of candidates, and a full-fledged agreement with the Radicals and even the Christian Democrats, which was buttressed by a promise of governmental accord if they were to win the election (an eventuality which no one took very seriously). Finally, with considerable reluctance, the party endorsed the candidature to the Presidency of Gaston Defferre, long before the election was to take place, and perhaps, in the minds of many, with the hope that it would indeed never take place: too many oppositions had arisen between Guy Mollet and Gaston Defferre for the former to feel comfortable at the idea of the latter gaining popularity. But the Party was thus coming back to the fore, and an inconclusive attempt by the Socialist Mayor of Marseilles would, if thwarted by other parties, have the advantage of accruing to the Socialist Party while not undermining the authority of the Secretary General.

Gaston Defferre indeed had to withdraw, partly because of a Communist veto, and largely through the intransigence of the Christian Democrats who, at the last moment, felt that their electors could not support a Socialist candidate. But this intransigence was manifest because Gaston Defferre, not content with being merely a candidate, started an entirely new process, which, despite his own disappearance from the front of the stage, has remained very much alive. Realizing that alliances such as those of the Fourth Republic or even of 1962 were soon to be broken when coalitions came to power, he insisted on the constitution of what amounted to a new party, the *Fédération démocrate et socialiste*. During the course of 1965, he made his own party agree with some difficulty (after his reelection as Mayor of Marseilles had proved that, whatever pains his opponents, Communist and Gaullist, were taking, he was still a votegetter) to a Federation, which would comprise the Radicals, the Christian Democrats, and representatives of some of the many new political "clubs" which had developed in the Fifth Republic, and which would be as firmly anti-Communist as it was anti-Gaullist. This was a momentous achievement, since it could have meant—and could indeed still mean—that the Socialist Party as such would disappear, and become the nucleus of a new coalition resembling that of Britain's Labour Party. The Radicals did agree, but the small United Socialist Party, worried about not being at the center of a Communist-Socialist arrangement, and the Christian Democrats, unsure of their conservative voters, opposed the project. The old anti-Catholic reflex which is rampant among Socialist militants and which Guy Mollet is never hesitant to exploit, partly genuinely, partly as a useful tactical instrument, was revived by this intransigence of the Christian Democrats. After a conclave in which the party leaders tried unsuccessfully to hammer out the differences, Gaston Defferre resigned his candidature, but the next few months were to show that he had, to a large extent, won the day. In September of 1965, a member of a small center-left group near to the Radicals, François Mitterrand, announced that he would fight the election. He was swiftly endorsed by the Socialists, Radicals, and Communists (and by the United Socialist Party as well), on the basis of a program which was not vastly different from that of Gaston Defferre, and under an arrangement which smacked of the tactics of the Mayor of Marseilles. Indeed, after the presidential election, the *Fédération* was reborn as the *Fédération de la Gauche Démocrate et Socialiste;* it was to be nicknamed the "small" Federation, because this time it did not comprise the Christian Democrats. But it was a Federation all the same, and the Socialist Party has agreed to work jointly with other groups; indeed, it came to the 1967 election as the component body of a larger unit.

Time will tell whether the Federation is to be merely an electoral alliance under another name. Its relative success at the 1967 General Election was followed by some decline in unity and some internal bickering. Since it does not include the Christian Democrats, however, it is not likely to be labeled a "centrist" organization; it will have as a result slightly more authority vis-à-vis the Communist leadership. It may therefore not suffer from the complex of the lesser partner which characterized the Socialist Party in all its dealings with the CP since the end of World War II. In a period in which parties are attacked for being too old, too numerous, too concerned with idiosyncratic problems, the Federation may appear, to the Socialists, to be a relevant way out of their difficult predicament. If this is the case, Gaston Defferre will indeed have started a process which may alter the character of French politics in future decades. There are, admittedly, many problems: the Radicals are not likely to be easy partners any more than they were in 1936 when Blum tried his first Socialist experiment; and for some time at least, the leader will be François Mitterrand, a man who, though progressive in his outlook, has never concealed that he was not a Socialist, so that frictions between Guy Mollet and François Mitterand are likely to increase as time goes by. But there is some hope, too, that a rejuvenation of the leaders and rank and file of the Socialist Party may take place in this way. If this happens, old-style difficulties may be solved by being bypassed. If, on the other hand, the Federation breaks or comes to have a mere formal existence, the Socialist Party will probably survive, but its ability to lead future French politics will be greatly decreased; only a reunion between an entirely remolded and liberalized CP and the remaining faithful of the SFIO, perhaps under the auspices of the United Socialist Party, could, if the Federation breaks, lead to a revival of the Left.

THE RADICAL SOCIALIST PARTY AND THE CENTER-LEFT GROUPS

Probably the most French of all the French parties is not a party at all. For many, and not only abroad, the resilience of the Radical Party is a baffling phenomenon. Together with a number of small groups at the Center-Left of the political spectrum, the *Parti Républicain Radical et Radical-Socialiste* (as this is its official title) managed to dominate the governments of the second half of the Third Republic and was scarcely less successful during the Fourth. Bitterly riven by the vote of 1940 which gave full powers to Pétain, and seemingly doomed to the wilderness, the Party recovered and produced from its thinned ranks scores of premiers and prominent ministers.

Far to the left in the early days of the Third Republic, its real period of glory was just before the First World War, when, after having been organized as a united party in 1901, it was prominent in its fight against clericalism and achieved the separation of Church and State in 1905. From then on, radicalism was on the decline: the religious question was the main issue which still united—at least in words—all Radicals, but the sources of division began to increase as problems connected with capitalism and the development of the welfare state created cleavages between the *"grands bourgeois du radicalisme"* and some of its more obscure petty-bourgeois elements. Its greatest figure of the interwar period, Edouard Herriot, epitomized almost all the characteristics of the Radicals. Brilliant, somewhat literary in his instincts and interests, prone to considerable oratory, Herriot was probably more the victim of the system which he adored than he himself realized. In a situation of stable and disciplined parties, Herriot might have conducted foreign policy, and even perhaps financial policy, on the basis of sound principles. But he used his principles mainly in his speeches; his presence in the Government was associated with troubles and with problems which he could not solve. He gave the world and France the image of an impotent Government, an impotent Chamber, and an impotent system.

It seemed for a while that the Radicals would never recover from the events of the Second World War. They left 130 in 1940; they returned twenty-eight in 1945. They were then the smallest of all parties, even smaller than a new party which had just been created as a result of the *Résistance*, the *Union Démocratique et Socialiste de la Résistance* (UDSR), which had twenty-nine deputies. This Party, allied in the first instance to the Socialists, with whom they shared the desire to rejuvenate French social structures without being as tainted with anti-clericalism as the Socialists or Radicals, came to be nearer to the Radicals in the course of the debates on the Constitution of 1946. The Radicals succeeded in realizing their first great coup of the postwar period by concluding negotiations with the UDSR and building a federal organization, the *Rassemblement des Gauches Républicaines*, thus losing some of the opprobrium resulting from their war record. They managed to return, jointly with the new group, seventy deputies at the election of November, 1946. The road to recovery was open. With ministerial coalitions becoming shakier as a result of the Communists' being pushed into opposition, the Radicals came back to power, and in 1948, France had once more a Radical Prime Minister in the person of Doctor Queuille, who ran the country for over a year and achieved stabilization, both political and financial. For many the return of the Radicals symbolized the return to normalcy and showed that the *Résistance* had been only a brief interlude.

Despite the influx of new blood coming from the UDSR, however, "normalcy" was not to last long. First, the UDSR was becoming more and more like the Radical Party: its "socialist" outlook became less visible and the personal ambitions of its divided leaders more apparent—Pleven's UDSR was different from that of Mitterrand. Second, the electoral strength of the Radicals scarcely increased at all (it remained at 8 percent), and only the electoral law of 1951 could conceal what was actually a slight decrease in the percentage of votes cast. The electors were old (65 percent were above fifty); mainly composed of men (64 percent—Radicals have always been prone to think that women cannot understand the intricacies of political behavior, whether locally or in the Assembly), composed in the majority of peasants and shopkeepers, and therefore mainly located (for three-fifths) in places of less than 5,000 in population. This was not a particularly promising springboard for future advance, though Radicals, being more concerned with problems of Assembly manipulation, were probably unwilling to consider—or indeed even incapable of understanding—the importance of these characteristics. But, even in the Assembly, difficulties had begun. The impact of the first large Gaullist wave, in the late forties, was hard on the Radicals; it forced them to decide whether they would agree that their deputies—traditionally free to vote the way they wanted, and indeed exercising this freedom with great eagerness —should be allowed to belong both to their own party and to a Gaullist group. This was solved in a characteristically confused Radical manner, but the ranks of the Party were somewhat depleted. By then, the impact of the alliance of the UDSR had been wholly lost. The Radical Party was not changing; it was instructing others in its own techniques.

Yet, for a short moment, it seemed that the Party was indeed going to change: one of its leading members, Pierre Mendès-France, who left De Gaulle's Government in 1945 because he advocated a policy of austerity, and who had been mainly prominent for his criticisms of French policy in Vietnam, became popular overnight, not only in the Assembly, because he seemed the only one who was prepared to take the responsibility of a peaceful settlement, but in the country, because he practiced a style of politics which the French had not been accustomed to seeing in their Premiers; his "fireside chats," direct and devoid of rhetoric, were immensely successful, and he promised a regeneration of politics, not only in foreign affairs, but in internal matters as well. In order to accomplish this, he began considering the possibility of streamlining the Radical Party, and when he came to be defeated in Parliament, partly thanks to the passionate speech of another Radical, he tried to do what no Radical had ever done before: he wanted to create a rank and file membership which would pay dues, go to meetings, and discuss politics in broad national terms; he also wanted to make the parliamentary party obey the orders of the national organization. For some months, he seemed on the verge of winning, and of achieving the impossible. He was helped by the General Election of 1956, called by yet another Radical, Edgar Faure, who had succeeded Pierre Mendès-France as Premier and was defeated in Parliament at the end of 1955 thanks to the votes of many Radical deputies on the subject of electoral reform (a matter which Radicals take very

seriously indeed). At the polls, there was a considerable upswing
of the Radical forces in such unlikely places as Paris and other
large towns: the young, the white-collar workers and skilled
engineers, even the women had started to vote radical. The popularity of Pierre Mendès-France had led to an unprecedented
success for the Party, which gained over a million votes above its
previous level. But the old Radical spirit did prevail in the end:
Mendès-France did not succeed in streamlining the Party, which
first split, then expelled him (on the occasion of his joining
forces with anti-Gaullist groups in 1958) and eventually came
back to its ways. By the beginning of the Fifth Republic, the
Radical Party had returned to being the Radical Party of the past
—but with one difference, namely that the presence of De Gaulle
at the helm made it impossible for the Party to think, at least for
the time being, in terms of parliamentary manipulation and of a
speedy return to power.

Thus, of necessity, the Radical Party came to be part of the
opposition. Gradually, during the course of the 1960s, it looked
with less disfavor at the alliance with some of its former partners
of Fourth Republic coalitions: on the one hand, the Socialists, with
whom it shares anti-clericalism, now anti-Gaullism, but not much
else, except a common concern for the return to a more traditional political system; and on the other the Christian Democrats
and even the Conservatives, with whom it does share a concern
for only limited experiments in the social and economic fields.
But, as we saw in the previous section of this chapter, the Socialists forced the Radicals to choose; somewhat reluctantly—
and with the usual divisions—the Radicals agreed to enter the
Fédération. In it they are very much the junior partners, with the
Socialists providing the organization, and François Mitterrand and
his immediate advisers providing the leadership. But the Radicals
are electorally weak (they can really count only on some deputies in parts of the Southwest) and they have become more aware
of electoral constraints; their voters, after the Pierre Mendès-
France fever receded, are still mainly the old, the men, the residents of small towns. Perhaps, in the depth of their hearts, Radicals think that they will, as after 1945, regain prominence, if they
stoop for a while and wait sufficiently. This may, indeed, once
more happen. But the probability is smaller than in the past, for
France has moved fast, economically and socially, and the base of
the Radical Party has shrunk more in the 1950s and 1960s than
in the whole first half of the twentieth century.

THE CONSERVATIVE GROUPS: INDEPENDENTS AND PEASANTS

Students of French politics often analyze the Christian Democrats after the Radicals, and leave the Conservatives for the end, but the similarities between the "Independent" and "Peasant" organizations on the one hand, and the Radical Party on the other, are such (they both represent so strongly the traditions of the Third Republic) that both groups should be considered in sequence. In both the Radical Party and the Conservative organizations one finds the same lack of discipline in Parliament (or perhaps, more precisely, the same total lack of concern for discipline, except for occasional outbursts which soon fade); both Conservative groups and the Radical Party suffered from having been compromised by the Vichy régime—though the Radicals suffered more, while the Conservatives were more compromised; both Conservative groups and the Radical Party are preponderantly elected by old people and residents of small towns (but the Conservatives draw much more than average from the woman vote); both attract peasants and shopkeepers, but the Conservatives also receive considerable support from employers. If France had only two parties, the Conservatives and the Radicals, they could be analyzed together, and together they would constitute a party "system."

Distinctions have to be made, nonetheless, between Radicals and Conservatives. We noted some differences in the sources of electoral support: broadly, the Independents (if not the Peasants) are more affluent, more bourgeois, and somewhat more Parisian than the Radicals. They also come from the North of France, while most Radicals are located in the South. Thus, not unnaturally, the Independents are also pro-Church, though not aggressively so. They are, also, less "politicalized"; that is, they do not try to turn politics into a fine art as the Radicals do. They are "conservative" either because they mainly want to keep things as they are or, if they are less prudent, because they want to return to the past. Most accepted Vichy, but few were really convinced; compromised by the Corporate State, they did not really believe in it. Only a minority—which manifested itself once more on Algeria—really wants to overthrow the regime. For better or for worse, most are mildly in favor of a liberal regime, though more out of a conservative and complacent attitude toward politics than out of a profound belief in the virtues of modern democracy.

This conglomeration of groups was so shaken by the electoral defeat of 1945 (though Conservatives of all kinds gained sixty-four seats—more than twice the number of deputies obtained by the Radicals) that efforts were made to streamline, unify, and organize. A first attempt, under the name of *Parti Républicain de la Liberté*, was not really successful; the Peasant deputies (mostly from the Massif Central area) organized themselves outside the PRL. But the following effort, under the leadership of Roger Duchet, was much more longstanding; it led to the creation of a rather loose federal body, the *Centre National des Indépendants et Paysan*, which most Conservative deputies joined. By the 1951 election, the CNIP was recognized as a group and it was at least as homogeneous as the Radical Party. It won almost a hundred seats at the election, though this was largely the result of the electoral system, as the number of votes decreased, largely under the Gaullist impact. It was soon to attract more deputies, as the Independents were about to achieve, with Antoine Pinay, their great coup of the Fourth Republic.

Antoine Pinay was a relatively little known deputy of the Massif Central, who was called in February of 1952 to solve a ministerial crisis which seemed in complete deadlock. Nobody expected a Conservative to become Premier, and he was designated by the President more in order to placate the Conservatives than because it was thought that he would win. Yet he did win the investiture of the Assembly, after having made twenty-seven members of the Gaullist party defy their tight discipline; they were soon to form an autonomous group within the CNIP. Thus Gaullism seemed to follow the fate of the Christian Democracy, a section of whose supporters had come back to the Conservatives by 1951. As the Radicals had done but much more successfully— and without appearing to have used consummate skill—the Conservative groups were making a strong comeback. Indeed, during the remainder of the 1951 Parliament, except for the seven-month period of the Pierre Mendès-France experiment, they were to dominate the scene, and, though the 1956 election marked a swing to the Left, the Conservatives benefited from the almost total collapse of the Gaullists and came back almost a hundred strong. Within a few months, they were to operate on the new extremist group of the Right, the Poujadists, the third successive "breakup" operation. If the Radicals had shown resilience, mainly during the middle part of the Fourth Republic, the Independents were even more successful; they were able to undermine, divide, and take over.

In the Fifth Republic, however, the Independents have been much less successful. The Conservatives returned almost 130 in 1958, helped by the Gaullist tide; they seemed, in the first few months, to be about to benefit from Gaullist splits, as they had done seven years earlier. Algeria proved to be a bone of contention among Gaullists, and the Conservatives, though profoundly split, were clever enough not to play up their differences, at least in the open. But De Gaulle in power was more difficult to circumvent than his supporters had been when in opposition. The Conservatives were members of the Government, but merely as epigones. By 1962, with the end of the Algerian war, they hoped for a real comeback; they concurred in voting against the Government over the change of the procedure of the election of the President of the Republic. They were faced with the immediate dissolution of the Chamber, and forced to choose: those who had voted against the Government joined forces with Radicals, Christion Democrats, and even Socialists. Whether liberal or not (some of the opponents of De Gaulle were among the staunchest supporters of French Algeria), most of them were defeated: 108 left the Assembly; twenty-eight returned. Even the Independents who supported De Gaulle (renamed *Républicains Indépendants*) lost some seats: the twenty-eight who had left the Assembly had thinned to twenty after the election. With fewer than fifty seats, the Independent Conservatives had suffered their worst defeat of the century, worse even than that which the war and Pétain had brought on them in 1945.

Since 1962, the Independents have seemed slowly to recover, largely because their Gaullist wing, under Valéry Giscard d'Estaing, Minister of Finance from 1962 to 1965, appeared able to challenge Gaullism and provide an alternative, more liberal, less anti-American, more European, to a Government which Conservative electors were unlikely to abandon for a Socialist policy. But the electoral test is of a different kind. At the presidential election, Independents were unable to find a strong candidate. Conservative voters split their votes four ways: some voted for an extreme right-winger, Jean-Louis Tixier-Vignancour, who catered mainly to the French Algerian supporters, and received 5 percent of the vote; others to a solitary Conservative senator, Pierre Marcilhacy, who received 2 percent; yet others to the Christian Democrat candidate, Jean Lecanuet, while the great mass plumped for General De Gaulle himself. At the second ballot, all had to vote for the General, unless they were prepared to join forces with the Communists in supporting François Mitterrand.

Whether Valéry Giscard d'Estaing, whose support for Gaullism became conditional when he was dismissed from the Government, will find that he can rally the Conservative vote before Gaullism ends is very doubtful indeed; he may be an alternative to Georges Pompidou or Michel Debré after the General disappears from the scene, though even then his cold personality is unlikely to attract as much support as that of Antoine Pinay. But unlike the Radicals and whether they are temporary advocates of Gaullism or mild opponents of the new regime, the Independents can expect to reap benefits and profit from the spoils. Their hope lies in a Gaullist split, though this may be more unlikely and more difficult to provoke than in the early fifties. They could, admittedly, organize themselves and become more disciplined, but they would then no longer be the Independent Party of the past —and a disciplined party of the Right is more likely to come, if not from the Christian Democrats, at least from the Gaullists.

THE CHRISTIAN DEMOCRATS
(*Mouvement Républicain Populaire*)

France was the last Roman Catholic country of continental Europe to have a Christian party; it is also the country where it has always been weakest. Indeed, had it not been for the war, the defeat, and Vichy, the MRP would probably never have existed. Traditions of anti-clericalism are stronger in France than in any other Roman Catholic country; Catholicism is also rather laxer; and only certain limited sections, either geographically circumscribed (Alsace-Lorraine and parts of Brittany) or defined in narrow social terms (Christian Social progressives among workers and farmers), have had a long-standing tradition of Christian Democracy. It is indeed symbolic that the French Christian Democrats (unlike the Christian trade unionists, for a very long period at least) should have chosen to give themselves a title which does not formally include the word "Christian," though the *Mouvement Républicain Populaire* has never hidden the fact that it was a Christian Democratic Party. Starting from obscure origins in the early part of the century, moving slowly in the interwar period, and mainly in its regional outposts, the MRP emerged suddenly, at the 1945 General Election, with almost five million votes, a quarter of the electorate, and 150 deputies: it had swept all over France, replacing the Independent Conservatives where they used to be strong, but allegedly supporting a program of social reform which Conservatives never advocated.

The success was brief. The MRP found itself almost immediately faced with the contradictions of remaining in power against De Gaulle, after having presented itself as a "faithful" Gaullist party, of opposing Socialists and Communists on the first draft of the Constitution while remaining in the tripartite alliance, and, more dangerously for its future fate at the polls, of agreeing to progressive social policies while relying mainly on a conservative electorate. Divisions started inside; some deputies left to join the Independents, while others became Gaullists. The Assembly of 1946, where the MRP had 169 deputies, was to be the last where the Party was to have a commanding position; reduced to ninety-six seats in 1951 (and only remaining that large thanks to an electoral system which the MRP opposed in principle since it stood for full proportional representation), the Party was to decline at every successive contest. With 1.6 million votes, it was to obtain only thirty-six seats at the General Election of 1962.

In many ways, the MRP is an unlucky party. It has supported liberal institutions against the unrealistic and possibly dangerous first draft of the Constitution which was rejected by the voters—and by its stand in the Assembly it did, perhaps, save the Republic; it defended the Fourth Republic in its difficult early period, when it was subjected to the combined violence, not only oral in the Chamber, but even physical in the street, of the Communists and the Gaullists; it did much to reintegrate the Church in the nation, educating the hierarchy, the mass of the Catholics, and especially the youth into thinking in liberal and even somewhat progressive terms; it was among the first to preach European unity—and the name of Robert Schuman will probably for a long time be a symbol of European integration; it was one of the main proponents of the idea of modernization in the economic and social fields. Yet it gained little credit in the minds of Frenchmen and has been constantly assailed by politicians of all sides. In the nation as a whole, it has been associated with the stigma of the Fourth Republic; the last Prime Minister of the regime, Pierre Pflimlin, was a member of the MRP. In Parliament, it came to be attacked by the Socialists, because of the latter's long-standing anti-clerical animosities as well as because of the fear that it might not want to be sufficiently progressive in social terms; it came to be attacked by the Radicals and Conservatives because it was felt to be too progressive; Gaullists competed for its electors and the quarrel over subsidies for Church schools was at least in part revived in order to embarrass the MRP and make the Party choose between its Roman Catholic electors and its progressive views.

Accident prone, the MRP thus found itself in the unenviable position of appearing more responsible then most other parties for the fall of the two popular Prime Ministers of the Fourth Republic, Antoine Pinay, because he was too conservative, and Pierre Mendès-France, because he was not European enough.

Since the beginning of the Fifth Republic, the MRP has continued to have the same unhappy destiny. It first supported De Gaulle firmly (though the new President did not rate their support very high, the precedent of the MRP betrayal in 1945 probably having something to do with the new coolness), but it became more and more estranged from the new regime. Not only did Gaullists and Christian Democrats compete strongly for the same electors in the constituencies, not only were the attacks against the Fourth Republic too numerous to be pleasant to the leaders of the MRP, but the regime embarked on conservative social policies which the progressive wing of the Party found distasteful and on a nationalistic foreign policy which the whole of the Movement thoroughly disliked. Opposed to the "confederal" twist given by the Government to European policy, Christian Democrat ministers resigned in 1962, and the Movement joined, somewhat half-heartedly, the opposition. But the result of the subsequent General Election showed that the electorate did not support the Party on this stand, and, not unexpectedly, the more conservative leaders (including Pierre Pflimlin) prevented the MRP from joining the *Fédération démocrate et socialiste* in the spring of 1965. Some comfort was taken from the fact that at the 1965 presidential election a Christian Democrat candidate, Jean Lecanuet, fared relatively well, gaining third place and 13 percent of the vote. The idea of a new federal arrangement (the *Centre Démocrate*) centered around the MRP and including some non-Gaullist conservatives seemed to gain ground, and hopes were even expressed that this new group might become the key to all future coalitions.

These hopes are, almost certainly, exaggerated or at least premature. Jean Lecanuet's 13 percent of the votes is a far cry from the 25 percent of the late 1940s which the MRP alone could muster; the European policies of the Government—and also some aspects of the farming policy, the two being in fact linked—were probably responsible for part of the Lecanuet protest vote. Thus the MRP, whether alone or with the *Centre Démocrate*, may not find these electors again: the result of the 1967 election was to give very little encouragement indeed. The Secretary General of the Socialist Party once said that the MRP was a party which ought not to have existed; of all the French parties it is certainly the one which has proved the most difficult to create, the least successful in its tactics, and the least able to keep a solid hold on its electorate. Admittedly, Christian Democrats will not, whatever the future of the MRP, disappear from French Assemblies: there are too many pockets of Christian Social thinking, in Brittany and Alsace alone, to prevent the Movement from dying. But the Party has shrunk to a point where it may have to be content with a peripheral position among major party alignments, unless considerable skill and maneuvering talent are to help where strength is lacking. But throughout its short history, the MRP has not shown such talent—it has often taken pride in not thriving on tactics. It may regret this attitude, and politics in France may be the poorer for it, as the most imaginative policies of the Fourth Republic often had a Christian Democrat origin (although in the details of the parliamentary game, and in the midst of its personal animosities, the MRP did not always back the right candidate at the right time and indeed even supported weak men and defended weak policies for some higher motive).

THE GAULLISTS: *Rassemblement du Peuple Français* and *Union pour la Nouvelle République*

On December 2, 1958, the French woke up to find to their surprise that the newly-created *Union pour la Nouvelle République* could muster, together with the deputies elected by Algeria, a majority in the first Assembly of the Fifth Republic. But the surprise quickly passed, and the jump made by the Gaullists from 18 to 26 percent of the votes between the first and second ballots was often ascribed by commentators to the peculiar conditions of the new regime, the fears of the unknown, and the dangers of a military plot; moreover, only 26 percent of the electors had voted for Gaullist candidates, and the electoral system could be said to be responsible for the disparity between seats and votes. Observers noted that the previous Gaullist Party, the *Rassemblement du Peuple Français*, had obtained four million votes and 22 percent of the votes at the 1951 General Election, only to collapse lamentably to less than 4 percent at the next election. But when the French woke up, on the morning of November 19, 1962, to find that at the first ballot the UNR had 32 percent of the votes, they were already witnessing the beginnings of a major breakthrough, since no party in the whole of French political life had had as many as 30 percent of the votes at a General Election. The results of the second ballot, the following week, were even more astounding: the UNR received 40 percent of the votes, and had 229 deputies for metropolitan France, among whom many were elected in direct competition with supporters of French Algeria, sometimes originating from the Gaullist group of the first Assembly. For the UNR to have an absolute majority in the new Parliament 242 deputies were needed: with some overseas supporters, the UNR could muster 234, and about two dozen deputies were elected with Gaullist support, mostly among the Independents but also from the MRP. France had come near majority government in 1958 without noticing it; she was consolidating the trend, four years later, to everyone's amazement; and if the 1967 result was in part a setback, the Gaullist Party did remain stronger than in 1958 and stronger than any party in the Fourth Republic.

Yet, as observers often note, the UNR is scarcely a party at all. In this, it differs markedly from the RPF of the late forties. When De Gaulle retired from the Government early in 1946, he spent some months in total silence in his retreat of Colombey and came out in the open only once the French people—pressed by the MRP—had rejected the first draft of the Constitution. He first let a *Union Gaulliste* emerge in the Assembly, spoke his mind about the role of the President in his Bayeux speech, saw with pleasure a third of the population abstain on the second draft of the Constitution (adopted none the less, but by a slim majority), and, in the middle of 1947, launched a new movement, a "Rally," which was not to be a party (hence the suggestions made by some Radicals that they could belong to both the Radical and Gaullist organizations) and which was to be open to all Frenchmen who were not "separatists" (the term which De Gaulle used at the time to qualify the Communists). The Rally was an immediate success, and seemed to pose a direct threat to the liberal institutions of the regime, at the time when the Communists, having just been thrown into opposition, were starting their massive protest strikes. At its first electoral contest, the municipal elections of 1947, the Gaullists swept in most large towns, often obtaining as much as 40 percent of the vote. De Gaulle started his claim for a dissolution of the Assembly and organized his Rally to fight the election he asked for.

The organization of the Rally smacked dangerously of fascism. Authority and power were concentrated at the top and subordinate bodies were asked only to show discipline. Admittedly, some notables, whether Conservatives (particularly in the West), Radicals, or Christian Democrats, joined the new movement. But the structure was one of hierarchical leadership flowing through a network of professional "cadres" enlisting thousands of rank and file members. At one time, the Rally claimed to have a million members, more than any French political movement had ever had before or was to have afterwards. Ideological discussions were limited; the one original plank of the movement was the idea of a profit-sharing scheme between capital and labor, with which the name of Louis Vallon, a progressive Gaullist, was associated, but the details of which were scarcely worked out in practice. The bulk of the thinking was nationalistic, strongly anticommunist (support came to the Rally mainly for this reason), and somewhat reactionary in colonial matters (particularly on Indochina), though the position of the leader on this question was kept ambiguous. What was more apparent than ideology was the physical presence of the movement. French political life, normally complex, individualistic, and tiresome, is not usually ugly, but with the appearance of the RPF, fighting started to break out, local Communist headquarters were burnt, even thugs appeared (later the Poujadists and even later, of course, the supporters of French Algeria were to do rather worse, though they did not quite reach the level of German pre-Hitler politics; but it could be said that the Gaullists had shown the way). Some Communist retaliation took place and a repetition of the last years of Weimar or of the pre-Mussolini Italian Republic seemed in process.

But the skill of Doctor Queuille, the resilience of the Center parties, and the good sense of the French appeared to prevail: by 1951, the tide had receded. Somewhat handicapped by the new electoral law, the RPF elected only 120 deputies (less than a fifth of the Assembly), many of whom were old parliamentarians who were simply hanging onto Gaullist coattails; when, as we saw, Antoine Pinay proposed a solidly conservative program, a quarter of these latter-day Gaullists left the Movement and joined the Independents. The rest began to lose their discipline. In the country, members ceased to pay their dues, failed to turn up at meetings, and finally left the Rally. By 1953, De Gaulle realized that he had failed and disbanded the Movement, leaving his supporters in Parliament free to support the regime. The Social Republicans, as they were to be known, entered coalitions (including that of Mendès-France) and behaved like Radicals or Independent Conservatives. Only twenty-two were to return after the 1956 General Election, Poujadists having, for a while, become the "tough" party of the Right in the eyes of the electors.

Thus, on his return to power in the summer of 1958, De Gaulle had no party and little trust in movements. But as an election had to be fought in the autumn, a new group had to be created. Politicians of the old guard were not to be permitted to enter the organization, since in 1951–52 it was through these politicians that the RPF had been lost. Almost from nothing, a supporter of De Gaulle, Albin Chalandon, who was a businessman entirely new to politics, formed, from above, the Union for the New Republic. It was to be more democratic than the RPF, with executive committees and congresses, but it was also to be much smaller, with no appeal to a mass rank and file, as this could not be trusted; De Gaulle could, through various forms of patronage, hope to manipulate deputies, but hundreds of thousands of members could be dominated by factional groups and prove a powerful machine, even against De Gaulle. At the time, with the Algerian war, simple demagogic slogans (as were those of Jacques Soustelle) could easily be used to take over the Party. Indeed, almost immediately, at one of the first UNR Congresses, an attempt was made to take over the Party, and it might have been successful had the membership been larger and Albin Chalandon's men less skillful.

The UNR is thus not even a movement in the sense that the RPF was; it has little grassroots organization, except for constituency and town committees which tend to meet mainly to nominate candidates. Even after the end of the Algerian war and the consequent disappearance of all danger for the political position of De Gaulle, no serious effort was made to turn the Union into a real party. There is nothing "fascist" in the UNR; it resembles the *Centre National des Indépendants* more than the Nazi movement. But this non-organization, which inherited from the RPF the non-ideology and the non-program of Gaullist groupings, nonetheless managed to cohere and be disciplined behind and because of the President. While profound difficulties, mainly over Algeria, agitated the UNR parliamentary party in the first Assembly of the new Republic, only minor riddles—of the kind which trouble the British Conservative Party from time to time —were to be seen on the smooth surface of the parliamentary party of the second Parliament. Not that discussion is forbidden; much happens in the backbench committees of the party, and even competition for the leadership of the backbenchers was sometimes noted. But, in a curious way, there is unity among UNR deputies. It is obviously based on trust in De Gaulle, without whom most of the present members would not sit in the Assembly, but it also includes nationalistic foreign policy attitudes and expansionist views on economic affairs (interestingly enough De Gaulle chose his two "deflationist" Ministers of Finance from among the Independents, while Michel Debré became the first

Minister of Finance of the Fifth Republic to be both UNR and avowedly expansionist). The UNR outlook or approach also includes a desire to reform, and perhaps over-reform, all the traditional administrative institutions; it is based on the firm belief that past sectional attitudes have to give way to a new national thinking. It is clearly more a frame of mind than a dogmatic approach to politics. But it undoubtedly does exist, and the eight years of the two Assemblies have given opportunities and time for the development of common views, the weeding of unacceptable elements, and the buildup of comradeship.

Will the UNR last, however, and will it survive De Gaulle? The question would have been preposterous in 1959; at the time, it seemed obvious that the UNR was merely De Gaulle's poodle. By the late 1960s, while the question had become real, the answer was still not clear. Much depends on how much time will be given to enable members of Parliament, both inside and outside the UNR, to become aware of the new party's unity. Conservatives of other parties (in the MRP and more so in the Independent groups) must be convinced, even after a further defeat in 1967, that there is little hope of winning in opposing the UNR line and that infiltration from inside is more likely to succeed than outright competition. Members of the old guard must gradually fade out, and a new class with no patience for past attitudes and a simpler view of the political game must slowly replace them. Above all, leaders with a sufficiently high status above that of ordinary deputies to be recognized by all must gradually emerge; nothing would break the UNR more quickly than the setting up of factions inside the Party and the organization of joint groups with other parties. But in the late 1960s these leaders are not really in sight. Only if they come smoothly, without creating difficult succession problems, can the UNR hope to survive and a new style be imposed upon the Right and Center-Right of French politics, and indeed, indirectly, on the Left as well.

CONCLUSION

The future seems open. It may or may not include the major traditional groupings; it may show a decrease in the number of important political groupings and also a simplification in modes of behavior. What does seem clear, however, is that the future of the French party system depends largely on the UNR, though this is perhaps the most paradoxical of all French political groupings. What also seems clear is that, in France as elsewhere, the future of politics is based on political parties. After De Gaulle criticized parties in the late 1950s, and after the parties' failure, it seemed for a while that politics was about to take a different shape; political clubs, mainly of the Left and Center-Left, among whom the most successful was the *Club Jean-Moulin* (from the name of a higher civil servant who died in the *Résistance*), appeared to many to be the only way of influencing a political system in which the strength and power of one man had replaced traditional processes of government. Clubs soon had many members, issued pamphlets, and published books on the reform of the political system, on economic and social problems, and on foreign policy; they even hoped to nominate candidates and almost succeeded since Gaston Defferre's candidacy was, if not provoked, at least helped by a Club. Clubs even came to join with each other, and, at a common Congress, appeared to want to have a policy and act as the only living and relevant political pressure groups of the Fifth Republic.

But the success was, in the end, short-lived. Members of the Clubs themselves realized that their membership was, compared to the total electorate, very small; multiple membership was widespread; discussions were somewhat highbrow. In the last resort, the political parties, not the Clubs (though they were included in the discussions), decided on the fate of Gaston Defferre's candidacy and approved of François Miterrand's stand. On the Left, the two major organizations, Socialist and Communist, were scarcely influenced by the Clubs, and if the small United Socialist Party was somewhat more open to their influence, this was to be only for a time. With the presidential election of 1965, politics became more normal again, in that politicians had come back to the fore, but this was a new normalcy, based on eager expectations for some and great fears for others of what the future might conceal. Never before, during the whole of the Third and Fourth Republics, had the question of the party system been so much in the news. The change is gradual; it takes place by little moves which even specialists find difficult to detect, let alone to understand. Observers are baffled, and jump within a year from one expectation to the next, from one model to its opposite. But the trend toward simplification—Gaullists, Center, Socialists, Left, Communist—is becoming clearer. The link between behavior and structures is indeed difficult to grasp; nowhere perhaps as clearly as in the contemporary French party system can the difficulties of this analysis be more clearly perceived—but nowhere perhaps are there more opportunities to begin a real understanding of the underlying forces in a political system.

7: The Administration, the Judiciary, and Local Government

France is primarily a centralized State; it has been so for generations, partly because French political regimes were not sufficiently well established to allow for large measures of decentralization, partly because traditions of "enlightened despotism" have always had a considerable appeal in the country. In the seventeenth century, the King's ministers, and Colbert in particular, set out to implement what amounted to "plans of development" in various sectors of the economy. When Napoleon took over in 1799, he reorganized administrative institutions with the aim of making strong direction from the center possible, but he also directed his officials to carry out large projects of public works. Though agents of the Government in the provinces have traditionally been primarily concerned with making sure that political troubles did not arise, the political, economic, and social activities of the State were always closely linked, and even to the present day, it is not always easy to distinguish between officials operating in the various fields.

Between Napoleon and the Fifth Republic, few changes took place in the structure of most administrative institutions. While the country changed its Constitution on an average of every fifteen years—and perhaps because of this—the underlying organization of the "State" (a legal expression which in France embraces all public bodies, whether in Paris or in the provinces, whether central or local, whether created by the government or elected autonomously) did not vary much. The territorial units of the State—the *département* (county), the canton (rural district), and the commune (the basic local unit, whether town or village)—were scarcely affected by any boundary changes after the Revolution had created them and broken the traditional "provinces" which were said to embody the reactionary tradition of the past. It is during the Fifth Republic that the first reshuffle of *département* boundaries for over a century and a half took place when the Paris area was reorganized in 1964. Only the *arrondissement*, an intermediate division between *département* and canton, had a difficult life; considered too small for effective action, many *arrondissements* were abolished but the powers of the enlarged remaining *arrondissements* nonetheless decreased to almost nothing. Nor did many variations affect the principles of the organization of Government departments, whether in Paris or in the provinces, though new ministries were created and existing ones expanded. But the hierarchical arrangements and the role played by some highly trained and highly prestigious corps of civil servants remained broadly based on the Napoleonic model; one of the two most important training schools, the *École Polytechnique*, created by the Revolution and reorganized by the Emperor, was to remain the main way by which highly skilled engineers entered the higher civil service—and indeed business as well. While the judiciary, modernized and liberalized by the Revolution, was profoundly reorganized on less liberal lines by the Emperor, most of the features of its territorial organization, of its procedure, and of the substance of the law were kept throughout the nineteenth century and indeed up to the Fifth Republic.

Stability did not mean immobility, however. Some changes did take place, particularly in local government and to some extent in the judiciary during the Third Republic. These were aimed at liberalizing the aspects of administration which appeared too authoritarian; they made it possible for France to have, for the first time in centuries, a really thriving local government, at least at the level of the commune, if not at that of the *département* (county). But the changes took place within the framework of the system inherited from Napoleon: mayors became elective, instead of being appointed, and powers hitherto exercised by Government agents came to be given to the elected councils. The link between council and central administration was never wholly severed; control from above and authorization by Government agents were still required frequently. In the judiciary, while criminal codes were being modified in order to help the defendant, the main structure of the procedure and in particular the heavy reliance on examining magistrates rather than on juries to establish a case were kept barely altered. Even the most startling French achievement of the nineteenth century in the field of justice, the development of administrative law, originated from the Empire; by a slow and typically "British" process of transformation beyond recognition, what had begun as an advisory council designed to help the Government out of its many problems, the *Conseil d'Etat*, began to act more and more like a court and came to the defense of aggrieved citizens, on the basis not of codes, as in the rest of the French judiciary, but of case law.

The Fifth Republic is thus exceptional in having made perhaps more changes, in the course of a few years, than previous regimes had made in the course of many decades, but even these changes are mostly technical and pragmatic; they do not affect the spirit and principles of administration. Perhaps the most extensive changes concern local government, with the creation of all-purpose new bodies at the lowest level and of economic bodies at the regional level—that is, at a new level between the *département* and the central government. Justice was reorganized; the number of courts was drastically reduced and many outdated codes were amended and modernized. Finally, many Government departments were remodeled, the most conspicuous transformation being, as we noted in Chapter Four, the disappearance of the three service ministries. But overall, one can still define French administration as Napoleonic in its origins and in its broad centralized character, though the growth of self-government and of liberal institutions has tempered most of the excesses of the imperial machine and made the administrators not only highly competent but responsive to pressure, if not always accountable to the nation.

THE ADMINISTRATION

Apart from its centralization, French administration is perhaps mainly characterized by the competence and prestige of its personnel. Over a million Frenchmen (6 percent of the active population) belong to the civil service, though this figure is particularly high because it includes teachers and many other employees who, in other countries, would work for local authorities (which employ only 400,000 men and women). Not all of these Government agents are skilled and highly trained; the great majority are, as in every other country, engaged in clerical or industrial jobs which do not require much preparation. The renown of the civil service comes from its higher grades (the equivalent of the administrative and similar status classes in Britain, or of ranks above fourteen in the U.S. federal service). This reputation is based mainly on two grounds: dedication and indeed enthusiasm for the job (the tradition of "enlightened despotism" to which we referred earlier in this chapter) and technical competence acquired through a tough preparation in specialized schools of the civil service. The long-standing tradition dating from the *Ancien Régime* accounts for the dedication; it is unquestionably helped by the fact that the administration does not only advise and control, but can act on the spot. There are numerous "external services" of the Government departments in the localities, whether agencies of long standing of the Ministry of Public Works engaged in road building or of the Ministry of Agriculture engaged in land drainage, rural development, afforestation, or the like, or more recent but perhaps more important agencies of economic coordination, preparing and implementing the details of the Plan, which we shall examine in the next chapter. The technical competence of these agents comes from the relative weakness of private enterprise as well as from the belief in State intervention, both of which incited the Government, from very early on, to train its technical recruits itself. By the 1960s, a network of Government-run schools sets the pace in much of French higher education, provides training for future managers in all walks of life, and gives the civil service a position of undisputed prestige.

The two main *"grandes écoles"* (as these schools are known) are the National School of Administration (ENA), created in 1945, which prepares candidates for higher management jobs in all the Government departments (including the foreign service), and the *École Polytechnique*, created, as we saw, by the Revolution, which prepares technical administrators (a school of similar status, the *École Normale Supérieure*, trains the most brilliant of the future secondary and university teachers). Competition for entry into these schools is fierce. The School of Administration is a postgraduate school, which provides students with one year of training in the field *(stage)*, usually in the provinces, a year of study in the school itself, and a further *stage*, usually in a large firm, before the new administrator is posted where he has chosen to go (in fact, only top candidates can choose, and the others are left with the remaining places). The final examination, which leads to the posting, decides in particular whether the student is to become a member of a *"grand corps,"* that is, whether he will belong to one of the small elite groups of top administrators and is likely to be, in the next twenty or thirty years, among the leaders of the civil service. Nominally, these *grands corps* provide the staff of only a limited number of sections of the administration: the Council of State—the administrative court which we shall discuss later; the Court of Accounts—which reviews *ex post facto* the accounts of Government agents; the Inspectorate of Finance—which is in charge of the inspection of administrative (including local) financial transactions and can do spot checks; and the Prefectoral Corps—prefects are the agents of the Government in the *départements* and their role can be very important in promoting local activities, as we shall see later. The diplomatic corps of the foreign service is left somewhat separate. But the members of the *grands corps* do not remain in the original service all their lives. Over the years, the *grands corps* have tended to acquire such prestige that their members are sought by most if not all the branches of the civil service to head divisions or take over key positions; thus, after a few years in their organization, members of the *grands corps* come to be "detached" (the official expression) and are posted over a wide range of public bodies (including nationalized corporations). Inspectors of finance do not merely serve in the Inspectorate; they are in charge of practically the whole of the Treasury, of many sections of the Planning Commissariat, and of numerous other divisions and branches in which financial or economic expertise is required. The situation is broadly similar on the technical side; the graduates of the *École Polytechnique* who have achieved particular excellence enter one of the two technical *grands corps*, the Corps of Mines and the Corps of Roads and Bridges, and they often come to be "detached" later in order to run, not merely the mining or roads and bridges divisions of the ministries, but other Government departments and various nationalized industries. In the Planning Commissariat, "miners" and inspectors of finance collaborate to form the core of the top decision makers.

Technical excellence and skill can thus be achieved; this is done at some cost, however. Not only is the selection based on examination and competition to an excessive degree, but it also tends to create too early, too permanent, and too rigid a distinction between the potentially very high fliers (the members of the *grands corps* are almost certain to reach the top whereas those who are not in these corps are unlikely to go much further than the middle ranges of the administrative class) and the bulk of the members of the higher civil service. This is not because the service has anti-democratic attitudes; as the administrative and particularly the diplomatic sides of the administration had a bourgeois and even somewhat aristocratic tone before the war, the School of Administration was created precisely in order to broaden the base of recruitment and it has achieved this aim to a substantial extent; moreover, the *École Polytechnique* and the *École Normale Supérieure* have always been filled with young men coming from the petty-bourgeoisie; finally, reforms leading to the establishment of "second" or "limited competition" examinations have enabled civil servants from other grades to enter the higher civil service at a later age. But the overemphasis on examinations rather than experience as a basis for selection has other drawbacks. It tends to lead, if pushed to extremes as is sometimes the case, to a wastage of early efforts and to disillusionment with jobs obtained after such efforts. It also creates an undue sense of security, though, of course, opportunities for promotion exist and give purpose to the more ambitious men; the civil service, in France as elsewhere, does institutionalize security, in the form of tenure, regular (and regularized) promotion, generous leaves, and pensions. To add to this the chance of being almost certain, at the age of about twenty-five, of reaching the upper echelons of the higher civil service later in life if one is successful in a series of examinations is perhaps going too far and being in danger of turning civil servants into "mandarins"; particularly before the war, this accusation was fairly widespread. The fact that private enterprise does attract many civil servants who have gone through the *grandes écoles* is thus of great value, since it provides many of the fliers with an added incentive and many of the disappointed ones with the opportunity of a new career.

The move from the civil service to various sectors of private enterprise (known as *pantouflage*) also has another advantage: it creates links between the two sectors. Leading businessmen who were previously trained as civil servants are likely to understand more easily (though they may well criticize) the constraints which operate on the public sector; they are likely to know their whereabouts well when confronted with problems involving Government departments. Before the war, the weight of the civil service was perhaps too great as a result of the Malthusian attitudes from which the economy was suffering. With the rejuvenation which followed the Liberation, dangers of stultification of the private sector are much less serious. Combined with various other means of communication between the civil service and the rest of the community, which include numerous advisory councils, composed partly of Government representatives, partly of representatives of local authorities and interest groups, and which were, even in the *Ancien Régime* and the Napoleonic period, fairly common in the French system of administration, the traffic of personnel between Government agencies and private businesses prevents the administration from being closed to movements of opinion in the country. If the National Assembly has been labeled the "house without windows" (which it is concretely and often is metaphorically), the civil service is very sensitive to changes in the country's temperature and mood. Its leaders are recruited from many social groups; in many cases they are posted in the provinces, and they move around often; they have school friends in many walks of life and are themselves often lured into the business world. It is no surprise that France should have often been in danger of being the perfect type of the administrative

State—with all the implications, good and ill, which the expression connotes.

The controversy over technocratic power gathered momentum with the advent of the Fifth Republic. Civil servants entered the Government for the first time for generations, as we saw. Under the shadow of De Gaulle, officials were less bothered with requests, whether petty or highly motivated, trivial or important, from members of Parliament. They appeared able to make openly, normally after consultation, but finally nonetheless, the crucial social and economic decisions affecting the nation. The governmental system seemed to move toward an equilibrium in which a vast, paternalistic, but anonymous machine, sure of its own right, was replacing the democratic forum in which public debates led to clearly defined outcomes understandable to all. In reality, however, as was to be expected in such a large organization, neither complete unity nor total anonymity have been able to prevail. Officials have different views, either because the social and economic ministries want to act, and thus to spend, while the Finance Ministry is more likely to be parsimonious, or because styles of thought vary very markedly among civil servants in general and in particular between generations; semiautonomous public enterprises are also centers of independent power. Moreover, in the major divisions and in the major public agencies, civil servants have long ceased to remain anonymous; their attitudes are known, and so is their character and dynamism. Though they cannot be said to be "controlled" in the same public way as ministers would be by an Assembly, their policies (or "subpolicies") are discussed by colleagues and specialists both inside and outside the service. They become, in some way, accountable. Clearly, this is not a substitute for democratic check, but democratic checks, in an age of governmental intervention, can be rather formal if they are exercised solely, as they so often tend to be, at the level of governmental action and of decisions applied nationally. Both techniques must be used, if control is to be effective; the French political system has still to find the means by which a responsible government can be both really maintained in power and effectively scrutinized; for its part, however, the French administration does provide the country with a system of responsible administration which is broadly adapted to the needs of the twentieth century.

THE JUDICIARY

The French judicial system differs in many ways from the Anglo-Saxon. It is, first and foremost, divided into two sections: the "ordinary" jurisdiction is concerned with private and criminal actions, while all grievances of the citizen against the State (in the broad French sense which includes local government but not nationalized corporations, since Parliament wanted to give these a status similar to that of private firms) go to administrative courts. There are not only separate hierarchies of courts in each of the two sections, and a Court of Conflicts, composed of judges of both hierarchies, to settle difficult cases of jurisdiction; there are also differences in the whole spirit of the administration of justice. "Ordinary" courts decide on the basis of codes, but administrative courts, while using the statute book, give case law and general "principles" considerable weight. Thus the second difference between French (and indeed Continental) justice and its Anglo-Saxon counterpart. The Revolution was determined to abolish the traditional importance of custom and precedent and to replace these by clearly defined, written rules. It left Napoleon to promulgate the Codes (the Civil Code of 1804 being the first and perhaps most prestigious of a whole series), but codification is perhaps a less important principle in French law than the idea that courts should not substitute themselves for the legislator. In point of fact, however, "interpretation" of the law, particularly as enunciated by the highest court of the land, the Court of *Cassation*, tends to carry much weight and plays, in some way, the part of a "precedent." Thirdly, and associated with this attempt to prevent a takeover by the Courts, as under the last phase of the *Ancien Régime*, justice was organized as a "public service," made to implement the law (and not, for instance to decide on its constitutionality), and staffed with officials who would not be given such privileges as to make them believe that they are above the State. Reforms of the nineteenth century did give a wholly secure status to the judiciary (provided they are not members of the Corps of Prosecutors), but they are civil servants in all other respects (promotion was classically a means by which pressure was—and still technically could be to some extent—exercised on them). Indeed, members of administrative courts, not having the technical status of judges, are in no different position from that of other civil servants. Thus, in contrast to its counterpart in Anglo-Saxon countries, the French judiciary does not have a really exalted position, though by the second half of the twentieth century, dangers of governmental interference have, in fact, totally receded. But the principle of the separation of the judiciary from the other "powers" is more a practical arrangement than the consequence of a formal provision, despite the fact that, as we shall see, the Constitution does mention the "ordinary" judiciary and regulate the main lines of the judicial system.

Ordinary Courts

Civil and criminal cases are tried by a common body of State servants, known collectively as the "*magistrature*," in which there are clearly defined ranks and schedules of promotions, and which is entered through a specialized school, the *Centre National d'Études Judiciaires*, open to law graduates successful in a competitive examination and modeled on the School of Administration. The judiciary is in every sense a career service. In addition to judges, the service includes the prosecutors (known as *Parquet*), who do not have the same guarantees of tenure, but are nonetheless part of the corps (they form the *magistrature debout* —standing—while judges are the *magistrature assise*—sitting). One category of judges, though very much judges with a difference, are the *juges d'instruction*, or examining magistrates, who decide, on the basis of police evidence, whether a case has been made and committal to trial is to be allowed. These judges have always been at the center of one of the main difficulties of French justice (another being slowness); though examining magistrates are technically independent from the police, they are career civil servants whose reputation tends naturally to be based on the establishment of good relations with the police and who are therefore reluctant (despite various attempts made by the law to make them truly independent) to take a strict and close look at police operations. Appeal does exist, however, from the decisions of the *juges d'instruction* to a *chambre d'accusation* of the Court of Appeal (which in any case has to decide when one of the most serious crimes is involved) and the right to bail was extended in 1958, as one of a series of technical reforms aimed at diminishing the power of examining magistrates.

A major reform in the number of courts, both civil and criminal, also took place in 1958. Since this reform, the 3,000 or so Justices of the Peace have been abolished. The lowest civil court is now the *tribunal d'instance* of which there are only 454 throughout France (an average of about four per county but in fact distributed in relation to the size of the population in the area). For most important cases, plaintiffs go to the *tribunal de grande instance*, of which there are 172—less than two on average per *département*. This court also has appeal functions, especially from the judgments of some of the specialized courts, which have tended to multiply and which, though often criticized by experts, are usually simpler, less expensive, and more appropriate in technical cases. The most important are the *tribunaux de commerce*, which deal with commercial disputes, and the *conseils de prud'-hommes*, which deal with disputes between employers and employees over the implementation of labor contracts. While these specialized courts are elected by and from among businessmen and workers, the *tribunaux d'instance* and *tribunaux de grande instance* are entirely staffed by members of the career judiciary. *Tribunaux d'instance* have one judge, who in addition to his more formal powers also acts much as a Justice of the Peace did in the past, settling domestic and other minor disputes by conciliation. The *tribunaux de grande instance* have three or more judges, and neither court has a jury. The specialized courts are the only civil courts in which lay members are called to decide on cases.

Criminal law is dispensed in one of three sets of courts, depending on the gravity of the offense. Police courts function in almost all localities of any importance (in fact in the same way as the *tribunaux d'instance*). More serious offenses are brought before the *tribunaux correctionnels* where judges (the same as those of the *tribunaux de grande instance*) decide on cases without juries. Finally, the most serious crimes are tried at the periodic sittings of the *cours d'assises* (one per *département*) which consists of three judges and nine jurors. Eight votes of the twelve are required for the conviction and French judges normally bring their influence to bear on the jurors. Indeed, the French judge is not assumed to take a back seat in criminal trials; he actively participates in the questioning of defendants and witnesses (this is known as "inquisitorial" justice, while the Anglo-Saxon system, where the judge remains passive, is known as "accusatorial").

Appeal on matter of fact is generally allowed in civil cases (unless the matter is trivial), but not in criminal cases; appeal on interpretation of the law is always allowed. Appeal of both types normally goes to a Court of Appeal, of which there are twenty-five throughout France, unless, as mentioned earlier, the *tribunal de grande instance* is statutorily competent, or unless, on the contrary, the law decides that appeal on a point of law will go directly to the highest court in the hierarchy, the Court of *Cassation*, which sits in Paris. This Court is empowered to decide only on points of law; it can only "confirm" or "quash and send" for a retrial to another court of the same category, but not the same one, as the court which decided on the case (the formal expression is "*casse et renvoie*," hence the name of the Court). If the court which tries the case again does not follow the lead of the Court of *Cassation* on the point of law involved, the plaintiff can go to the Court again. While a case which comes to the Court for the first time goes to only one Chamber (seven judges at least), a case which comes for the second time goes to a bench composed of judges from all the sections (*toutes chambres réunies*); if the Court of *Cassation* once more states that the point of law was incorrectly interpreted by the lower court and thus quashes and sends for yet another retrial, the lower court to which it sends the case for this second retrial has to follow the line of the Court of *Cassation*. Thus unity of interpretation of French law is maintained and the view of the Court of *Cassation* can prevail, though only after due attention is paid to the viewpoint of the lower courts.

Since 1946, the whole judicial structure has been supervised by a constitutional body, the High Council of the Judiciary, but the powers of the body were substantially diminished by the Constitution of 1958 and its independence from the Government reduced. Formerly staffed mainly with members elected by the National Assembly and the members of the judiciary, it is now composed of the President of the Republic (chairman), the Minister of Justice, two appointees of the President, six members chosen by the President from a list of twelve drawn by the Court of *Cassation*, and one, also chosen by the President, from a list of three proposed by the Council of State. Lower courts have no representatives and the President has considerable scope for intervention. The powers of the Council were reduced at the same time, mainly because the Ministry of Justice felt that the Constitution of 1946 had unduly limited its scope for action, particularly on promotion questions. Since 1958, the High Council has no longer prepared the annual promotion lists; the work is now done by a special committee composed of the prosecutor general in the Court of *Cassation*, six representatives of that Court, and six officials of the Ministry of Justice (the High Council merely gives an advisory opinion). The High Council did retain, however, the disciplinary powers which it acquired in 1946, and in this respect at least, the independence of the judiciary is better ensured than before the war.

Administrative Courts

Administrative courts, as we saw, emerged only gradually from the status of advisory bodies to the Government which was theirs under Napoleon. These advisory bodies had two functions. First, they were to help the Government in Paris, the prefects in the *départements*, to draft regulations (decrees and *arrêtés*); in some cases the law even compelled the relevant executive authority to submit the text for advice, and in a small minority of cases, formal approval of the text had to be forthcoming. Second, Napoleonic councils were to advise the Government and prefects on complaints coming from citizens about administrative actions. While the first advisory function remains almost unchanged (and it does occupy a substantial proportion of the personnel of the councils), the advice about administrative actions transformed its character; during the nineteenth century, the Government came, as a matter of course, to agree with and automatically implement the suggestions made by the councils. The "advice" had become, by a process of evolution through custom, a real decision. In 1872, the situation was formalized by a law which decreed that the councils would have the status of courts and be competent to decide on complaints involving the administration.

The administrative courts are thus true courts, organized hierarchically, some of which deal with general administrative matters, while others are only concerned with particular problems (special bodies tackle disputes over national assistance, for instance). The general administrative courts are by far the most important. At a lower level, the ninety-odd *Conseils de Préfecture* of Napoleon were reduced to twenty-three in 1926 and were renamed *tribunaux administratifs* in 1953, while their powers were increased in order to speed up cases. At the upper level, sitting as an appeal court in many cases but directly competent for the more important problems, is the famous *Conseil d'État*, about which much has been written and which has become the model administrative court in large parts of the world. Composed of over 150 members, almost entirely recruited through the School of Administration (as we saw, those who belong to it form one of the prestigious *grands corps*), the Council of State is divided into several sections, the main distinction being between four advisory (so-called "administrative") sections and a judicial section (*section du contentieux*). This section is in turn divided into a number of chambers in which normally five *conseillers* decide on cases on the report of more junior members (*maîtres des requêtes* and even sometimes *auditeurs*), but very important cases can be decided by as many as ten or fifteen *conseillers*.

Three characteristics of the administrative courts, at least, need to be mentioned. First, the separation between the "advisory" and "judicial" functions is, even now, not complete—and the link is deliberate. Members of the *Conseil d'État* may move, for instance, from one section to another; they may also be "detached" for a period, as we noted earlier, to take a post in what is officially known as the "active" administration (i.e., the administration which makes decisions); when "detached" in this way, members obviously do not participate in the judicial (or indeed advisory) activities of the Council. But they are likely to come back after their period of "detachment" and will sit again among their colleagues to decide on cases. The status of members of administrative courts is indeed identical in all respects to that of other civil servants; there are in particular no differences in the tenure position, at least in theory. Such arrangements are considered both logical and beneficial. If the separation between administrative and ordinary courts is to be justified, it is because government work has a special character; if judgments on administrative decisions are to be taken on the basis of a realistic appraisal of the situation, members of the administrative courts must be aware in a practical sense of the specificity of civil service action. This does not mean that the administration is more likely, as a result, to win against the citizen. The converse is often true: civil servants are less likely to be able to cover their decisions with mystery and to deceive members of the court with a high-minded presentation of difficulties which could easily have been overcome.

Second, administrative courts also have a different procedure from that of ordinary courts. As we saw, the Council of State has always felt free to invoke precedents and to use general principles as grounds for its judgments. In many respects, administrative courts tend to decide cases on the basis of equity (in the literal sense of the word), of what seems honest and reasonable, rather than on the basis of the letter of the law which, particularly in the past, tended to define governmental powers loosely for emergencies. Moreover, plaintiffs find in the administrative courts, and particularly in the Council of State, some of the characteristics of the Scandinavian institution of the Ombudsman; the *maître des requêtes* who is given the task of preparing and reporting on a case will do all the work himself, dig through the administration's files and find out what happened, on behalf of the plaintiff who, in some cases, has nothing more to do than merely file his complaint and pay a very small fee. Administrative courts were created to advise (and presumably help) the Government against undue complaints; they have turned out to be the citizens' best (though at times somewhat protracted) friend.

Finally, and most importantly, administrative courts are competent to decide on the validity of executive decisions. The Council of State, in particular, can be asked to state whether governmental decrees are legal and should stand or illegal and be quashed. While full constitutional control is still not established, almost all the documents issued by executive authorities can be challenged in an administrative court. The procedure, known as *recours pour excès de pouvoir*, is limited only by two general conditions: the plaintiff must show that he is in some way affected, at least potentially, by the regulation (and this is interpreted very liberally) and the case must be filed within two months of the decision—so as to limit uncertainty about the validity of documents, uncertainty which can be very worrying to others and in some cases dramatic, as can be demonstrated by examples drawn from United States Supreme Court decisions. The Council of State has taken very seriously this power of scrutiny and it has to convince itself, before passing judgment, not only that the text was issued by the legal authority under appropriate powers, but that the spirit of the document does not go against the real meaning of the law; the *détournement de pouvoir* (use of legal powers in a distorted manner) is one of the grounds on which administrative courts can and often do annul decrees or *arrêtés*.

The development of the role of the Council of State is truly remarkable, particularly in a country which took some pains to limit the status of the judiciary and obliged judges to decide on cases within the rigid framework of elaborate codes of law. Administrative courts are, in many ways, the most effective counterpart to executive power and administrative centralization; this is so not only because they can and do take the side of the citizen when decisions of central and local bodies are unjust or go beyond the law, but because the fear of the decisions of the *Conseil* and other administrative courts may and do lead central and local authorities to be more prudent, less arbitrary, and altogether more reasonable. Administrative courts are thus true defenders of the rights of citizens and, though they are not mentioned in the Constitution, they are as important to the real and living Constitution as many of the bodies mentioned in the formal document. Indeed, perhaps it is because the Council of State is not given a place in the Constitution (and seldom was given a place in any French Constitution), that it has succeeded in becoming, slowly and unassumingly, so vital to French life; not even a change in the Constitution can affect its powers and the only changes to which it has been subjected were mere formalizations of an authority which had already, by custom, long since been acquired.

LOCAL GOVERNMENT

French local government is a curious mixture of considerable political importance and limited social and economic action, of great simplicity in basic organization and complex distribution of powers, of vast scope for local initiative and areas of tight governmental control. It is, at present, moving very fast. Often sleepy in the interwar period, local authorities have been caught since the 1950s by the idea of development; they have, as a result, experienced more clearly than in the past their own financial limitations. They have asked for more government help; subsidies have begun to flow and traditional forms of control (known as *tutelage*) have ceased to be as prominent. But local authorities have started to realize that size was a key to development and that parochial patriotism could lead only to stagnation. Really and truly, French local government has experienced a "takeoff" problem: the reforms of the Fifth Republic, limited as they still are (though they may seem, to some, already rather drastic), have opened the way to further development. Structurally, French local government still needs a major rehauling, but the prospect of this change is no longer as remote; the consciousness of the defects has become more acute and new experiments have already shown some success.

The basic unit of local government is, as we noted, the commune. It was created by the Revolution. There are 38,000 of them (they have on an average 1,300 inhabitants). A typical commune might well have a population of only four or five hundred and it cannot therefore be expected to have the same scope of action as a town of 100,000, let alone a city of a half million or more. Yet formal arrangements and powers are almost identical. The electors of all the French communes choose, every six years, their municipal councilors (from nine in very small villages to thirty-seven in the large cities, except Paris, Lyons, and Marseilles, which have even more); the council elects a mayor and assistants (*adjoints*) who act as the parliamentary government of the council (except Paris which has, as we shall see, a special organization). The council adopts the broad policy and votes the budget; the mayor and his assistants implement this policy, take the necessary executive measures, and supervise the municipal officials. If there is conflict between mayor and council, during one of the four sessions which the council holds every year (for instance over the budget), the mayor may be led to resign; the Government is then likely to dissolve the municipal council and call for new elections.

Powers of mayors and councils are regulated by a law of 1884, which finally organized modern local government and states that the municipal council "deals with the business" of the community: this is understood to be broad and enables communes to run services, start new undertakings, and provide amenities, though under some governmental control, and provided the administrative courts do not deem such actions to be invalid if they go against, for instance, the freedom of ordinary citizens (a number of cases were related to "municipal socialization"). The mayor who, before 1882, was appointed by the Government has retained some of the status of a State representative: not only does he deal with births, marriages, and deaths and electoral registration, but he has "police powers" which he can be directed by the Government to use in case of threats to law and order, if he does not do so on his own. But he is essentially the first citizen of the commune and the post has very important political undertones, not, of course, in small villages, but in medium-sized and large towns; as we saw in the last chapter, political careers often start at the municipal level and the mayoralty of cities is an important springboard from which to move to a higher destiny.

The other important unit of local administration is the *département*, of which there are now ninety-five, as a result of the 1964 reorganization of the Paris area. Between the commune and the *département*, the Revolution had created two intermediate steps, the canton and the *arrondissement*, but neither has survived as a unit of local self-government. *Départements*, on the contrary, quickly became important, but at first more as points of penetration for the central government than as means by which local representatives could exercise their action; they have indeed retained some of their original structure. While the government of the commune has become wholly autonomous, the *département* is still ruled in a somewhat "colonial" fashion or, at best, enjoys a limited form of separation of powers. The council of the *département*, known as the general council, is elected for six years, with half of its members retiring every three, on the basis of one member for each canton. This electoral system has serious defects since cantons are very unequal in population, urban areas are at a great disadvantage, and changes in the distribution of cantons are very rare. This somewhat unrepresentative council has been given, by a law of 1871, the power to "deal with the business affairs" of the *département* and, in particular, to vote the budget, as the municipal council does; it is also empowered to appoint a standing committee, the *commission départementale*, to oversee the actions of the executive between the sittings of the council (there are only two sessions during the year, each of which lasts about two weeks). But the executive is firmly in the hands of an appointee of the Government and a member of one of the *grands corps*, the prefect.

The prefect has a dual role. In the first place, he is responsible for the external services of the central government in the *département*, whether outposts of the Ministry of Finance, Public Works, Agriculture, Labor, Interior, or any other. He is made to coordinate the activities of the representatives of the ministries—and this task has indeed proved increasingly difficult, officials of the various Government departments usually preferring to by-pass the prefect and deal directly with their superiors in Paris about major problems. In recent years, decrees and circulars have repeatedly attempted to restore the position of the prefect over his civil service colleagues, but practices have markedly changed since the nineteenth century (the Second Empire of Napoleon III, from 1851 to 1870, can be said to be the period when the authority and prestige of prefects reached a climax), when the pomp and status of the office made the holder of the post the true "governor" of the *département*. Increases in the strength and number of external services of the ministries are partly responsible for the decline of the prefect's role. But the development of representative institutions also contributed to the loss of power.

In his other capacity, the prefect is the "executive" of the council of the *département*. He implements the decisions of the council and he therefore has to use political skill and acumen as well as strong-mindedness. The more he is confronted with local politicians of importance—mayors of large towns (indeed whether they sit or not on the council of the *département*), deputies and senators, sometimes even ministers—the more the prefect has to try to persuade and compromise rather than command. Moreover, the pressure exercised by local politicians (outside meetings of the council, as much as inside) does not merely concern those matters, mainly roads and social aid, on which the *département* spends most of its money; it extends to the governmental activities which, under his other hat, the prefect comes to supervise. The prefect does not have to bow to this pressure, admittedly; formally he is responsible only to the Minister of the Interior and, through the latter, to the Government as a whole. But, in fact, he cannot afford to be opposed by too many people; his action would be prejudiced and that of other officials in many other fields would also be impaired, and his career would in turn be prejudiced, as the Minister who can remove him (indeed prefects are typically moved from one *département* to another every three or four years) could come to consider that only posts of lesser authority could suit such an unlucky or unsociable official.

Local government in the *département* thus has to be seen as a maze of activities and pressures; some of these originate in Paris and, through outposts in the provinces, try to influence local development down to the commune (sub-prefects in the *arrondissements* help prefects and other officials in this respect); some of these pressures stem from the commune and take the form either of requests for more governmental help or of opposition against administrative encroachments; some, finally—and perhaps not the most important—come from the *département*. A knowledge of the precise legal power of each body is not always helpful; indeed, in many cases, the law organizes the "sharing" of the services between central government, *département*, and commune. Social aid is the clearest case but, with the operation of subsidies, and if one takes into account building and upkeep, other services such as education, fire protection, transport, and, of course, the police, are run in various degrees and on the basis of various principles by all three levels of central and local government. Education is usually said, for instance, to be essentially a responsibility of the central government, but most of the work is done in the external services of the "*Académie*," whether in the region or in the *département*, and communes are directly concerned with much of the school-building program. The police services are also traditionally shared, though the State police has grown in importance both because law and order have always been major problems for usually insecure French regimes and because the mobility of criminals has, in France as elsewhere, made the centralization of police forces a practical necessity. Thus, while the State always had its *gendarmerie* posted in the provinces, and while since the early 1920s it has had a mobile reserve force (known since 1945 as *Compagnies Républicaines de Sécurité*), powers of mayors over the town police have gradually shrunk.

The 1966 reform of the police unifies the various police forces, once more at the expense of the communes, which lose all the powers they had over recruitment though they are still, but to a limited extent, able to give orders to the members of the new police force.

The centralization of the police forces is somewhat untypical, however, of the evolution of French local government. The two major changes which took place in the course of the 1960s—regionalism and consolidation of existing authorities in larger units—are much more likely to be indicative of future developments. Regionalism is still rather limited, based on appointed and not elective consultative councils, and mainly concerned with broad economic development. We shall see in the next chapter some of the content of this economic action, but the creation of the *comités de développement économiques régionaux* (CODER) in the twenty regions into which France is divided and the granting of powers of coordination to the "regional prefects" seem to forecast a more general move (though these coordinators existed before, they did not seem to be given means of exercising pressure, except over police questions, on the ordinary prefects). As early as 1959, a district of the Paris region was set up with much wider powers: the head of the executive, the delegate general, has, at his disposal, considerable resources voted by a council appointed by the various local councils of the region, and he can intervene in planning, housing, and transport matters. It will take time for other regional organizations to be shaped on this model; it will also take time for these institutions to be given councils directly elected by the population. But both central government and local authorities have now realized that the *département* is clearly much too small; thus on the one hand, supporters of "enlightened despotism" and technocrats, on grounds of efficient government, and on the other, defenders of local self-government, on the grounds that only large units can have sufficient resources, tend gradually to agree and combine their forces to quicken the pace towards regional government.

The consolidation of communes into larger units is an equally slow process. Communes had always been authorized to come to special agreements with a view to creating joint boards to run special services, but the problem is more general. In rural areas, many powers have been taken over, in practice, by officials of the external services of the ministries, acting on behalf of the communes, simply because these do not have the specialized staff to man undertakings on an efficient basis; in urban areas, the problems of conurbations create difficulties between adjoining local authorities. While no solutions to rural difficulties have as yet been contemplated, some efforts have been made in relation to conurbations. In 1958, communes were authorized to form "urban districts," which are effectively multi-purpose joint boards run by representatives of the various local councils. In 1966, new conurbation authorities were created for some of the major cities, where, despite the law on urban districts, no action had been taken. But the major reform took place in 1964 and concerned the Paris area; it resulted in a drastic rearrangement of the *département* boundaries (the first to take place since the Revolution). Since 1789, except for a short while, Paris had been a commune, in the *département* of Seine; it was run not by a mayor, who seemed to be a potential challenge to the Government, but by two prefects (Prefect of Seine, and Prefect of Police), operating with a council for the Seine *Département* and a municipal council for Paris. Meanwhile, the population grew, not so much in Paris proper (which still does not reach three million), but in many surrounding areas of the adjoining *départements*. Thus the Prefect of Seine was not only in charge of a large administration; he was running services for six of the eight to nine million people who live in the Paris area. With the creation of the District of the Paris Region, in 1959, *département* boundaries became even more out of date and burdensome. Thus, the law of 1964 divided the Paris region into seven new *départements* (instead of two), each of about equal size, except for Paris proper which is raised to the status of *département*. It is hoped that the new local authorities will be able under the guidance of the regional office to administer the services of the area more efficiently. Thus, new institutions have come to develop below the regional level. They are still limited in scope and representative character. But they give some opportunities to the large local authorities. Self-government may no longer be associated with restricted horizons; the self-government of the future may indeed develop against traditional parochialism.

CONCLUSION

French administration thus experienced transformations in the postwar period, and particularly since 1958. It shelved most of the bureaucratic and authoritarian characteristics which it still retained from the past, under the combined impact of social and economic development and of the desire for democracy. More changes are likely to come, though one does not see yet how an administration can be made accountable to the nation in the direct, precise, and public fashion in which a Government elected by Parliament can be accountable to national representatives. But, probably unconsciously, French civil servants have made good some of the deficiencies of the representative machinery and nobody can clearly see how far the movement will go: advisory councils may be taken increasingly into the confidence of officials; consultation at the levels of the region and of the *département* may lead to a greater sharing of the decisions by which public money is distributed locally; administrative justice may enable the citizen to become even more protected from the abuses of the State. But, in the last resort, the most helpful development is perhaps the revival of local government in the 1960s. This may have taken place because many politicians, frustrated at not being able to influence, let alone overthrow, ministers and premiers, turned to consider more carefully the opportunities presented by local action. If politics at the center were once more to have the unwieldy and hectic character which it had in the past, interest in local government may correspondingly decrease. But new forces, mainly concerned with economic development, have also led the move; the decentralization of economic decision-making is behind many new demands. If local government is to be truly revitalized in this way, France may no longer have to choose between a weak and often inept self-government and efficient bureaucratic command. The two might be joined in a way which would have seemed wholly unfeasible to observers of the interwar period.

Government, Groups, and
Social and Economic Policy

The centralization of the French administration has traditionally been linked to two other characteristics: the individualism of the citizens of a nation in which associations were relatively few, and the relative smallness of the average business or farm. There were indeed close connections between all three points. The Revolution was fought in part against the "corporate State" prevailing in the *Ancien Régime:* "intermediate bodies," mainly in the economic field, were said to be too strong, and they did indeed prevent free enterprise and large scale industry from developing in the eighteenth century. They were abolished in 1789. On the other hand, the Revolution achieved some land redistribution, though more as a result of political or religious accidents than because of a clear social policy. Having broken the power of factions and groups, having brought about a modicum of equality, the Revolution could thus leave Napoleon with a country in which the centralization of administration would be both necessary and relatively easy.

The perpetuation of this state of affairs did lead to serious consequences when, added to the losses of many and the strains felt by all during the First World War, the depression made Malthusianism appear a virtue and the occupation during the Second World War turned the self-contained one-man farm into a haven of prosperity. Organization seemed synonymous with control; joint action was less useful than a clever "muddling through." Indeed, the more individualistic the French were, the more organization had to be imposed. The Vichy regime seemed to trigger once more the anarchistic traditions of the French by instituting a corporate State, modeled on Italian fascism, which alienated workers because it denied employees any means of expressing their grievances, businessmen because it limited free enterprise, and all Frenchmen because production was simply insufficient. The unreal economic policy of the government could be maintained only by the power of German occupation; as soon as this cracked, repressed demands were sure to explode violently and galloping inflation consequently to occur. At a time when the needs of sheer war reconstruction would have required discipline and self-denial, governments were faced with mounting tension at a level unknown perhaps for generations. It was questionable whether the country's morale and energies had not declined to such depths that it would never recover.

In this situation, the centralization of the French State was thus, once more, of great value. But this centralization proved valuable only because administrators seized the opportunity which was offered and decided to embark on a major reconstruction, not only—and indeed not primarily—of the houses, plants, roads, and bridges destroyed by the war, but of the whole fabric of the French economy. The political collapse of big business, the almost total disruption of the capital market, indeed the demands for nationalization of major undertakings were all to help government officials in this operation; it would become possible to control, more than in any other Western country (except perhaps Italy) the level and direction of investment. Somewhat paradoxically (as many American businessmen were to notice) the program of U.S. aid, channeled through the Government, was to be a major determinant of this successful takeover, as only large sources of capital, which the United States did provide, could finance the reconstruction. Inflation, too, was to be deliberately used, with almost complete ruthlessness, by the new economists; since social demands were large and governments of the early postwar period were willing or obliged to meet them, inflation was to play the role of deterrent which could not be obtained from a self-imposed discipline or from an authoritarian government. From 1945 to 1949, a repeatedly devalued franc lost 85 percent of its value and only since 1958 has the currency become not only "strong" but really defended by a nationalistically-inclined government determined to be able to look the dollar in the face.

Such was the basic philosophy at the root of the first French Plan, which started modestly, almost under cover, in 1946. But, in the course of the next twenty years, the Plan did not only help "reconstruction and equipment" (the objectives given to the program at its inception); its effect was not only economic in the narrow, or even broader, sense of the word. It created a new climate of movement, development, progress, which had been almost totally absent for at least a generation. This, in turn, led to a break with the two classic traditions of individualism and of stagnating small business. From the late 1950s on, France ceased, very suddenly, to cultivate the "*petit*" and came to consider with admiration and pride things big and expanding. Whatever effect Gaullist nationalism and anti-Americanism may have on foreign policy, France has never been so American, in its economic attitudes, as in the 1960s. And as big things cannot be done alone, Frenchmen started to cooperate in order to achieve them: businesses began to merge, and takeovers were a common feature. At the juncture of the social and the economic fields, collective organizations also started to spread; trade associations and consumer groupings, and even to some extent the trade unions, became more accepted, more pragmatic, and also more relevant. Even the peasants, long held as the backbone of French individualism, proved collectively-minded. Pluralism had come at last, not on paternalistic grounds as under Vichy, but on free, "Anglo-Saxon" lines. Thus the economic transformation originated by the centralized State and its administrators had started a new multicentered society in which decision-making processes were becoming more complex. Much, as we shall see, is still to be done; but industry, commerce and agriculture, employers and workers, economic and social relations all have now been infected by the new germ.

THE STATE AS PLANNER

Ambitious efforts had been made from time to time to adopt logical programs of economic and social action that would chart new courses for the French society. But before 1945, the only one which had begun to function was that of the Popular Front of 1936, which was to be a massive assault on economic institutions which had for decades, or so it seemed, maintained the domination of "two hundred families" at the real center of economic power. The Popular Front program was in part a compromise; it was by no means comprehensive or integrated; its stress was on social change, rather than on economic rejuvenation, though many framers of the program felt that economic rejuvenation would "naturally" proceed from a change in the structure of the economy and in the climate of industrial relations. Yet, in one year, the Socialist Government of Léon Blum did push through, in the midst of considerably difficulties in the country and fairly soon in Parliament, an impressive array of legislation. This included the nationalization of the Bank of France and of the armament industries, the imposition of a sharply-graduated income tax, the establishment of a National Wheat Board to provide the Government with a lever for controlling crop production and guaranteeing minimum incomes to the producers, and the institutionalization of a government-protected system of collective bargaining, of the forty-hour week as a rule, and of two-week paid holidays. Perhaps such a mixed bag should not be labeled "planning"—even social planning, let alone economic planning. But the measures did contribute to creating the feeling that the working class was, at last, being socially enfranchised (the *"congés payés"* became such a success that it can perhaps be argued that a new form of working-class behavior began in 1936) and that the power of business was no longer beyond the pale of the law. It was possibly the first time that France had achieved so much social change in such a short period without a revolution.

The year 1945 was different. Whether it was a revolution in the technical sense of the word is debatable, but the Vichy regime had created a gap in the continuity of French politics. Much social thinking had gone through the conclaves of the National Council of the *Résistance* during the occupation; this had led to the production, in March of 1944, of a blueprint for France's future which called for the nationalization of primary resources of energy, State direction of banks and insurance, elimination of trusts in private business, and the participation of labor in industrial management. These were radical aims which could have paved the way for a planned economy, if fully implemented, and the enthusiasm was such (and the representatives of traditional business so discredited) that the Charter of the *Résistance* was accepted by most political elements in France and endorsed by General De Gaulle.

Following the Liberation, the plans of the Charter were put high on the agenda of the provisional government of 1944. Most of the nationalization measures were enacted by the end of the following year, and by mid-1946 coal, electricity, gas, five major banks, and dozens of insurance companies had gone into public ownership (the railways had been taken over in 1937). A reform of the firm had taken place, which led to the creation of committees, known as *comités d'entreprise*, empowered to make suggestions on various aspects of the business and to manage funds set aside compulsorily for amenities and cultural activities. But the enthusiasm was receding; the population as a whole remained rather passive (in sharp contrast to the situation of 1936, when the atmosphere was electric), possibly because it was easier to see the inflationary effects of these various measures (to which, as we shall see, social security is to be added) than the long term political or social benefits which might accrue from transfers of power. Divisions between Communists, Socialists, and Christian Democrats started to grow, and were exacerbated by the conflict over the Constitution. When the first regular National Assembly of the Fourth Republic met in November, 1946, the revolutionary fervor was over; the "social" phase of the regime had ended.

Its economic phase, however, was only beginning. The First Plan had just been devised—it was to start operating on January 1st, 1947, and was made to last four years (in fact, it was extended to the end of 1953). The *Commissariat Général au Plan*, a small braintrust of a few key experts, with only some telephones, much enthusiasm, and little effective power at their disposal, was being installed under the leadership of Jean Monnet, a strong-willed ex-civil servant and ex-businessman, who was to be the key to the psychological success of the operation and who was indeed later in much the same vein to foster European unity. From the start, it was clear that the Planning Commissariat (which was to have only four heads in about twenty years) would remain a flexible and informal operation; it was to be a "team," not a hierarchical and bureaucratic organization. Its strength was to come from its intellectual authority, which had to impose itself gradually on both businessmen and workers, farmers and industrialists, private and public enterprise. At the beginning, of course, the Commissariat could count on the prevailing "socialistic" mood of the country and of its leaders; its first move was in the area of basic investment —and this concerned mainly nationalized corporations, whose cooperation was easier to obtain. But from the start, the Planning Commissariat was adamant about using persuasion rather than command. It was never given powers to order (hence the expression of "indicative" planning); only the Treasury could order and direct investment—and for its own independence (indeed fearing the conservatism of the Treasury), the Planning Commissariat was placed directly under the Prime Minister. Gradually, its best weapon came to be its ability to forecast; by providing employers with trends in the various branches of industry, it gave them, free, a basis on which they could decide the lines on which to develop. And as employers did follow forecasts, the Plan became, in many ways, a self-fulfilling prophecy; this, in turn, increased the authority of planners.

Between the First and the Fifth Plan (1966–1969), however, considerable changes did take place. First, naturally, the objectives became different. The First Plan was concerned, as we saw, with the structural reconstruction and development of the basic industries. The documents which followed were concerned with the whole of the economy; the end of the Second Plan (1957) coincided with the last inflationary spell, and the last balance of payments crisis of postwar France, and the emphasis of the Third

Plan was on greater stability. This was indeed a period in which the Government was so much concerned with monetary rectitude and so little with development that by 1960–1961, it seemed that the whole of the planning machinery might be in question, if not in jeopardy. However, after 1962, the Fourth Plan showed a return to greater inventiveness: the drafters of the scheme emphasized regional development and an expansion of the social (and not simply economic) amenities offered to Frenchmen from all classes and groups, within the framework of financial stability. From that time dates the concern with decentralization and the real look at life in the provinces, which had been neglected before; the rejuvenation of local government, which we discussed in the previous chapter, coincides with that period.

Second, the preparation of the Plan became a much more complex operation. The First Plan was almost wholly prepared by officials of the Planning Commissariat. It was approved by the Government; it came to be mentioned to Parliament, rather than discussed by the elected representatives. The enthusiasm for the principles and proposals was great, but few were consulted. Gradually during the Second Plan, and more so during the Third and Fourth, the idea of involving large sections of the community, and not merely Parliament, came to be regarded as normal. The Planning Commissariat divided the study of the specialized targets and programs among numerous committees, simply because the Commissariat could not do the work itself; thus, for the Fourth Plan, twenty-seven commissions were created, mostly dealing with vertical branches of industry, commerce, or the social services. On these committees, "outside" representatives naturally came to be appointed; thus employers, leaders of nationalized industries, and trade unionists were associated in the preparation. It was hoped that in this way the Plan would be both more realistic in the targets suggested (the less planners were dealing with basic industries, the less it was possible to make *a priori* assumptions about the behavior of firms) and more readily accepted by the sectors of the economy concerned with these targets. In the latest Plans, the procedure lasted many months, concerned thousands of persons, and led to numerous procedures of conciliation and arbitration between various interests. The staff of the Commissariat is nonetheless always there, guiding and advising, reminding everyone of the overall growth target (4 or 4½ percent per year), of the general objectives of the Plan, of conflicts of suggestions, and of the consequences of certain decisions. In the end, the Plan, described in detail in one overall document, is presented for approval to the Planning Council (one of the advisory bodies comprising representatives of the various branches of the economy and of which the working committees which have just been mentioned are nominally sections). The Plan then becomes official; it is forwarded to the Government, which agrees to it and sends it in turn to the Social and Economic Council, a professional chamber created in 1926 and given constitutional status both in 1946 and in 1958. This body, which is composed of representatives of the various economic and social sections of the community and has competence to give advice on bills and even decrees, has come to take the discussion of the Plan with increasing seriousness, though attitudes of members are to some extent decided in advance on the basis of the "line" taken by the unions or employers' associations on the overall targets. After the Social and Economic Council has given its advice, the Plan is sent to Parliament (it was not even sent to Parliament in the first few cases); the discussion there remains rather limited in scope and length. Clearly, none of these bodies can "change" the Plan in more than minor details, as none of the arrangements are truly independent and as it is too late to rethink the economy of the whole document. Discussion amounts more to letting off steam, and the Plan thus becomes law between two and three years after the Planning Commissariat began discussing preliminary projects.

Third, while the preparation of the Plan was becoming more complex and involving many more people, discussion and criticism of targets and even procedures was also becoming widespread. It is difficult to imagine how limited the discussion of the First and Second Plans was, when one considers what happened to the Fourth and Fifth. In the case of the Fourth Plan, which had accepted pluralism both in practice by enlarging the committees, and in theory by insisting on targets of "decentralization" and of participation of all the groups in the nation, the criticism was that too few trade unionists were engaged in the preparation process and could therefore express the demands and fears of the working class (9 percent of the members of the committees were workers as against 41 percent who represented employers). But the Fifth Plan was attacked for its targets as well, in a much more elaborate way, by left-wing groups, and in particular by members of the United Socialist Party, who published a "Counter-Plan," aimed at showing that the growth targets were too low and could easily be increased—indeed had to be increased, if necessary social reforms (in the field of education, for instance) were to be implemented. Thus the "debate" and contestation (to take an expression very commonly used in French political circles) has greatly expanded. It is an indication of the increased economic culture of the nation, or at least of that of the politically-minded circles; it is also a measure of the interest which people show in the Plan and of the importance which they attribute to planning problems. These "debates" probably have little influence on the Plan immediately under discussion (though they may lead to some changes at the level of the committee), but they may have an impact on the targets of the next Plan. What the planning process shows is that discussion of a technical and lengthy document can and does take place and that technocracy and political confrontations may commonly be associated.

Finally, the machinery through which the Plan is implemented has also come to be more complex. We did note that, from the start, the Plan was not conceived as compulsory; it is officially known as "indicative"—and the more it is concerned with consumer goods, with changes in patterns of behavior, the more it has to be content with being indicative. But the interest shown by the Fourth and Fifth Plans in decentralization and in the social "substructure" of the nation meant that machinery had to be created, in the provinces, to supervise in detail the implementation of the Plan. The creation in 1964 of the twenty *Comités de développement économique régional* (CODER) mentioned in the last chapter corresponds to this necessity. The CODER have not had, as yet, much opportunity for action; neither they nor the regional prefects have had time to acquire influence over the authorities of the commune and the *département* and to control the distribution of funds effectively. But changes are likely to come as various public bodies must act on behalf of the planners and as ideas of decentralization are, as we saw, gradually becoming widespread. Together with the *comités d'expansion régionale* (created earlier, and possibly somewhat in competition with them), the CODER are likely to become instruments of regional planning as well as meeting places where feelings of "regionalism" will develop and possibly ultimately prevail over purely local sentiment.

The French approach to planning methods is thus unquestionably successful, whatever difficulties it went through in the past and is likely to go through in the future. The French Plan has sometimes been considered as a modern and typically French experiment in Fabian socialism. It is less empirical than British Fabianism; its emphasis on social engineering is to be taken literally, as many of the men in charge of the planning process are or were engineers (following in this the tradition of the French social thinker of the early part of the nineteenth century, Saint-Simon, and of his part-disciple, Comte). It is a modern experiment in that it uses the latest mathematical techniques in order to understand and forecast economic and social trends; it is indeed also modern in that, unlike traditional Soviet planning, it is flexible and realistically adapted to a complex economy. Whether it aims at socialism is debatable; this claim would indeed probably be rejected by many of the planners and by most trade unionists, and even the employers, who have come to accept the Plan, would be likely to deny that they are being "socialized." Yet, whether socialist or not, the French Plan certainly helped to make French society more collectively-minded, more conscious of the value of discussion and debate, more prone to pluralistic attitudes. It has started an entirely new form of political, social, and economic confrontation, not only in France, but in the whole of the developed world.

THE STATE AND BUSINESS

The new French pluralism has begun to modify markedly the behavior of business in relation to the State. Before World War II, industrial pressures on the government were common, but they tended to remain somewhat secret at the top and disorganized at the bottom. The Socialist administration of 1936 was not only interesting in its attempt to diminish the power of the *"haute finance"*; it also set a precedent by discussing openly and coming to an agreement (the *Accords Matignon*) with the representatives of big business, the CGPF (*Confédération Générale de la Production Française*), which was to be renamed, in 1945, the CNPF (*Conseil National du Patronat Français*). The new Council started its life in an unfriendly environment; although it decided to elect as its President a man who had suffered in deportation, Georges Villiers (he was to remain its President for twenty years), the stigma of collaboration, both political and economic, was attached to French employers as a class. Nineteen forty-six was a year when the Communists were still in the Government, when nationalizations were still taking place, when the capitalist firms were being reformed. Most important of all, employers seemed to be divided among themselves about their objectives; though the new Council was technically a federation covering all types of firms, small and medium-sized enterprises were organized under Léon Gingembre into a semi-independent Confederation, the *Confédération Générale des Petites et Moyennes Entreprises* (CGPME), which, because of the large number and the smaller incomes of its members and the general cult of the "*petit*," could afford to be more militant. Employers of large firms were themselves somewhat uncertain of their rights; a section of the *patronat* organized into a *Centre des Jeunes Patrons* was aiming at more progressive attitudes and criticized typical bosses for their conservatism.

The return to normalcy which characterized the early 1950s benefited the employers; indeed, big-business leaders appeared politically more reliable than many other sections of the middle classes. They had been less infected with Gaullism in the late forties than the petty-bourgeoisie; they were not, unlike the shopkeepers, to be amenable to Poujadism in the middle fifties. On the whole, the CNPF and the men in charge of large scale industry behaved responsibly. They accepted the Plan, possibly in the first place out of opportunism as they quickly realized that, in view of the dearth of capital for investment, only State-supported schemes would be likely to expand. They renewed the links which they had had with officials in the economic departments; the comradeship of the members of the *grands corps*, on both sides of the fence, came to be reestablished. But, perhaps more importantly, they soon realized that State-led development, far from being detrimental to them, would produce direct benefits. Their firms would expand, both nationally and internationally. They would increase their profits by increasing their activities. If they could have a say in the investment and fiscal policies of the Government, they could make sure of participating fully in a continuous boom. And they came to discover that by the time of the Second Plan, in order to develop the whole of the economy, and by the time of the Third, in order to develop exports and a "Common Market Spirit," the planners and the State needed the collaboration of business.

Thus began a partnership which led to constant discussions over subsidies, preferential rates for certain businesses in government-operated transportation, and selective export licensing. Through these, the Government hoped to achieve the objectives of its overall economic policies as it hoped to encourage business by gradually changing the system of indirect taxes, and by shifting from a strict turnover tax to a production tax which applied successively to the various stages at which "value" is "added" to the product (*taxe à la valeur ajoutée*). While business taxes are high in total volume (the French have always been notoriously unwilling to pay high direct taxes—and the various forms of consumer taxes therefore have to be heavy), and while social security benefits are financed, in large part, by a fixed percentage of the salaries and wages paid by employers, concessions have in general been made in favor of business, though firms of a large, complex, and highly technical nature are still at some disadvantage.

Private business has to compete, in France more than in most Western countries, with a large number of public and semi-public bodies. Nationalizations mainly affected basic industries, but they also covered, sometimes for accidental reasons (as in the case of Renault, which was taken over because the owner had collaborated with the Germans), parts of the car industry, most of the aviation industry, many shipping firms, many aspects of petroleum research and exploitation, as well as, through State-owned banks and insurance companies, an important section of the financial world. In the early 1920s, the State started being involved in many new ventures and the "mixed economy" company became fashionable. Complex networks of financial participations (through mixed companies in turn creating new mixed economy firms) can provide exciting material to lovers of jigsaw puzzles. Among the most elaborate are perhaps the Sofirad, which is involved in the activities of radio and television stations operating just outside the French border, in Andorra, Monaco, or the Saar, and the extraordinary *Caisse des Dépôts et Consignations*, a huge lending organization which, under the leadership of one of the most talented economic administrators and "technocratic" managers of postwar France, François Bloch-Laîné (an Inspector of Finance by origin), was made to conduct on its own and almost on the side a large-scale operation of regional and local development (many of the housing estates around Paris, and in particular the controversial *"grand ensemble"* of Sarcelles were financed by the *Caisse des Dépôts*).

Not unnaturally, small business found itself much less favored by these new large-scale business undertakings. While, as we saw, the small and medium-sized enterprises were those which could afford to be most vocal in the late forties, they came soon to be considered dysfunctional in the prevailing economic philosophy, to be less and less favorably considered by the public as a whole, and to lose some of the privileges which the French tax system had given them in the past. For a while, in the mid-1950s, opposition mounted and direct action prevailed among large sections of shopkeepers, particularly in the least developed regions of the

Center and South. Directed first against tax inspectors, Poujadist-type outbursts soon threatened the whole machinery of the State. When the fifty-one members of the movement of "Defense of Shopkeepers and Small Traders" (UDCA) came to the 1956 National Assembly, they appeared more violent (and ill-mannered) than any revolutionary group had ever been and they seemed to be engaged in the total disruption of a State with which they did not want to cooperate. The Confederation of the Small and Medium-sized Enterprises, with its leaders torn between "responsibility" and pressures for direct action, became more violent in words, though less anxious, in practice, to break with the Government. By the end of the 1950s, however, the movement was dead, direct action was over (at least among shopkeepers), and a new pattern of relationships with the Government had started to develop. Clearly, the weight of small business has declined markedly; its influence in governmental quarters has diminished to a point where, having ceased to be a threat, or even a problem, shops and small business are treated as a sector which has to be integrated into the general pattern of the economy. Though slowly and somewhat reluctantly, the Confederation of small business has agreed to this new role. Still divided from employers of large organizations by their outlook on life, their education, often their background and their place of residence, leaders of small firms have realistically come to recognize that, for them too, collaboration with the State is necessary and economic development valuable. This is probably an intellectual "reconversion"; it was perhaps not easier, and is perhaps also no less remarkable, than the changes in attitudes which were to be noticed elsewhere in the French social structure, among peasants and even among workers.

THE GOVERNMENT
AND AGRICULTURE

The French Government has concerned itself traditionally with the agricultural problem, as the farming community (the "peasantry") always had a special place in French life, and was supposed to be, up to very recently, the backbone of the French nation. We noted in Chapter Two that the flight from the land was rather slow up to the early 1960s; on the contrary, the political system, as we saw, was, up to and including the Fourth Republic, geared to the inbred and sectional characteristics of the quasi-self-supporting small village. No wonder that many members of Parliament came to Paris with the aim of fulfilling the demands of the peasants and of stopping any schemes which the "bureaucrats" might have conceived. No wonder, too, that the Ministry of Agriculture should have remained for a long time—indeed up to very recently—the Ministry of the Peasants, acting on behalf of those it was supposed to control.

Though one always talked of a peasantry, however, the desires and the demands of members of the farming community were vastly different. In the North and in the Paris area, the wheat and beetroot growers had for a long time constituted an aristocracy. Plots were large, mechanization widespread, and incomes rather high; many agricultural workers were employed by what often amounted to firms dealing with their problems in a capitalist fashion. Most of the rest of French agriculture was run by small farms, sometimes efficient (particularly when they were dealing with fruit, wine, or vegetables, as often in the valleys, especially the Rhône valley) but often quite inadequate in size and producing small incomes for large amounts of human work seldom relieved by machinery. This inefficiency was increased by the fact that many peasants worked on very small strips, sometimes separated by long distances, and though legislation had for a long time attacked the problem, it had not succeeded before the late 1950s in bringing about a rearrangement (*remembrement*) of the parcels which had come to each family through accidents of inheritance. As a result of this diversity, the individualism of the peasantry was rather reinforced, and the main pressure group of the farmers, the *Fédération Nationale des Syndicats d' Exploitants Agricoles* (FNSEA), found itself very often landed with suddenly-expressed demands from the rank and file which it had great difficulty in channeling and turning into a coherent program. Even the creation of this body, in 1947, was progress, however; before World War II, the farming community had known a number of attempts at organization which generally had political origins (from both Right and Left), which never had much impact in the farming community as a whole, and which usually foundered after a few years. The FNSEA emerged out of a governmental attempt at organizing in 1945 an all-embracing *Confédération Générale de l'Agriculture* (CGA), which quickly proved incapable of resolving the oppositions between the various aspects of the agricultural world; in the middle of these difficulties, the organization of the "farmers" proper became a powerful body, supported by the membership of at least a third of Frenchmen working on the land, and though it tended for a while to be dominated by the richer and more pressure-group-minded northern farmers, it tried to represent all agriculture and clearly succeeded in giving the peasant community an appearance of unity which it never had had before.

Three factors of great moment have tended to transform the relationship between agriculture and the government and indeed to change drastically the place of farming in the nation. The first was mechanization, which was a direct consequence of the action of the *Commissariat au Plan*. Convinced that French agricultural production, since the land was generally rich, was very much below the levels which it could easily reach, the planners decided as early as the First Plan to develop (and indeed almost to create) the French tractor industry. Through governmental credit institutions (the *Caisses Nationales de Crédit Agricole*), funds were to be made available to farmers in order to enable them to improve and modernize their plants (a stride was made at the same time to increase the amount of fertilizers used by French agriculture; in most cases, French farmers were using three or four times less fertilizers than Belgian, Dutch, or German farmers). Government-sponsored extension services were used to break the distrust which the average peasant had of the "bureaucrat" trying to teach lessons to people who knew better and whose fathers had always survived without getting themselves involved in the heavy repayment commitments which the new gadgets entailed. For a long time, the work was difficult and opposition was widespread. Gradually, however, the ice came to be broken—and nothing was more interesting to note than the fact that at protest demonstrations in the late fifties (including road blocks) peasants came with their tractors and other expensive machinery to explain that they were dying!

The second transformation was the development of organized and collective action, originating from discontent but going much further than classic "peasant revolts" as a result of the influence of groups of progressive young farmers, mainly Roman Catholic. On the surface, the demonstrations of farmers which took place, in several instances, from the early part of the 1950s, were having the same character; they were aimed at increasing the price paid by the Government for some of the products which it controlled (such as wheat and milk), or at obtaining a better deal from the Government in terms of "parity" between industrial and agricultural prices. But a transformation in depth was also taking place. Many younger French peasants had begun to understand better the basic structures and problems of the economy.

The necessity of mechanization was becoming clear, but mechanization implied more capital per head, larger farms, more efficiency all round; this could be obtained, in the French context, only with the development of the cooperative idea which, indeed, could be extended to almost all aspects of the farmer's life and include, for instance, certain aspects of marketing (it would thus be possible to avoid some, or all, of the middlemen). These new ideas, based on a reflection on the character of the peasantry, were the direct consequence of the educational efforts (mainly technical originally, but expanding into the social, economic, and political fields) brought about by the *Jeunesse Agricole Chrétienne* (JAC), one of the various youth organizations set up by the Roman Catholic Church, and indeed the only one which was a real success. The JAC trained thousands of young farmers to think differently from their fathers; it also trained hundreds of young leaders, some of whom seemed about to be, in the early 1960s, the potential leaders of the whole farming community, after having run for several years the *Centre National des Jeunes Agriculteurs* (CNJA); they did indeed manage for a while to take over the FNSEA. The traditional leaders succeeded in coming back to power after a temporary eclipse, but their hold on the FNSEA is no longer secure and they have to be much more progressive in their outlook, much more concerned with the reform of the farm and the position of the farmer in the nation, than they had been in the past.

The third dramatic change was the flight from the farm. The title of a book which appeared in 1965, *France Without Peasants*, symbolizes the great transformation: a quarter of the population engaged in agriculture left the land between 1954 and 1962; for men under twenty-five, the percentage of departures reached 45 percent. This movement probably helped to bring about some of the reforms asked for by the young farmers of the JAC and CNJA; it explains why farmers have eventually been much less unwilling to agree to the reparceling of land, and to mechanization. The conditions for a new climate had been created; expansion (a small "New Frontier") was at last possible and the farmers who remained could hope to receive higher incomes for less work on larger plots of more selectively chosen land.

Thus French agriculture, at a time when the Common Market will probably enable it to sell some of its basic products more easily, has come to see its position in the community in a wholly different fashion from the one which it had in the years before World War II. Governmental influence is no longer either looked

F

at with distrust or directed at purely sectional and immediate aims. The pluralism which has developed among the French farmers goes beyond the immediate demands of ordinary trade unionism, though the emergence of a really alive peasant trade unionism has already constituted a great change compared to the prewar period. The role of the Government has probably come to be simpler, as the pressures exercised by peasant organizations, and particularly by the CNJA, go in the same direction as those of the "technocrats" with whom the previous generation of peasants would never have conceived of an alliance. For many leaders of the Left, French agriculture may indeed become a source of interesting political and social experiments. On the question of leadership of the FNSEA, the optimists had perhaps hoped for too much too quickly. But French agriculture has ceased to be a backwater and this change alone is perhaps a small miracle.

TRADE UNIONS, THE GOVERNMENT, AND INDUSTRIAL RELATIONS

While socialist elements have played a large and at times melodramatic part in French political developments since the mid-nineteenth century, organized labor has only intermittently been able to assert any significant degree of direct political power. Legislation has therefore always been one of the main ways by which working-class advances have taken place in France. But as left-wing governments often came about as a result of revolution or traumatic developments, left-wing legislation has tended to come in large doses during small periods of time, while most of the intervening periods amounted to "consolidation" and "arrangements," and rarely to a reactionary abandonment of dramatically-won "victories."

Labor's political ineffectiveness stems from many factors, but the two principal causes can probably be traced to the relatively late development of an organized working-class movement and to the tendency of French trade unionists to divide themselves between rival, if not warring, ideological camps. French trade unionism had a difficult early history and was legally "tolerated" only in 1868 and frankly recognized only in 1884. It was virtually wrenched into full life by the aggressive efforts of the anarcho-syndicalists, who believed in direct action and who managed to displace from the leadership by the turn of the century the more reformist or even Marxist elements who could have gradually turned the organization into a powerful force directed against the employers. Syndicalists (who were by no means prominent only in France at the time, but who succeeded in having more strength in France than in other large Western countries) believed in an uncompromising attitude toward the "politicians," and they were not prepared to enter into any agreements with the Socialist Party. Indeed the basic Charter of the *Confédération Général du Travail*, the CGT, created in 1895 as a federation of all major French trade unions, was modified at Amiens in 1906 in order to prevent any longstanding arrangement with the Socialist Party. The official policy was based on the belief that working-class victories would be won not piecemeal through parliamentary means, but in one major push, through the general strike. But the union was never powerful enough to launch any such action—and indeed, when war broke out in 1914, trade unionists, whether syndicalists or not, defended the "bourgeois" State.

After World War I, the majority of labor leaders adopted a more reformist attitude, but the appearance of communism brought about a split and introduced politics into the trade union movement. The CGT followed more closely the Socialist Party, under the leadership of Léon Jouhaux, while the more extreme elements entered the communist-led *Confédération Générale du Travail Unitaire* (CGTU). This was not very successful, however, and it was disbanded in 1936 when the Popular Front alliance came into being, its members rejoining the CGT. Communist trade unionists gradually acquired more influence in the newly reunited body, and by 1945, thanks to the *Résistance*, the CGT had come under their overall domination. Socialist trade unionists tried unsuccessfully to recover some of the lost ground, but, in 1947, when the unions came to be more openly used for political reasons (we noted in Chapter Six the extent to which strike action was revolutionary in that year), they broke from the CGT and created a new CGT—*Force Ouvrière* (the name of their paper). Meanwhile, Catholic trade unions had gained considerable ground; created in 1918, the *Confédération Française des Travailleurs Chrétiens* (CFTC) gradually increased its following from among the white-collar employees and the strongly Christian parts of France (Alsace in particular) to manual workers and the whole of the country. By the 1950s, it had become the second trade union, easily beating the *Force Ouvrière* and producing a strong challenge to the CGT in many areas. In order to widen its appeal, it decided in 1964 to drop the word *Christian* from its title and to rename itself *Confédération Fran-*

çaise et Démocratique du Travail (CFDT); a small element refused to follow, but, on the whole, the change seemed beneficial.

There are thus three main trade union organizations catering
to the manual and white-collar workers, plus a number of independent or "autonomous" unions (including a very strong pri-
mary-schoolteachers' union, the *Fédération de l'Éducation Nationale*, grouping members from all political tendencies) as well
as associations catering to middle management (*Confédération
Générale des Cadres*). This division has been detrimental to the
working class, as it has enabled governments to pay less attention
to workers' demands by playing one union against the other, led
each union to get involved in more demagogic proposals in order
not to be "overtaken," and convinced many French workers that
unionization was not necessary. Admittedly, the division is not
everywhere as clear cut as it might appear on paper. We have
already noted that in some cases (as with schoolteachers) all the
members of a group belong to the same union. In many firms
and offices one or at best two unions tend to predominate. The
CGT is strong mostly in the coal mines, on the docks, and in
mechanical engineering (particularly around Paris); the CFDT's
strength tends to be in light industry and among white-collar
workers; *Force Ouvrière* predominates among textile workers in
the North and among civil servants everywhere. But competition
between two unions is common and, at the national level, all three
unions take stands and are involved in consultations between
themselves, with the Government, and with the employers. But
their following is relatively small; though French unions are
rather secretive about their (limited) achievements, it seems clear
that *Force Ouvrière* does not reach half a million, that the CFDT
has perhaps three quarters of a million members and the CGT
between two and three times as many. In all, about three million
French workers are unionized—perhaps 20 to 25 percent of the
working force, with considerable variations between groups.
The typical French worker still does not appear to be convinced
that he needs to give his commitment to his union which, in turn,
is totally unable to help him with strike funds and other facilities.

The combination of this traditional weakness of unions and
of the legislative efforts to integrate working-class representatives
into the society led to a characteristic though paradoxical mixture
of compulsory cooperation at the top and of semi-anarchistic and
often ineffective outbursts at the bottom. Laws, particularly since
1945, have organized working-class representation in a large number of bodies. The social security system is largely run by the

trade unions; firms, as we saw, have a factory committee (*comité d'entreprise*) which is in charge of large sums of money devoted to leisure and cultural activities; boards of nationalized industries have union representatives. Many advisory committees of the government, both in Paris and the provinces, include union men; the committees of the Planning Council, as we noted earlier in this chapter, and the *Comités de développement économique régional* have trade unionists. This has sometimes led to considerable troubles with the CGT, as this organization has tended to follow the CP line of non-collaboration; more recently, however, it felt this attitude to be of little value and, probably under rank and file pressure, decided to participate much more. Thus, on the whole, the French State has achieved a greater degree of formal government-union collaboration than most Western states, and indeed most states all over the world, as Soviet-type unions can scarcely be deemed either to represent the workers or indeed to be made to participate in any serious sense in the leadership of the country (possibly only the Yugoslav experiment may appear to be more advanced).

Meanwhile, however, trade unions are in a weak position when it comes to pressing for demands at the level of the firm, factory, or office. They often find it difficult to agree on a common stand. They cannot promise members any financial help in case of strike; workers are likely to think that they might as well work during the strike since they will thus be able to benefit whatever the outcome. The divorce between workers and leaders can easily be exploited by the Government or private employers, while it contributes to the increased bitterness of industrial relations. As a result, strikes tend to be typically of two types. Either unions resort to one-day stoppages, slowdowns, and the like, which are always supposed to be warnings of worse things to come, but are normally followed by other one-day stoppages or other slowdowns since unions are unlikely to have the whole of the workers behind them if they resort to longer actions; or strikes come from the bottom, almost unorganized, sometimes on a vast scale, as in the summer of 1953. Then unions do not appear able to control the rank and file, any more than the *Fédération Nationale des Syndicats d'Exploitants Agricoles* appeared able to control peasant demonstrations or than the *Confédération Générale des Petites et Moyennes Entreprises* would act decisively when confronted with large-scale direct action from the mass of shopkeepers. Waves coming from the bottom are perhaps the last remnant of old-fashioned syndicalist attitudes of the early part of the century. But these do not profit unions, are often of little advantage (except perhaps psychological) to the workers, and do not constitute a major threat to the life of the nation; they are merely the best that organized workers can traditionally achieve.

As among the shopkeepers and peasants, however, a change among the manual workers has come about in the 1960s; and as with the agricultural unions, the main driving force behind the change was the Christian leadership. The CFTC (now CFDT) has done more than any other organization in politics or in industry to reintegrate the worker in the nation, on the basis not of old-fashioned and ambivalent paternalism, but of equality of rights and of democratic socialism. As their colleagues in agriculture did, Christian leaders in the working-class movement recognized, at least from the mid-fifties on, that something had to be done in order to understand the real character of the fight and the gains which could be made in the short, medium, and long term. Rather than placing all of their hopes in a long term which was never coming, leaders of Christian unions started educating workers into thinking in terms not of the end of the capitalist system, which was not in sight (and whose alternatives were either not clear or not very pleasant), but in terms of a gradual betterment of their lot through the means of tough discussions, responsible action, and direct confrontation with employers—instead of the usual calls on legislative measures. Collective bargaining had been legalized only in 1936 (a fact which in itself indicates much about the psychology of industrial relations in France); another law relegalized the machinery in 1950. Yet only by the end of the decade can it be said to have come about when, thanks to the efforts of the CFTC and to the bafflement of everybody, including the CGT, a collective agreement was signed in 1958 between the Renault works and the Christian union; this was later to be followed by agreements with other firms (on the basis of the type of tactics used by the American UAW to extract concessions from employers) and the success was such that even the CGT had to agree to accord with what it had originally dismissed as a capitalist plot. Gradually, workers' attitudes in the 1960s seemed to change—strikes became less common, but tougher (like the coal strike of the winter of 1963 or the boat strike of the summer of 1966), except in the civil service and in the utilities, where the one-day token strike still tends to be the norm. Gradually, too, Government and officials have come to recognize the change among working-class representatives: these are no longer shunted aside (as indeed they often were rightly in the past) as irresponsible leaders who had not done their home-work; collaboration has become normal, and is actively sought. The spirit of pluralism has infected practically all sectors of the economy and all parts of the country.

SOCIAL SECURITY

In the struggle between revolutionaries and reformers which characterized the early history of French trade unionism, one of the major objectives promised by the reformers was a compre-hensive system of social security to provide for the sick, the indi-gent, and the unemployed worker. Certain sections of the scheme were adopted at various periods, partly before the First World War, partly between the wars. But in 1946 an overall scheme was enacted: Social Security was legalized as one great network of benefits in kind and cash, covering medicine and hospitaliza-tion, as well as allowances for loss of work, retirement, or death. Most of these measures had been obtained in response to pressure from the left-wing parties, though the beginnings of the social security system can be found among the "paternalistic" and often Christian employers of the North, particularly in the textile in-dustry. Family allowances, on the other hand, had been introduced by a conservative Government and were aimed essentially at stimulating a birth rate which had been the lowest of all Western countries for several decades and did not provide replacement of the existing population. (The birth rate did subsequently rise very markedly and indeed more steeply than the normal "war boom" would have allowed for.)

Social security is run, in a semi-autonomous fashion, and under the supervision of the Ministry of Labor, by a number of regional *Caisses* (technically "Fund" or "Exchequer," in fact meaning "Board") which both control the flow of cash payments going to the members of the social security system and manage the various hospitals, clinics, convalescent homes, etc., which the *Caisses* see fit to have. The system is much more complex than the British social security system; it is also less generous. Except for major operations and long stays in hospitals or clinics, the patient has to pay first and is not wholly reimbursed, both because the law felt that 30 percent of the medical and pharmaceutical costs should be paid privately in order to reduce irresponsible recourse to medicine and because doctors have tended in practice, despite long-standing battles between the *Caisses* and the medical profession, to charge more than the agreed fees. Moreover, unlike the British system, little redistribution between rich and poor is achieved in the French system, as the *Caisses* receive no money from the taxpayer but are financed from contributions, mostly paid by employers, as percentages of the basic wage. Family allowances are a particularly heavy burden, though they have come to be a proportionately smaller part of the total social security bill as the Government systematically decided to let their rate drop while wages were being increased; they correspond less to a social need, let alone to a demographic need, and though the issue is potentially explosive politically, they are likely to be even more reduced in the future.

CONCLUSION

The study of social welfare in France is obviously difficult; social security is only one, though the most obvious, aspect of the numerous social activities in which the Government, local authorities, and (though less so than in Anglo-Saxon countries) voluntary organizations participate. It has also been analyzed less systematically than the economy. The reasons for this relative lack of interest shown for social welfare are not wholly clear, though they are not entirely due to the fact that, the economy being in such bad shape in 1945, economic reforms were by far the most urgent; the French, as a nation, are not primarily concerned (at least not yet) with the welfare of their fellow citizens. Sudden outbursts of compassion (as when the fate of the *clochards*, those strange Parisian tramps, was revealed publicly one winter) do not replace the lack of continuous interest in the problems of the poor, the sick, the disabled. This, clearly, will have to be the next major advance in the revival (or perhaps simply birth) of a genuinely national conscience.

Meanwhile, however, the strides made in the economic field have been perhaps more striking than in any other country. Increases in production have been large, though some of other European countries can easily match them. But changes in behavior—more difficult to measure adequately—have been particularly striking. The old socio-economic structures have started to break up, and new classes have come about: not only a new class of workers, but of peasants, shopkeepers, and managers. The country seems to have regained a vitality and an optimism which the mass of the population ceased to have perhaps in 1914, perhaps even before—only the Second Empire, in the 1850s and

1860s, showed such dynamism. In the middle of this change, the Government is to find a new role—and it has, up to now, kept well in front of others. Having precipitated the change in the midst of major difficulties, the "technocrats" are able to understand the new requests, to apply new techniques of advice, and to treat as partners those who, up to recently, were still grappling with out of date problems in their organizations. The move has gone so far, by the late 1960s, that a reversal of the trend is unlikely to take place; the momentum is too great for further changes not to come about in the social field, and indeed probably in the political field as well. Only a war or major international difficulties could lead to a break, or at least a halt in the economic advance of the country, to the withdrawal of the technocratic planners, and to the renewed sclerosis of the "cadres" of the nation.

9: From Union to Community and Beyond

With the end of the Algerian war in the spring of 1962, France ceased to be at war for the first time in a generation; she also ceased to have colonial problems on her hands, though she still has a number of small overseas possessions in the Caribbean, Africa, and the Pacific. "Decolonization" had come to an end, but in a more painful and protracted fashion than in the case of Britain, Holland, or Belgium. This was partly because the defeats in overseas France followed the defeat in 1940 and added to the bitterness of the French political leadership. It was also for other reasons; the Empire was sufficiently large to give France a first-class international status which she felt she would lose with the end of colonial rule; it also offered a wide network of military bases and an almost bottomless reservoir of recruits for the French Army; some of its land did bring wealth to investors from metropolitan France, though, on the whole, France did "less well" out of her colonies than Britain, Holland, or Belgium. Indeed, the Empire was becoming a burden to the Treasury, which had to pay for the "infrastructure" of roads, schools, health, and welfare.

At first problems were confined to the rivalry between competing colonial powers for influence in Africa and the Far East. In 1911, the visit of the German fleet to the port of Agadir in the French protectorate of Morocco intensified the tensions between France and Germany prior to World War I. Great Britain had a continuous antagonism toward France over territorial claims in Africa, and the settlement of 1904 had not taken away all of the bitterness. But new problems arose during the interwar years; the first of the nationalist revolts occurred in the Rif part of Morocco and was finally subdued after much bloodshed in the desert and political disenchantment at home. On the eve of World War II, it was becoming clear to many Frenchmen that the Empire—or parts of it—constituted an expensive luxury and that a reexamination of its ties with the motherland would be necessary when peace returned. By the time General De Gaulle took the lead of the Free French forces, the fundamental loyalty of the colonies to France had become a crucial national question, since the authority of a Government in exile had to be established by consolidating its power and rallying support in the overseas territories. But the difficulties which De Gaulle encountered were mostly with French administrators and military officers who supported Pétain.

After the war, the problem of loyalty became quickly more acute. Whole native peoples turned either violently against France, or marched off into independence while retaining cordial relations of varying degrees. The successful rebellion of the Viet Minh in Indochina cost France her principal holding in the Far East, debilitated and humiliated her armed forces, and gave birth to some of the ugly political discord in the metropolis that culminated in the collapse of the Fourth Republic. The protectorates of Tunisia and Morocco won their independence with less bloodshed and bitterness, but in both cases France paid a price in internal political distress. But it was to be Algeria which was to sap French morale most, bring about De Gaulle's return to power under the pressure of a potential military takeover, and threaten for several years the very existence of democratic government. Meanwhile, most of the huge colonies which constituted French Black Africa gained their independence without bloodshed (though in one case with great bitterness on both sides), largely because France could not carry two wars, one to the north and the other to the south of the Sahara desert. But only with the end of the Algerian war have relations between France and her former possessions become really harmonious, thus giving De Gaulle an apparent freedom to play a part in world affairs which did not seem open to him before 1962.

FRENCH COLONIAL POLICY IN PERSPECTIVE. THE FRENCH UNION OF 1946

French empire-building was achieved by and large in two phases. The first was in the seventeenth century and it saw the French flag planted in the New World (Canada and part of what was to become the United States) as well as in India and the South Seas. In the territories acquired during this wave of imperialist expansion which have remained under French control—Guadeloupe, Martinique, Guiana, Réunion, and Saint Pierre et Miquelon —there is a general disposition to accept French tutelage; the relationship between colony and administrative power has had time to mature and solidify. The first four became overseas *départements* of Metropolitan France in 1946; their inhabitants enjoy universal suffrage and elect deputies and senators to Parliament. Saint Pierre et Miquelon, along with other colonies acquired later either in the Pacific (New Caledonia for instance) or in Africa (French Somalia) are overseas "territories" with some degree of home rule (and representatives in Parliament), though most of the legislation is still in fact passed in Paris.

The second great wave of colonization took place in the nineteenth century. Algeria was first to come under French rule, after a bitter "pacification war" lasting almost fifteen years, from 1830 to 1845; Black Africa, Tunisia, and Indochina were acquired in the second half of the nineteenth century; Morocco, the last possession to be acquired in Africa, was gained in the years before World War I; Syria and Lebanon were to be obtained under League of Nations mandate in 1919. These were the territories which French leaders of the 1880s hoped would make France great (though there was much opposition to many of the colonial "adventures," on the grounds that they were diverting attention from Europe and from the duty of recovering Alsace-Lorraine, which Germany had acquired in 1871). Colonial policy was devised primarily with these larger and newer colonies in mind, yet it has been more successful in the smaller and older possessions, which, having lived with France longer, and having been better assimilated, have had less longing for independence.

The key word to French colonial policy was indeed "assimilation." The notion was that the cultural, social, and economic characteristics of the mother country should gradually be extended to the overseas dependencies. The idea was that the native peoples would become French and that their countries would either become part of France or be closely associated with Paris; the French assumed that the natives would want to become French—indeed that nothing better could happen to them than to become Frenchmen. In fact, before World War II, only a few Africans and Indochinese had become citizens, and most of these had acquired this status by virtue of having served in the French Army. In Algeria, administrators from the mother country found the durability of Moslem customs, institutions, and practices so formidable that it was necessary to make many adjustments and to maintain the principles of Koranic law. But many Africans, Indochinese, and even Arabs were virtually turned into Frenchmen through being educated, first locally in primary and secondary schools built on the French model, and later in French universities. These constituted an elite, which often went into administration (local administration run on French lines and under French aegis) or teaching (President Senghor of Senegal was for a long period a teacher in a French *lycée*). The mass of the people, however, often remained completely untouched by the "gallicization" process, even in Algeria, where colonization lasted longest and "assimilation" was most pronounced.

The basic fallacy of the policy was clearly the belief that the indigenous population wanted to become French. But there were also three major weaknesses in the implementation of the idea. First, in many cases, wide gaps existed between theory and practice, between the enunciation of a colonial policy in Paris and its local enforcement. Few settlers or colonial administrators living in the midst of what were for the most part backward populations really agreed with the notion that these were actually or even potentially their equals. The notion of equality, when it existed, tended to be theoretical and abstract; the reality of daily life was, at best, enlightened paternalism, at worst (though not very commonly, except in some quarters in North Africa) an unpleasant racism. Second, French colonial administrators often found it expedient to support and identify themselves with traditional local leaders. This the French did primarily because at the moment of colonization these were the only leaders on the scene, but also because local chiefs (*caids* in North Africa) usually proved more receptive to the immediate benefits available in accepting favors and protection against rival interests and because it was often simpler, for the colonial power, to support than to undermine them. When, particularly since World War II, new generations, often educated in France, came to question the right of the French to rule, traditional leaders gradually became discredited and the colonial power was associated with this discredit. Finally, the assimilation policy came too late, and at too leisurely a pace, to compete with the development of nationalism. The collapse of the traditional French colonial policy suggests that time was running out; the real drive toward complete assimilation came in Algeria when the war had already shown that demands for independence could no longer be reversed.

In 1944, while the fighting still raged in Europe, General De Gaulle convened a conference of colonial administrators at Brazzaville in French Equatorial Africa to discuss the future of the Empire. Although no representatives of the indigenous population were on hand as delegates, the conference laid down liberal principles hailed everywhere as great advances. Equal rights and privileges for all regardless of race or creed were proclaimed, the development of local administrations was promised, and the entry of the native-born to the highest ranks of the French colonial service was speeded up. In addition, steps were taken to set up a large investment institution in Paris for the development of overseas territories. But there was no mention of training of local leaders for responsibilities in ultimately independent states. In fact, the possibility that a goal of French colonial policy might be to prepare territories even for autonomous status within the Empire was specifically excluded in the public declaration issued at the conclusion of the conference.

The Constitution of 1946, which established the Fourth Republic, did follow the principles of Brazzaville, at least inasmuch as it marked an advance over previous French policies. Equality of rights was proclaimed—though in practice, and indeed in law as well, important differences obtained between the rights and freedoms of colonial populations and the rights of the French in metropolitan France. The words "colonies" and "Empire" were abolished from the official vocabulary and French possessions were organized into a French Union, but the bulk of them still came legally within the "Republic," with a status of overseas *départements* (the old and small colonies, which had equal status with metropolitan *départements*) or of overseas territories (in particular the whole of West and Equatorial Africa). The "Republic" thus composed was linked through the Union with associated territories (the trust territories of Togo and Cameroon) and associated States: this last category was due to include Indochina and the protectorates of Morocco and Tunisia; in fact, the latter two refused to enter the new legal arrangements, and the States of Vietnam, Laos, and Cambodia only agreed to be included because France was waging a war in Indochina which gave the Governments of the three States little room for maneuver. Moreover, within the Union, powers were concentrated firmly in the hands of the President of the Union (*ex-officio* the French President) and his Government. The other two organs, the High Council and the Assembly, had a consultative role and remained relatively uninfluential. Thus the French Union was to be a semi-artificial experiment; by the end of the Indochinese war, in 1954, it had become almost wholly a paper organization, while the "Republic," comprising the whole of the African territories, tended to be as centralizing and unitary as the Empire had been in the past.

By 1956, however, with the loss of Indochina, independence given to Tunisia and Morocco, and the beginning of the Algerian war, it was clear that even the "Republic" had to change its character. The newly-elected and Socialist-led Government of

Guy Mollet decided that, if the Algerian war was to be fought, peace in Black Africa was necessary. Gaston Defferre, then Minister of Overseas France, thus produced an "outline law" aiming at drastically revamping the structure of colonial administration in the overseas territories. Despite some opposition (though this was less strong than might have been expected), Parliament adopted the scheme, which recognized African demands for the creation of political institutions and for the direction of these institutions by the Africans themselves. This law was crucial; it marked the first real abandonment of the policy of assimilation and it manifested the victory of a current of opinion, hitherto small and less vocal, in favor of association. The institutionalization of specifically African political entities implied recognition that non-French arrangements were acceptable and that local populations might not want to develop as Frenchmen. Moreover, as right-wing critics correctly pointed out, the grant of autonomy (even though limited in various ways) would simply be the first step in a rapid march to independence.

The reform was, indeed, somewhat limited. The territorial assemblies (created long before as governors' councils, and made elective after 1945) in the overseas territories (and in the associated States of Togo and Cameroon) were given new authority and increased jurisdiction over domestic affairs. They were to elect a Government council, which was still to be nominally headed by a French official, but whose locally-chosen Prime Minister was to be the real leader. But France retained control of foreign relations and defense, some aspects of justice, and higher education. Moreover, local governments were to be set up only in each territory, and not at the level of the two federations which had been created by the French administration, French West Africa and French Equatorial Africa: in these, appointed Governor Generals were to remain and to keep, almost intact, the powers which they had gradually acquired. Hence the cry of "balkanization" of Africa; in order to keep some power, so some nationalist critics said, France had decided to give autonomy to the smaller units (some of which, for instance Mauritania or Gabon, had only about half a million inhabitants) and not to foster moves towards federation.

Nonetheless, Africans quickly established functioning regimes and began almost at once to extend the authority and appeal of the new political parties which had been created in the last years before autonomy. Ideas of larger communities became widespread; congresses and conventions of parties took place.

But the movement split, usually on a territorial basis (the local Prime Minister managing to keep a complete hold over his party apparatus) but sometimes within a territory (with consequent feuds which were to be carried into the 1960s and account for the numerous coups which have taken place in ex-French Africa). It was these new congeries of semi-autonomous States—some of which had intensely nationalistic Premiers such as Sekou Touré in Guinea, while others had more conservative leaders who had served in several French governments, such as Leopold Senghor of Senegal and Felix Houphouet-Boigny of the Ivory Coast—to which De Gaulle appealed for support in endorsing the last experiment in the evolution of French colonial policy before complete independence, the Community.

THE COMMUNITY

The French Community was to be the shortest-lived institution of the Fifth Republic. In name it still exists, but the purpose for which it was planned (to keep overseas France in some formal association with France) ceased to be acceptable within two years of the promulgation of the Constitution, and the institutions devised to embody the purpose lapsed and seemed to be simply forgotten. By 1960, practically all of French Africa had become independent and ties with France were to be simply economic and cultural. Paradoxically, however, the Community may have succeeded far better than any of the previous experiments, in that it provided means by which to smooth the necessary transition from assimilation to free association. Goodwill was probably never higher and, even during the Algerian war, when relations were naturally more strained, African States which had belonged to France were usually somewhat more "understanding" than other developing nations.

The Community was in many ways a mere constitutionalization of the outline law of 1956. When one looks at it in detail and from the point of view of its prescriptions and prohibitions, one sees that it did not go very much farther than Parliament had gone with the 1956 law. The Constitution did allow overseas territories to adopt the status of "States of the Community"; to that extent there was formalization of an existing situation. But these States were not to be responsible for foreign policy, defense, currency, or economic and financial policy; the Community also undertook the supervision of justice, higher education, national transportation, and communications. It was only stated that the

Community could transfer common policy obligations to individual members or vice versa, a feature which gave substance to De Gaulle's promise that the African States could develop fully autonomous regimes at their own speed. But, for the present, the States were to remain strongly dependent within "the Community"; they could not expect independence on the Commonwealth model, since the Constitution specifically stated that States of the Community had the right to secede, but if so automatically ceased to belong to the Community—with the financial and other consequences which would follow.

The President of the Republic was given wide powers in the new institutions. The President of the Community (*ex-officio* the French President, though in the 1958 arrangement, States of the Community did participate in his election) headed an Executive Council of the Community, which included not only representatives from the various States, but also the French ministers in charge of Community affairs. This indirectly tended to increase De Gaulle's power over the French Government, as he could maintain that the heads of various important ministerial departments were responsible to him, *qua* President of the Community. The Council was authorized to organize the political and administrative arrangements, which would institutionalize the new form of cooperation between France and her overseas territories, but in practice, the Council listened to formal presentations of French policy made by the President (who was helped by a strong staff dealing with Community affairs) and tended to serve as a convenient body for the negotiation of problems arising between France and lesser members of the Community. The Constitution also called for the creation of a Senate of the Community (in charge of the discussion of financial and economic inter-relationships between the members as well of treaties involving Community obligations), and of a Court of Arbitration to settle disputes between member States. The Senate had only one session, and its deliberations were of no significance; the Court was never convened.

Though the new arrangements gave considerable power to the President and helped to maintain the French administration and the French Government in a superior position, and though, indeed, many important changes had already taken place through the Defferre outline law, the symbolic role of the Constitution was great. It was recognized as such by many African leaders, among whom one of the most prominent was Felix Houphouet-Boigny, who helped to draft the Constitution as a minister in

De Gaulle's Cabinet of the summer of 1958. Indeed most Africans agreed to the plan. First, the leadership elites of most of the States involved were moderate in politics and had strong ties with France through education and often through career training in the French civil service. The strength and monolithic character of the political machines which many of them headed in their territories were sufficient to produce a favorable vote for the Community arrangements when the referendum took place on the Constitution, in the overseas territories as in metropolitan France, in September, 1958; only Guinea voted, and overwhelmingly so, against the new system, at the call of its leader, Sekou Touré. When De Gaulle made a tour of French Africa before the referendum, the Guinean Prime Minister had stated in the frankest and clearest terms that he wanted independence now; the leader of the Fifth Republic, enraged by what appeared to him to be the irresponsible attitude of a naughty child, replied that Guinea could take independence by voting *"Non"*: this did indeed happen and was followed by an immediate withdrawal of all French administration and the cutting off of all French aid. But all other territories "behaved" and voted for the Constitution; twelve were soon to become States of the new Community and have a right to the benefits. Hence the second reason for the acceptance of the system by most African leaders: territories were thus making sure of receiving the funds necessary to carry out their advancement to full maturity as independent States. Third, the flexibility of the new Community arrangements offered balm for everybody. Those States which feared that the Community maintained the "balkanization" process which the outline law had begun were reassured by the Article which said that States could change their status within the Community and, among other things, join with one another in federations or confederations. Changes in the powers of the States were deemed to be real possibilities. Finally, it was simply assumed that the Community would quickly have to change and to open up a third way between the quasi-federal structure which it organized and the secession which it brandished as punishment. To everyone's surprise (and probably thanks to the Algerian war), the change took place before the new system was even two years old.

During the first year of the operation of the Community, 1959, developments took place along the lines of the Constitution. The year was crowded with meetings of the Executive Council at which the institutions were set into being; the President quickly asserted the full powers of his office and indeed assumed responsibilities not explicitly contained in the Constitution. However, the real political battles went on in the distant African capitals: efforts at confederation, federation, and even merger were tried, failed, and attempted again, the link between Senegal and Sudan (under the name of the Mali Federation) being the best known of these attempts. Discussion of the natural and sometimes unnatural associations of States took place on a large scale, often based on rivalries between leaders as well as on the necessities of modern development. Meanwhile, however, negotiations between France and Senegal were gradually leading, in the early part of 1960, to a wholly different basis in the status of association. For several months, hopes of stopping short of independence were entertained in Paris. These were to prove unreal; in the end, a constitutional amendment had to be rushed through the French Parliament, which enabled first the Mali Federation, and in the summer of 1960, all the African States, to claim independence. Some states remained in the Community; others chose not to do so. By the autumn of the year, the whole of West and Equatorial Africa had ceased to have any formal ties with the mother country.

The ties which remained were economic and cultural. Gradually, during the course of the 1960s, differences between the status of Guinea (which was refused aid for a long time) and that of the other States ceased to be as clear. Various bilateral agreements enabled France to retain considerable influence in, and to give large sums of money to, her former possessions. Though the assimilation principle is wholly dead, cultural penetration is as intense as ever. The language ties with France (French is spoken more often in the United Nations since 1960 than it was before) help to maintain economic and technical links. Moreover, as De Gaulle's Government has taken postures of independence from the blocs and of championship of the rights of the smaller nations, countries of ex-French Black Africa, suspicious of Russian and Chinese intervention (Guinea's experience with Russian technicians was traumatic) as well as of American capitalism, about which they know little, prefer French technicians, whose mores they know and can perhaps more easily influence. Thus the image of France came to be strengthened to a point which few could have forecast in the early fifties. Coups and changes of government in the African States are unlikely to modify this "special" relationship.

ALGERIA

The Algerian problem was by far the most complex which the French Republic had to solve. First, as we noted, France had been in Algeria for over a century; in the minds of most Frenchmen, it was associated with French life more than any other part of Africa. Second, and as a result, the French were more numerous in Algeria than in any other region of the French colonial Empire; one million people, or one ninth of the population, were of French, Italian, or Spanish origin. For the great majority, Algeria was their home, as waves of immigration, from France from the 1850s to the 1870s, from Italy and Spain since, had tended to decrease; second or third generation French Algerians, who often had never been to France, felt that their farms, villages, or cities were really and truly theirs. They were not colonial administrators rotating from post to post and land to land, or businessmen sent for two years on contract by a metropolitan company. They were often small men, running their shops, employed as skilled manual or white-collar workers. They generally had a higher income than the Algerian Moslems, but the gap was often small, particularly in the towns, and differences in status often had to compensate for the lack of a real break in purchasing power.

Third, and most importantly, institutions of Algeria were sufficiently intertwined with French institutions to make major changes difficult. From very early on, the policy of assimilation had led to the creation of *départements*, complete with prefects and councils, and of communes, with councils and elected mayors. But assimilation had stopped short of the mass of Algerians—largely, it was argued, because Algerians did not want French law; the renunciation of Moslem customs and the acceptance of the Civil Code were the key to obtaining French rights. As most Moslems did not accept French law, they remained, throughout more than a century of occupation, second-class citizens. In 1946, by the Constitution, and a year later, by an Algerian Charter (the *Statut de l'Algérie*), they were given more influence. The Algerian Assembly in Algiers and the French Parliament in Paris had representatives from the Moslem part (or "second roll") of the population, but both rolls had the same number of representatives and the domination of the French minority was thus perpetuated.

The changes brought about by the 1946 Constitution and the 1947 Algerian Charter were partly the consequence of a rebellion which had taken place in 1945 and which was violently repressed and quickly liquidated by the French Army. Nationalist forces (particularly under Ferhat Abbas) came to be organized legally—and their representatives were elected in the French Assembly and in the various Algerian councils. For a while, it seemed that reforms might take place peacefully, though clearly the demands of the nationalists went considerably further than what even the most liberal Frenchmen were prepared to contemplate. By the early fifties, however, ballot-rigging by the local administration started taking place on a wide scale; nationalists "happened" to lose their seats and were replaced by more amenable and traditionalist leaders. The idea of peaceful change gradually lost ground among the Algerians, and a Revolutionary Committee (which was later to become the *Front de Libération Nationale,* or FLN) was set up in 1954 to fight, by whatever means, until independence came. On November 1st, the rebellion started simultaneously in various parts of the country. It was to take seven and a half years to achieve its aims—but few would have assumed that such a major change could happen in so short a period by a rebellion originally dismissed as likely to be crushed like that of 1945.

The development of the Algerian war added one further interested party to those who were anxious to prevent a change in the *status quo*. Originally fought on a small scale, by 1956 the war involved the bulk of the French Army, which, defeated in 1940 and just returning from eight years of unsuccessful jungle operations in Indochina, was determined not to suffer further reversals. As demands for more equipment and more men (the draft was extended at one time from one and a half to two and a half years) had little apparent result in the field, many officers turned more bitter, became involved in operations of "psychological warfare" (allegedly the war could be won only through applying in reverse the teachings of Mao Tse-tung, which had become well known through the Indochina war), and started accusing the Government, using it as a scapegoat. An alliance came into being between certain elements of the Army and some of the more extreme settlers. Though the alliance had to take place since both wanted to maintain the *status quo*, it was to remain uneasy since many members of the Army felt that major reforms—not merely social and economic, but in the relative status of Europeans and Moslem—were necessary to create the requisite "psychological impact." In three instances, revolt came to the streets. In May, 1958, the constitution of a new Government, headed by the Christian Democrat leader Pierre Pflimlin, was accused of preparing a "sell out." A "Committee of Public Safety" was created in Algiers, followed by others in other parts of the country; for two weeks, there was open rebellion—which only the arrival of De Gaulle to power and the end of the Fourth Republic succeeded in stopping short of the French mainland (Corsica was indeed taken over by rebellious forces). Thus De Gaulle had to act very cautiously, for the best part of the next two years—and yet, early in 1960, barricades went up in Algiers, and for a week challenged the Government, while confronting the Army with a tense and nerve-racking decision to take. The Army stood still and the barricades collapsed, but fifteen months later, in April, 1961, under four generals including Raoul Salan (who had headed the expeditionary corps at the time of De Gaulle's return to power), a mutiny took place which appeared to challenge directly the power of General De Gaulle. However, most of the regiments, largely under the fear that the conscripts would not tolerate a *coup d'état*, refused to support the move; the mutiny collapsed after four days, and the generals were eventually caught and tried. When, in April, 1962, after the Evian settlement, independence was granted to Algeria, revolt was wholly and exclusively a matter for activist European settlers and their French supporters; bomb outrages in Algiers and even in France, under the auspices of the OAS (*Organisation de l'Armée Secrète*) were the worst which France had known. But the Army supported the settlement, defeated the activists in Algeria, and returned to France to become once more what it had ceased to be for twenty-five years—a garrison Army.

As a result of the Algerian settlement of 1962, hatred of De Gaulle on the Right became widespread (there were indeed several attempts at the life of the President). Many felt that they had been betrayed, and betrayed by the man whom they had brought back to power. Almost certainly, De Gaulle's policy did indeed change, when it became clear that a French victory in Algeria was impossible and "integration" between Europeans and Moslems an empty concept which neither side would accept. Thus the French President showed realism in his approach to the Algerian problem, as well as a combination of toughness and skill in the realization of his aims. For the majority of the French, he succeeded in doing what no other politician was in a position to do

—solve the last colonial problem which faced the country, repatriate the Army (and indeed most of the Europeans too, in the summer of 1962), avoid a fascist takeover, and establish relationships with the new Algerian regime which did not differ markedly from those which France entertained with her other ex-possessions in Africa. Thus De Gaulle created for a time a consensus around him (as shown by the referendum of April, 1962, which approved the Evian settlement by a majority of nine to one) which gave the French President considerable scope in other sectors of government, and particularly in foreign affairs. The Algerian war was traumatic for a generation of Frenchmen; it raised questions of allegiance, of direct participation, of sheer morality. To that extent, more than the Indochinese war or the evolution of the rest of French Africa to independence, Algeria was an internal French problem as much as a colonial question. The solution of the Algerian crisis had perhaps as much effect on the country as many of the social and economic reforms of the Fourth Republic. Though the Empire originally gave nineteenth-century France greater possibilities of international action, only the economic recovery and the end of the Empire enabled the Gaullist government to take a forceful line in its conduct of foreign affairs.

10: Foreign Policy

French foreign policy in the 1960s derived its force, direction, and style from Charles De Gaulle. But it is not uniquely the General's creation: it is essentially based on an analysis and interpretation of French history by the President. De Gaulle has readily admitted at times that in the twentieth century France came to the bargaining table of international politics with no material of military substance, no assets in the accepted currency of international relations, and yet maintained her position and indeed often strengthened it. This does not mean that France dealt alone in the faded glories of past greatness—a manifest impossibility in the world of international diplomacy. What it does mean is that France demonstrated through De Gaulle that diplomatic technique, firm leadership, and world influence (if not power), although overlooked in recent decades, can (if skillfully employed) be indices of international status only slightly less formidable than vast populations, great national wealth, giant industrial complexes, and large standing military establishments. What De Gaulle has done is to emphasize the best of France's assets, all of which have their roots in the past: her world-wide cultural influence, the traditional intelligence of her people, the energy of her leaders, and a crucial geographical position at the crossroads of Western Europe. From this amalgam he created the image of a vibrant, living state with a special character and force that he is busily adapting to the requirements of an otherwise bipolar world.

There is no trickery in all this because France is accepted as a power on the international stage to an extent which nations of roughly comparable size and equivalent richness in historical tradition, such as Spain and even Japan, are not. One reason for this, of course, is that De Gaulle has insisted on asserting his claim for French *grandeur*. Furthermore, he has never desisted from forcing his claim on the other nations of the world which are sufficiently endowed with the natural and tangible elements of power to make their recognition of his claim decisive. Spain and Japan, on the other hand, have generally preferred the seclusion forced on them since the days of World War II; as their pretentions have been limited, so have their international positions been confined to secondary or even tertiary roles. While De Gaulle has not used sleight of hand in carving out a unique status for France, he has not hesitated to capitalize on the mystique of his own person to achieve the goals he has set for his country.

Although it is essential to the task of restoring the glory of France, the fact that De Gaulle's part in the effort is dominant constitutes its greatest weakness. Before analyzing the international drives of French foreign policy, one must always remember that after the disappearance of the French President, if it is not followed by the emergence of a successor who shares the same ideas and has the same drive (and the Gaullist Party does not seem to have succeeded in creating such men), French foreign policy is very likely to be of lesser moment in the world, though French international behavior may also be less frustrating to allies and less puzzling to foes.

EARLY POSTWAR FRENCH FOREIGN POLICY

As we noted in several instances, the defeat of 1940 was traumatic for France, both internally and externally. Although technically counted among the Allied victors against the Third German Reich, the country was only a shell when, five years later, the battle was over. In the process of fighting the German invader and in successive years of Allied bombings, much of the nation's wealth had been destroyed. The restoration of French sovereignty, moreover, had been largely accomplished by the force of American and British arms, and indirectly, by the Russian armies, which broke Hitler's Eastern front. France played only a secondary role in these events, despite General De Gaulle's success in fielding a Liberation army of surprising size, largely composed of Frenchmen from the overseas Empire in Africa, the Middle East, and Indochina.

Once the fighting ceased in Europe, France saw her holdings elsewhere threatened not by the erstwhile enemy, but by her allies and by the newly-born forces of native nationalism. Under British pressure she was quickly forced to dissolve her protectorates in the Middle East and shortly thereafter began dispatching troops to Indochina to quell the incipient native revolt in Vietnam. By the late 1940s, nationalist stirrings had begun in North Africa. Within a few years, Tunisia and Morocco had won their independence and the Indochinese war was succeeded by an even more agonizing struggle in Algeria.

Meanwhile, in Europe, France was involved in a somewhat footless search for security against the possible revival of German militarism, to which she had fallen victim three times in less than a century. At the same time she was seeking a means of maintaining the leadership of the continent, when totally ill-equipped to do so. Preoccupation with the German question made it difficult for French policy makers to grasp immediately the essential fact that in a world where an uneasy balance of power was delicately kept between the United States and the Soviet Union, neither of these two superpowers would allow Germany to become a pawn of the other. Hence the only solution from the point of view of *Realpolitik* was to see to it that the West's particular part of Germany did not became dangerously weak relative to the other half and, more importantly, to commit positively the weight of the Bonn Republic to the power of the West. The long detour of French policy before this fact was seen to be complicated and delayed the effective building of a united Europe. It also caused antagonism against France throughout Europe and the Free World.

Nevertheless, considerable progress was made in the early years after the war toward bringing Europe closer together, and France instigated most of these moves. She was instrumental in initiating international discussions which led to the creation of the Council of Europe; she contributed effectively to the international planning which produced the Organization of European Economic Cooperation (with efficiently using American aid as its main purpose); and she launched the idea of European integration—the Coal and Steel Community was to be known for a long period as the Schuman plan, from the name of the French Foreign Minister of the period. However, although France moved with dispatch and provided ingenious leadership during the formative period of these organizations, the path was by no means smooth, and considerable European suspicion of French motives resulted as long as it seemed that France was using all her power to control a renascent Germany. It was only at the end of the 1940s that French policy can be said to have been wholly committed to Western defense against Russia and to a form of European integration which would include Germany on an equal basis. But the development of both these ideas was sometimes a difficult one, since French prejudices still remained near the surface and since colonial problems often came to interfere with the general aims of French foreign policy.

THE FOREIGN POLICY OF
THE FOURTH REPUBLIC

After France came to realize that the idea of partitioning, or even controlling, Germany could not be seriously entertained in view of Anglo-American opposition, her foreign policy came to take great pride in the construction of Europe. This was a way of integrating Germany in such a way as to make adventures of the Hitler kind wholly impossible; this was also, in the eyes of "technocrats" such as Jean Monnet, a means of forcing competition on a French industry which had been hitherto depressed through Malthusianism and protectionism. But immediate and full-blown European unity was impossible on a number of grounds. First, public opinion was scarcely ready for it. It was not even ready for it in some of the devastated countries of Western Europe, such as France or Germany; opposition was likely to be even greater in countries which were still confident of their own ability to survive alone in the postwar world, such as Great Britain. Moreover, any immediate European developments on a large scale would be dangerous for the economies themselves; protectionism had to be demolished gradually if countries were to be able to benefit fully from the change. Hence the discovery of the "step by step" method of European integration, which was at the root of the proposal made by France of a first Community which would be limited to coal and steel. It was to be a real "Community," not simply an agreement or an alliance; there were to be institutions (an Executive, a Parliament, a Court) which would have a "supranational" character; members of the Executive, in particular, were to take decisions on the basis not of the interests of the individual countries, but on those of European coal and steel as a whole.

Even this relatively modest suggestion for European "integration" was more than Great Britain was prepared to accept. While the British had taken part in the discussions leading to the creation of the Council of Europe, it became clear, when the proposal of a coal and steel community was made in the spring of 1950, that Britain was both convinced that she could solve her own problems alone and that she was not willing to bow to decisions taken on a supranational basis by a Community organization. The Europe of the Six (France, West Germany, Italy, Belgium, Holland, and Luxembourg) was born from this refusal—which was to have serious consequences, both psychological and practical, in the years to follow. European integration, as launched and propounded by the French (and in particular by the party which advocated European unity most consistently, the MRP), was to have a continental flavor—some said a Roman Catholic flavor. De Gaulle was later to use (or attempt to use) this situation to his benefit, and he was to find allies in some quarters of French politics which had become convinced that Britain would never really be prepared to participate in the building of Europe.

By the time the treaty establishing the European Coal and Steel Community was signed in 1951, however, the question of Germany had already been revived much more dramatically through an American proposal that the old enemy of France should be rearmed and brought within NATO. Opposition flared from various quarters—indeed it became clear very quickly that the move would not be willingly accepted by France. Various efforts at procrastination were made by the French government, but they failed against American determination. Something had to be done by the French who, by the early fifties, had recognized that NATO was necessary to their own defense (except for the Communists and a small neutralist section on the Left) and who were engaged in a war in Indochina in which American support was being increasingly sought and obtained. The French Government thus conceived of a plan, the European Defense Community, which used the European idea to limit the full weight of German rearmament: armies would be merged, there would be only contingents of each nationality at the lower levels, and the high command would be fully integrated. If the scheme had succeeded, France would have managed, in one move, to prevent Germany from ever recovering an army capable of waging wars, to bring forward the European idea of community, and to satisfy the Americans on basic defense requirements.

The plan was accepted in Washington, but the French were to be divided on EDC in a way which resembled some of the most bitter political fights of the early part of the century about the Dreyfus case or the separation between Church and State. Except for the Communists, who were predictably and thoroughly against the idea, all the parties were divided, some right down the middle. Most Christian Democrats, many Socialists, and some Radicals and Independents supported the scheme not because of its intrinsic virtue, but because of its contribution to European integration. De Gaulle and his supporters were strongly against the plan, mainly on nationalistic grounds, as was a large section of the Army which felt that the price was too high, since it might lead to the dismemberment of the French high command. The Government procrastinated for two years (between 1952 and 1954) before presenting the treaty to Parliament, while the climate of opinion in the country became more passionate and opponents gradually gained ground. In the end, it was to be Pierre Mendès-France who, after having solved the Indochinese war at Geneva, decided that the abcess had to be opened, however painful the operation might be. After a stormy debate (as a result of which the Christian Democrats were never to forgive Mendès-France for not having come down firmly in favor of the treaty), EDC was killed at the National Assembly by a coalition composed of all the Communists, about half the Socialists and the Radicals, a large minority of the right-wing Independents, and almost the totality of the Gaullists. The consequence was to be full German rearmament at the end of 1954, with, however, the guarantee given by the British that they would maintain an army on the Rhine for fifty years and that they would agree to the creation of a much less supranational Western European Union. The new treaty, though less pleasant in the eyes of the "integrationists," was at least acceptable to the French nationalists.

European integration did indeed appear at a very low ebb at the end of 1954. It seemed that it would be impossible to bring back to the fore an idea which had been so severely shaken by the crisis of EDC and which was not based on a genuine *rapprochement* between the French and the Germans. Yet the idea of "step by step" integration was revived in 1956, somewhat surprisingly, by the new Socialist Government of Guy Mollet. After a relatively easy negotiation (in view of the problems which were at stake) and largely because it was agreed from the start that most difficult problems would have to be solved during various transitional periods lasting up to fifteen years, a treaty was signed and ratified in 1957 by the French Parliament, and the Common Market was born (another treaty, creating a European Atomic Community was also signed and ratified). This decision was recognized as momentous at the time since it probably prevented the European idea from dying; in fact, the decision was perhaps even more momentous than was thought in 1957, for De Gaulle's policies on Europe might well have been very different and his room to maneuver much greater, if the last Parliament of the Fourth Republic had not landed him with a new child whom Frenchmen suddenly came to love, and were to continue to cherish during the whole of the subsequent period.

The legacy of the Fourth Republic was thus far from negative. The Franco-German problem had been solved, though indirectly. Commitment to the Western Alliance was perhaps less strong than in other European countries. France never practiced a militant form of "Atlanticism"; this was perhaps because there were many Communist electors; this was also because, even before De Gaulle, the French were somewhat uneasy about the Anglo-American leadership of the Alliance. But there was never any question of breaking the ties which most people agreed had been essential in preserving peace in Western Europe and perhaps in making the Soviet Union realize gradually that an aggressive policy would be of no avail. But it was in the field of European integration that the French contribution had been the greatest; despite the failure of EDC, it was the Fourth Republic which had provided leadership and started a movement which no one would be able to reverse. Admittedly, the cost had been the division of Western Europe, which became clear in 1958 when the European Free Trade Association was erected as a countermove to the Common Market, but, for the French "integrationists," this cost was both temporary and unavoidable; Britain would only respond if she were made to realize that the Common Market would be a success and that her economy would suffer from remaining outside. This the "Europeans" were determined to prove. By the late 1950s, they had already to a large extent made their case, as businesses everywhere were preparing for entry into the large new market. The failure of the Fourth Republic in Algeria can perhaps be said, in retrospect, to have been more than compensated for by the success of the European idea.

FOREIGN POLICY IN THE FIFTH REPUBLIC

When he came to power in 1958, De Gaulle stated plainly that he would respect French foreign obligations. Indeed, he went further: in relation to the Common Market he sought to lower tariffs sooner than the treaty required. Having devalued the franc (and created a "New Franc," worth one hundred of the old ones, partly for prestige reasons, since the franc became roughly equal to the Deutschmark as a result), he decided that France had to swim, from then on, in the same waters as the other five countries; it was indeed typical of his attitude to have anticipated, rather than followed, the first Common Market move—and it can only be surmised whether France would have so closely followed the treaty had the Fourth Republic remained in being. For De Gaulle, however, this was not out of real love for integration; it was a matter of honor—and a shrewd political calculation.

The calculation was essentially that, if skillfully used, the European movement and European organizations could become the means by which the French Government, or more precisely his own Government, could have a much stronger hand in international negotiations, particularly with the United States. From the start, De Gaulle was determined to increase French independence in respect to foreign policy—and, since the United States was the country on which France was, perforce, most dependent, French policy would aim as disengaging itself as much as possible from the United States. At a higher level, moreover, De Gaulle was convinced that the United States (and the "Anglo-Saxons" in general, as he called the Anglo-American community), were being both old-fashioned and naïve in their conduct of world affairs. They were old-fashioned in their stress of an anti-Soviet line which did not correspond to the realities of the post-Stalin world; Russia (as he always calls the Soviet Union) was returning to the fold of the European nations; to emphasize divisions between the communist and noncommunist parts of Europe helped the perpetuation of a division which was becoming daily more artificial. Americans were being naïve in forgetting too easily the requirements of power politics and in giving too much prominence to ideology in international relations; for De Gaulle nations are human beings, with their wills and passions, and whatever dress each nation is currently wearing makes little difference to "real" governmental behavior. Russia and China have "traditional" aims, and regimes currently holding power are bound, by some internal necessity, to act upon these aims. Nothing is gained in refusing to agree that these constraints exist; nothing, for instance, is gained in refusing to "recognize" a country on the grounds that one does not like a regime, or in refusing to accept the fact that large countries need buffer states to protect themselves. In the 1962 Cuban crisis, De Gaulle was one of the first to give explicit and total support to Kennedy; but, equally, De Gaulle deems American policy in Vietnam to be unrealistic since it is not based on the recognition of the "traditional" aims and needs of China.

The twin instruments of a foreign policy, in the Gaullist interpretation, were to be a position of basic strength and a skillful system of alliances. The position of strength was to be had through the atom bomb, envisaged as a credible deterrent which would force others to negotiate with the French Government. De Gaulle had not started the French atomic program; he inherited it from the Fourth Republic. But De Gaulle was to go further and give great emphasis to the *force de frappe*. He chose to reconvert the whole French Army and to divert as much money as possible to the construction both of weapons and of means of delivery. The Algerian war was a burden in this respect, as it forced the French President to maintain strong conventional forces which were of no relevance to the requirements of a modern system of defense, and, more importantly, to the aims of a global policy. As soon as the war was over, and despite opposition from a large section of the military, De Gaulle took steps to reduce the size of conventional forces both from a desire to redirect funds to the nuclear-weapon effort and to adapt the military establishment to modern defense concepts.

The system of alliances was to be built on the foundations of European integration inherited from the Fourth Republic. Instead of a European community, in which European countries would be merged (in De Gaulle's view a wholly unrealistic, or at best a premature idea), the French President wished to develop the "Europe of the Fatherlands." The aim was indeed a little too ingenious to be really successful. Briefly, it consisted in using what integration was already in existence to make sure that alliances would not be broken and to turn to France's advantage the cultural and economic potential represented ·by the combined strength of the European nations. On the one hand, the idea of European integration and the already existing institutions of the Coal and Steel Community, the Atomic Energy Community, and the Common Market would make the other five members of the Six wary of making moves which might lead to a break, and only France had an atomic force (indeed, Germany was prevented by the treaty of 1954 which allowed her to rearm from ever being involved in a nuclear weapons program). On the other hand, France (and De Gaulle) would be free to decide how to use the combined European strength; this could be employed to further aims specific to the French (or to De Gaulle's vision of what France needed). In order to establish French supremacy, at least in foreign policy, over the other five countries, it was even suggested that reunions of foreign ministers (or heads of governments) should take place periodically. De Gaulle hoped to play in them the part which he did succeed in playing, for a while at least, in the Executive Council of the Community. At the same time, failing the agreement of all five, a special arrangement was made with one partner: Franco-German friendship was pushed to a point which it had never reached during the Fourth Republic or before. Konrad Adenauer's passionate desire for European unity, as well as the strong influence which the French President had on the old German Chancellor, led to a temporary and apparent identity of views. A curious confederation seemed to be gradually born, which borrowed some of its features from the structure of holding companies; though she had only a share in the Europe of the Six, France appeared able to make the major decisions (or at least to speak in the name of the others) and the French leader, through his control of French policy, could lead European destinies.

While these arrangements were being skillfully constructed, De Gaulle was gradually disentangling France from what appeared to him to be the unacceptable constraints of the North Atlantic Treaty. In a first phase, he pushed for the establishment of a three-country directorate, in which France, Britain, and the United States would take the major decisions which other countries, not possessing nuclear weapons, would have to abide by. In the name of realism, De Gaulle claimed that only those three countries could carry out the threat of the deterrent and that a larger directorate would in any case be cumbersome and unwieldy. The American Government predictably refused (whether De Gaulle believed that his idea would be agreed to is difficult to know) on the grounds that the other members of the alliance were entitled to have as much a share as was permitted by the necessities of modern warfare. This was dismissed by De Gaulle as an obvious means of maintaining American (and to some extent Anglo-American) supremacy over the alliance. From 1960 onward, he became determined to gradually undermine the "integrated" character of the organization and hoped, with German collaboration, to reduce it to a conventional alliance in which U.S. predominance would be markedly reduced.

The year 1962 was perhaps the best year of Gaullist policy, the year in which it seemed that, however dubious the foundations, the system might be about to succeed. With the end of the Algerian war, the French President would at last be free of "trivial" colonial preoccupations and the French Army could be devoted entirely to being the prestigious arm of a grand diplomacy. Franco-German collaboration was at its highest point and the official visit of the French President to Germany seemed to manifest the European (as distinct from "merely" French) stature of the General. As the German magazine *Der Spiegel* said after the

G

occasion, "De Gaulle came to Germany as French President and left as European Emperor." A treaty was to be negotiated between the two countries (it was indeed to be signed early the following year) which would formalize the "special" relationship existing between them and would in particular lead to the development of regular exchanges and conferences at all levels of foreign policy making. But 1962 was also the year in which the British, at last, did recognize that EFTA was only a limited success, while the Common Market was an unqualified one: at Brussels, for several months, British ministers were gradually to make concessions on various aspects of economic policy, though perhaps not enough in the agricultural field. De Gaulle seemed on the verge of achieving what the "Europeans" had not been able to do: the old British "independence" was coming to an end and was being replaced by full participation. Though such a change might mean more policy-sharing on the part of the French President, British entry into the Common Market would mean the creation of the kind of powerful unit which Gaullist policies needed if autonomy from the United States was ever to be achieved.

De Gaulle did fear, however, the consequences of British entry. Clear independence from the United States was going to be more difficult. The two-person game with the German Chancellor would be replaced by a more difficult three-person relationship, with the last entrant in the team having long been expert at diplomacy and having practiced the balance of power for several generations. For once, De Gaulle clearly overplayed his hand, though he was quite possibly cornered into doing so; by vetoing British entry into the Common Market, he stopped any intrusion from complicating the elaborate system which he had so cleverly built, but he also quickly was to find that the system itself was about to crumble. With the end of the Adenauer era, in the summer of 1963, he was presented with a new German opposite number, Ludwig Erhard, who had less admiration for his talents, was less interested in maintaining at all costs a real Franco-German friendship, and was generally more convinced of German economic leadership in continental Europe. During the following years, France was as a result to pursue a more bitter and less successful foreign policy than during most of the postwar period.

The second phase of the foreign policy of the Fifth Republic thus opened in 1963. It seemed to be based on gradual withdrawal from all classic alliances with the hope of gaining a compensation, in the communist world and in the Third World, for the losses suffered in the Western world. Negotiations became increasingly difficult inside the Common Market; the toughness of French negotiators was not merely a reply to German efforts aimed at maintaining some special advantages to German agriculture. Though no desire to break was overtly expressed, at least in the first instance, warnings were more frequent and the attitudes of the French Foreign Minister, Maurice Couve de Murville, became increasingly less amenable to the idea of compromise. Yet there was surprise when in June, 1965 the French delegation walked out of a Brussels meeting and when France subsequently decided unilaterally to put the Common Market in cold storage. But the evolution followed logically from the events of the previous two years; the technical difficulties of the Common Market were no greater at the time than they had been in the past and particularly during the early period, when, thanks to the personal alliance between De Gaulle and Adenauer, the French President seemed to reap many benefits in the field of foreign policy. By 1965, De Gaulle had turned his back on a European Economic Community which he could not use for his own aims, since the other Five had shown little or no interest in the confederal and strictly governmental plans which the French Government had launched.

Thus De Gaulle abandoned Western Europe; he moved towards a policy of collaboration with the communist countries and attempted a new leadership of the developing world. The difficulties between Russia and China and the increased independence shown by Eastern European countries seemed to help the new line of the French President. The recognition of China, which took place in 1964, was presented as a piece of realism, which indeed it was; but hopes were also raised at the time, not merely of trade arrangements, but of a broader collaboration. These were quickly to prove groundless, but as the views long expressed by De Gaulle about a Europe stretching "to the Urals" seemed more realistic in view of the unfreezing of the Communist Bloc, the French President saw in various Eastern countries, in particular Rumania, a possible outlet for his new "global" policy. Yet it was in the Third World, and particularly in Latin America, that De Gaulle seemed to look for the real basis for his alternative policy. The 1964 Latin-American trip, organized with great pomp, appeared to be a clear success. While, during the Algerian war, France had had to use all her skill to keep the friendship of a section of the Third World (and while, indeed, as we saw, only the independence of West Africa enabled France to maintain her position in parts of the developing world), the new anti-American and apparently neutralist postures of the French Government seemed to lead, almost overnight, to a complete reversal. Admittedly, French aid, particularly in West Africa, did help to modify some of the attitudes. But De Gaulle's apparent determination to produce a middle way by capitalizing on the anti-American feelings of much of the Third World seemed to increase the prestige of a country which had always longed for status; it also injected attitudes of superiority among many diplomats who had been forced, through the 1950s, to accept rebuffs and to remain humble.

By the end of 1965, however, this policy had had little concrete effect. French morale might have been boosted; French diplomats might have felt life more bearable among their foreign colleagues. But the collapse of De Gaulle's European "master plan" in the early 1960s had not been replaced by an effective leadership of the Third World or an arbitrating position in East-West conflicts. In fact, even the French, more concerned with the future of the Common Market than with the potential of a *politique de grandeur*, came to signify to the President, when the election of December, 1965 took place, that Europe (an *integrated* Europe) was important to them; while the population as a whole remained largely unperturbed when foreign policy was concerned mainly with world questions (though perhaps secretly pleased sometimes, the majority of the French simply do not take very seriously the global vision of Gaullist policy), there were considerable rumblings over the Common Market breakdown. De Gaulle seemed to have realized that he might have gone too far. Drawing the lesson from his failure to be elected on the first ballot, he decided, slowly but unmistakably, to come back to Brussels and to start negotiations where they had been left. By mid-1966, all difficulties had been fairly easily solved and the European Economic Community had gone through the last phase of the negotiations of the transitional period.

Yet De Gaulle soft-pedaled only on European economic integration. On defense matters, his determination to replace the North Atlantic Treaty by bilateral arrangements went even further: he requested and obtained the departure from French soil of American forces and of the headquarters of the organization. But the move, however irritating and unwelcome to the other members, is not of great moment. By and large, NATO had accomplished its mission long before De Gaulle came back to power—and few of the countries had taken their duties seriously in the course of the 1960s. Convinced of the realism of his position, De Gaulle is indeed perhaps only hastening a move which would probably have happened by the end of the decade. Though it is too early to say that, disappointed with the small or indeed nonexistent effect of his Third World policy and his opening toward communist countries, De Gaulle might return to Europe, if not to the Atlantic, to look for further moves, there are signs of less grandiose and general a plan in French foreign policy of the late 1960s. As De Gaulle says himself, and as we so often noted, he is a realist; and realists cannot long pursue an unreal policy. From 1958 to 1962, the policy was real, but too clever to maintain; since 1963, the policy has been, for most purposes, except to boost internal morale, almost totally unreal. It was clearly beyond the means of French capability, even with a De Gaulle. While it may be less flamboyant in future years, it may become more permanent and profound, as was indeed permanent and profound the policy of economic integration which De Gaulle inherited from the Fourth Republic and which he, whatever his motives, carried to fruition.

II: Problems of the Future

The Algerian war is over; the French economy is flourishing; social tensions are diminishing; the international status of the country is high: France is by all accounts a prosperous nation. It has fewer structural problems than at any time during the twentieth century. Yet the new regime still appears provisional to many Frenchmen. The country does not hang any longer on the verge of a political precipice. The disappearance of De Gaulle would not shake the foundations of the State; it would simply be "politics as usual," however difficult and lengthy the process of transition might be. But the institutions do not *appear* stable; few seem to believe that the political problem is solved. Even the most forceful of the Gaullist supporters seem to praise the regime more loudly than their innermost convictions would warrant. Indeed, changes made by De Gaulle himself, whether through constitutional amendment (as in relation to the electoral college of the President) or through customary practice (as in relation to the powers of the President) seem to reinforce the feeling of transition. We noted that, from a strict interpretation of the Constitution, the system was not really made to fit De Gaulle; but we also noted that the twist to the institutions gave the President the room to maneuver which he intensely desired. Yet this change has increased the fragility of the new political system. Instead of providing France with institutions which he would support and help to grow by protecting them by his authority, De Gaulle has, more selfishly, been concerned with his own possibility of action; by contributing so much to shaping the present political arrangements, he has mortgaged his influence over the future of his country.

Thus the problems are, as usual, but this time almost exclusively, political and constitutional. During its early years the Fifth Republic hesitated at the crossroads. Disregarding the advice given him by numerous political scientists, leaders of political clubs (and in particular the *Club Jean Moulin*), the head of the new regime did not decide to take a firm line in the direction of presidential government. Various reasons have been given. Cynics said that De Gaulle wanted to have it both ways, namely to be able to run the executive and yet to have considerable control over the legislature, to have the elbow room of a U.S. President but the hold over the Chamber of a British Premier, or, in practical terms, to be immovable for seven years but to be able to dissolve the Chamber and to appeal to the people. Others claimed that De Gaulle was incapable of understanding and appreciating the importance of constitutional structures. There is, indeed, some truth to this view, though attitudes of the President on this matter are certainly complex: he seems at the same time to consider that constitutional arrangements are matters for lawyers who can always find solutions if they are firmly led, and yet to have a simple, naïve, and almost religious belief in the virtues of constitutional reform to redress the imperfections of a political "system"; his approach to political analysis is more "institutional" than "behavioral," to use the common expressions of modern political scientists. Still other students of the French scene have claimed that the country was not ripe for a presidential system (and that De Gaulle knew it, whether consciously or not); the memories of 1851 are said to die hard, and only if the move is made by stages (first an election by universal suffrage, combined with a *de facto* increase of powers, then a formalization of the system by the disappearance of the Prime Minister) will the country accept the transition. If De Gaulle did indeed make this calculation, he showed himself to be both more far-sighted and more mysterious in his ways than even his most fervent admirers claim. But none of his pronouncements seems to suggest that he visualizes (let alone visualized in 1958 or in 1962) a step-by-step transformation of the Constitution; the temporary and precariously balanced character of the system of government which he created does not appear to cause him great concern.

If De Gaulle had not wanted to establish a presidential system, he could have moved in the direction of a more "responsible" and more streamlined party system, as Adenauer aimed at doing and indeed succeeded in doing in Western Germany. As we noted earlier, there are signs that this is perhaps happening, though the evolution is taking place almost against De Gaulle's will and clearly without the President's realizing, more than purely empirically, the importance of the change. To be a true parliamentary leader, De Gaulle would indeed have to abandon many prejudices and reconsider many standpoints; he would have had to condescend to remain Prime Minister, rather than becoming President; he would have had to be prepared to go and discuss matters in the Assembly (he tried in 1945 and was thoroughly miserable and pained); he would, most importantly, have had to recover from his hurt pride at being betrayed by his political friends, first of the MRP, who continued the Fourth Republic without him, later of the RPF, many of whom broke away at the first sign of a "new" conservative policy. De Gaulle's attacks on parties (much more common in 1958 than in the mid-1960s, interestingly enough) prevented him from recognizing that a modern political system needs parties to operate at all and that a parliamentary form of government needs disciplined parties to work efficiently. Thus De Gaulle stumbled on the UNR because something had to be created (but he was too sore, this time, to organize the party himself); he used the new grouping in 1962 because his Government had been overthrown in the Assembly and some means had to be found of separating the sheep from the goats. But De Gaulle never *willed* the development of the UNR; he was never anxious to generate and favor regroupings; he did not seem happy to see better arrangements taking place on the Left. It may be that, despite its curiously undesired birth, the UNR will survive as a solid party; from the point of view of the stability of the French political system, this survival should be called for. But the dice are still loaded against it—and the leader of the country has done little to reinforce the permanent structure of the party.

Of course, the main stumbling block against a real streamlining of the party system remains: whether De Gaulle strongly supports the UNR or not, the Communist Party is responsible for the permanent division of the Left. Changes in the character of the CP are slow; the disappearance of Maurice Thorez and his replacement by Waldeck-Rochet did not affect the main line of approach, and indeed no move by the Party, short of voluntary disbanding, could really be a new deal. A whole way of life has been created; prejudices and taboos have erected a wall isolating Communist leaders, activists, and electors from the rest of the political community. Even if the Party wanted a change and was prepared to abandon its total and unconditional opposition to the "capitalist system," and even if, more importantly, it was to become committed to a liberal, democratic form of government, it would find itself, perhaps for decades, intellectually entangled in the maze of the enormous edifice which it built to protect itself. French political circles look for signs of Communist "liberalization"; they try to measure the size of changes, though these are often obscured by the almost hermetic jargon which the Party produces in attempting to popularize Marxism. But these changes are small, and they cannot be other than small. Only a sizable decrease in the Communist vote which would clearly give the Party second place among the forces of the Left will produce the real unfreezing. Socioeconomic changes may bring about this decline, but the signs are still weak, confused, and even contradictory.

The non-Communist Left may, nonetheless, come to constitute a greater electoral force than the Communists, before the CP declines appreciably, because the realignments which have taken place under the name of the *Fédération de la gauche démocrate et socialiste* have brought about in the mid-1960s an element of polarization which was scarcely noticeable before. Very cleverly, the leaders of the *Fédération,* and François Mitterrand in particular, decided to behave as if they were the only possible alternative. This change can perhaps indirectly be credited to De Gaulle; the presence of a Gaullist majority in the Chamber and the requirements of the presidential election increased the role and maximized the opportunities of the left-center. Perhaps the most important and durable move took place early in 1966 when, capitalizing on his relative success at the presidential election, anxious to keep the members of the *Fédération* together, and having to remain in the public limelight for the election campaign of 1967, François Mitterrand decided to create a "counter-government"—a shadow cabinet. This development is entirely new. Before the Fifth Republic, the opposition did not have a capital "O"; opposition was everywhere and nowhere; it took the form of guerrilla warfare, with no clearly-defined front line. Whether other groups and parties recognize it or not, and in particular whatever the feelings of the Christian Democrats and their allies, on the one hand, and of the Communists on the other, the counter-government of Mitterrand has taken the leading opposition place and has acquired some of the legitimacy of the British shadow cabinet. It has announced its election program in detail and long in advance; it makes pronouncements on current governmental policies, agrees to some and criticizes others in a "responsible" fashion. Out of fairness or simply because it is easier to do so, the press prefers to give prominence to the views of the counter-government rather than to the scattered range of views of individuals or groups which do not belong to the *Fédération.* The mechanics of the political system become more easily understandable and are likely to be more easily appreciated.

Thus the "system" has not stood still during the first two Parliaments of the Fifth Republic. But the prospects of further moves and the speed at which these moves might take place are difficult to ascertain. On balance, the Fifth Republic is still likely to return after De Gaulle to a style of politics not very different from the one practiced in the Third and Fourth Republics. Only if De Gaulle lasts for a very long period—at least to 1972—and has the opportunity to see the whole of the third Parliament and the beginning of the fourth through will the new system become accepted. What is indeed needed is a thorough renewal of the personnel and the arrival of new generations to the political lime-light; what is also needed is enough time for the effect of the profound social changes to be felt on the political structure. Even in the best of circumstances, the streamlining of politics might still be only temporary, and given normal expectations, the change is likely to be a modest one indeed.

Whatever happens to the political system, the role of the administration will remain profound in the economic field and perhaps decisive in many aspects of social development. The administration, as we saw, is also at the crossroads, though the question naturally receives less public attention and the dangers arising from any mistakes in direction may be, at first sight at least, less worrying. The administration is at the crossroads in that it is about to make a choice between "enlightened despotism" (or paternalism) and "guided democracy" (in the best literal meaning of the expression). The question of "decentralization," particularly in the form of regionalism, is one which is very likely to test the ability of the administration to steer, advise, warn—and yet let representatives act. The larger the groupings, the less the officials of the central government are likely to be able to impose their views and directly influence people; one cannot treat representatives of regions in the way one used to deal with the mayors of small villages. Moreover, "guided democracy" is also being attempted on other planes. It goes further than consultation; it does not simply mean hearing the representatives of the various groups, trade unions, employers' associations, and professional bodies; it means trying to enlist the cooperation of these representatives in the operations by which, for instance, the Plan is being gradually prepared. As we saw, the first experiments in this democratic form of corporatism led to numerous criticisms and met with only limited success. But French higher civil servants are obstinate. They have now been sold on the idea of a joint enterprise in social engineering, and they often have a personal stake in the success of the whole venture. Many more forms of participation and cooperation will have to be devised before a truly satisfactory formula can be found, but ingenuity and imagination are not lacking. Paradoxically, and unlike the more rigorous line adopted in economic planning, the French approach to social pluralism is even more empirical and less doctrinaire than the notions of Fabian socialism once devised by the British, and it is also accepted by more people in the top administrative circles. It has, thus, greater chances of success.

Observers around the world admire the British form of government, but they are fascinated by the French political system. For a while, under the Fifth Republic, it was fashionable to say that a new French political system, streamlined and dull, was developing. This was scarcely true at a time when the Algerian war was giving rather too much virulence and unpleasantness to the political fights of the French; this has not become true with the end of the colonial wars. The long search for an equilibrium in the constitutional powers still goes on, as lively as ever, in a rejuvenated country. The players are somewhat different—though one great personality dominates the scene, individuals have ceased to play as prominent a part as they did in the past; groups and forces now have the major role in a country which is reexperiencing pluralism after a century and a half in which it was proscribed, legally or in fact. The growth and tactics of these groups are fascinating to study; they are also more relevant to a modern society than the personal battles conducted in the "House without windows" of the old Parliament. The moves made by the associations—as well as those of the administrative or semi-administrative bodies—are perhaps somewhat more difficult to perceive than those of deputies, but they have more impact on the whole community. Neither in the Fifth Republic nor in the Fourth or Third has France been able to create a political model, easy to export, or ready for imitation; but parts of the inside machinery are brilliantly put together and should, after a closer look, be followed and used elsewhere. The main trouble with the French political system does not lie in a lack of responsiveness, or in an inability to forecast and meet new problems; it lies in the undue emphasis placed on unreal and unimportant elements of the political system at the expense of very lively and relevant structures which, often without being noticed, are slowly being created.

The French Constitution[*]

PREAMBLE

The French people hereby solemnly proclaims its attachment to the Rights of Man and the principles of national sovereignty as defined by the Declaration of 1789, reaffirmed and complemented by the Preamble of the Constitution of 1946.

By virtue of these principles and that of the free determination of peoples, the Republic hereby offers to the Overseas Territories that express the desire to adhere to them, new institutions based on the common ideal of liberty, equality and fraternity and conceived with a view to their democratic evolution.

Article 1

The Republic and the peoples of the Overseas Territories who, by an act of free determination, adopt the present Constitution thereby institute a Community.

The Community shall be based on the equality and the solidarity of the peoples composing it.

TITLE I: ON SOVEREIGNTY

Article 2

France is a Republic, indivisible, secular, democratic and social. It shall ensure the equality of all citizens before the law, without distinction of origin, race or religion. It shall respect all beliefs.

The national emblem is the tricolor flag, blue, white and red.

The national anthem is the "Marseillaise."

The motto of the Republic is "Liberty, Equality, Fraternity."

Its principle is government of the people, by the people and for the people.

Article 3

National sovereignty belongs to the people, which shall exercise this sovereignty through its representatives and by means of referendums.

No section of the people, nor any individual, may attribute to themselves or himself the exercise thereof.

Suffrage may be direct or indirect under the conditions stipulated by the Constitution. It shall always be universal, equal and secret.

[*] Adopted by referendum on September 28, 1958, promulgated on October 4, 1958, and amended in 1960, 1962, and 1963.

194

All French citizens of both sexes who have reached their majority and who enjoy civil and political rights may vote under the conditions to be determined by law.

Article 4

Political parties and groups shall be instrumental in the expression of the suffrage. They shall be formed freely and shall carry on their activities freely. They must respect the principles of national sovereignty and democracy.

TITLE II: THE PRESIDENT OF THE REPUBLIC

Article 5

The President of the Republic shall see that the Constitution is respected. He shall ensure, by his arbitration, the regular functioning of the governmental authorities, as well as the continuance of the State.

He shall be the guarantor of national independence, of the integrity of the territory, and of respect for Community agreements and treaties.

Article 6

The President of the Republic shall be elected for seven years by universal direct suffrage.

The modalities of implementation of the present Article shall be determined by an organic law.[1]

[1] New text adopted by referendum of October 28, 1962. The old Article 6 read as follows:

The President of the Republic shall be elected for seven years by an electoral college comprising the members of Parliament, of the General Councils and of the Assemblies of the Overseas Territories, as well as the elected representatives of the municipal councils.

These representatives shall be:

—the mayor for communes of fewer than 1,000 inhabitants;

—the mayor and the first deputy mayor for communes of from 1,000 to 2,000 inhabitants;

—the mayor, first deputy mayor and a municipal councillor chosen according to the order in which he appears on the council list for communes of from 2,001 to 2,500 inhabitants;

—the mayor and the first two deputy mayors for communes of from 2,501 to 3,000 inhabitants;

—the mayor, the first two deputy mayors and three municipal councillors chosen according to the order in which they appear on the council list for communes of from 3,001 to 6,000 inhabitants:

Article 7

The President of the Republic shall be elected by an absolute majority of the votes cast. If no such majority obtains at the first ballot, a second ballot shall take place on the second Sunday following the first ballot. May only stand at the second ballot the two candidates who received the greatest number of votes at the first ballot, if necessary after taking into account better placed candidates having withdrawn.

The Government shall be responsible for organizing the election.

The election of the new President of the Republic shall take place twenty days at the least and thirty-five days at the most before the end of the mandate of the current President.

In the case of vacancy of the office for any cause whatsoever or if the President is duly declared impeded from exercising his functions by the Constitutional Council, the matter being referred to the latter by the Government and the decision being taken by an absolute majority of the members of the Council, the functions of the President, except for those listed under Articles 11 and 12, shall be provisionally exercised by the President of the Senate, or, if the latter is in turn impeded, by the Government.

In case of vacancy or if the Constitutional Council declares the President permanently impeded from exercising his functions, the ballot for the election of the new President shall take place, except in case of *force majeure* officially noted by the Constitutional Council, twenty days at the least and thirty-five days at the most after the beginning of the vacancy or the declaration of the permanent character of the impediment.

In case of vacancy of the Presidency of the Republic or during

---

—the mayor, the first two deputy mayors and six municipal councillors chosen according to the order in which they appear on the council list for communes of from 6,001 to 9,000 inhabitants;

—all the municipal councillors for communes of more than 9,000 inhabitants;

—in addition, for communes of more than 30,000 inhabitants, delegates appointed by the municipal council in the ratio of one delegate for every 1,000 inhabitants above 30,000.

In the Overseas Territories of the Republic, the elected representatives of the councils of the administrative units shall also form part of the electoral college under the conditions to be determined by an organic law.

The participation of member States of the Community in the electoral college for the President of the Republic shall be determined by agreement between the Republic and the member States of the Community.

The procedures implementing the present article shall be determined by an organic law.

the period between the declaration of the impediment of the President of the Republic and the election of his successor, the procedures of Articles 49, 50, and 89 may not be invoked.[2]

Article 8

The President of the Republic shall appoint the Premier. He shall terminate the functions of the Premier when the latter presents the resignation of the Government.

On the proposal of the Premier, he shall appoint the other members of the Government and shall terminate their functions.

Article 9

The President of the Republic shall preside over the Council of Ministers.

Article 10

The President of the Republic shall promulgate the laws within fifteen days following the transmission to the Government of the finally adopted law.

He may, before the expiration of this time limit, ask Parliament for a reconsideration of the law or of certain of its articles. This reconsideration may not be refused.

Article 11

The President of the Republic, on the proposal of the Government during [Parliamentary] sessions, or on joint motion of the two assem-

[2] New text adopted by referendum of October 28, 1962. The old Article 7 read as follows:

The President of the Republic shall be elected by an absolute majority on the first ballot. If this is not obtained, the President of the Republic shall be elected on a second ballot by a relative majority.

The voting shall begin at the summons of the Government.

The election of the new President shall take place twenty days at the least and fifty days at the most before the expiration of the powers of the President in office.

In the event that the Presidency of the Republic has been vacated, for any cause whatsoever, or impeded in its functioning as officially noted by the Constitutional Council, to which the matter has been referred by the Government, and which shall rule by an absolute majority of its members, the functions of the President of the Republic, with the exception of those provided for by Articles 11 and 12 below, shall be temporarily exercised by the President of the Senate. In the case of a vacancy, or when the impediment is declared definitive by the Constitutional Council, the voting for the election of a new President shall take place, except in case of *force majeure* officially noted by the Constitutional Council, twenty days at the least and fifty days at the most after the beginning of the vacancy or the declaration of the definitive character of the impediment.

blies, published in the *Journal Officiel*, may submit to a referendum any bill dealing with the organization of the governmental authorities, entailing approval of a Community agreement, or providing for authorization to ratify a treaty that, without being contrary to the Constitution, might affect the functioning of [existing] institutions.

When the referendum decides in favor of the bill, the President of the Republic shall promulgate it within the time limit stipulated in the preceding article.

Article 12

The President of the Republic may, after consultation with the Premier and the Presidents of the assemblies, declare the dissolution of the National Assembly.

General elections shall take place twenty days at the least and forty days at the most after the dissolution.

The National Assembly shall convene by right on the second Thursday following its election. If this meeting takes place between the periods provided for ordinary sessions, a session shall, by right, be held for a fifteen-day period.

There may be no further dissolution within a year following these elections.

Article 13

The President of the Republic shall sign the ordinances and decrees decided upon in the Council of Ministers.

He shall make appointments to the civil and military posts of the State.

Councillors of State, the Grand Chancellor of the Legion of Honor, Ambassadors and envoys extraordinary, Master Councillors of the Court of Accounts, prefects, representatives of the Government in the Overseas Territories, general officers, rectors of academies [regional divisions of the public educational system] and directors of central administrations shall be appointed in meetings of the Council of Ministers.

An organic law shall determine the other posts to be filled in meetings of the Council of Ministers, as well as the conditions under which the power of the President of the Republic to make appointments to office may be delegated by him and exercised in his name.

Article 14

The President of the Republic shall accredit Ambassadors and envoys extraordinary to foreign powers; foreign Ambassadors and envoys extraordinary shall be accredited to him.

Article 15

The President of the Republic shall be commander of the armed forces. He shall preside over the higher councils and committees of national defense.

Article 16

When the institutions of the Republic, the independence of the nation, the integrity of its territory or the fulfillment of its international commitments are threatened in a grave and immediate manner and when the regular functioning of the constitutional governmental authorities is interrupted, the President of the Republic shall take the measures commanded by these circumstances, after official consultation with the Premier, the Presidents of the assemblies and the Constitutional Council.

He shall inform the nation of these measures in a message.

These measures must be prompted by the desire to ensure to the constitutional governmental authorities, in the shortest possible time, the means of fulfilling their assigned functions. The Constitutional Council shall be consulted with regard to such measures.

Parliament shall meet by right.

The National Assembly may not be dissolved during the exercise of emergency powers [by the President].

Article 17

The President of the Republic shall have the right of pardon.

Article 18

The President of the Republic shall communicate with the two assemblies of Parliament by means of messages, which he shall cause to be read, and which shall not be followed by any debate.

Between sessions, Parliament shall be convened especially for this purpose.

Article 19

The acts of the President of the Republic, other than those provided for under Articles 8 (first paragraph), 11, 12, 16, 18, 54, 56 and 61, shall be countersigned by the Premier and, should circumstances so require, by the appropriate ministers.

H

TITLE III: THE GOVERNMENT
Article 20

The Government shall determine and direct the policy of the nation.

It shall have at its disposal the administration and the armed forces.

It shall be responsible to Parliament under the conditions and according to the procedures stipulated in Articles 49 and 50.

Article 21

The Premier shall direct the operation of the Government. He shall be responsible for national defense. He shall ensure the execution of the laws. Subject to the provisions of Article 13, he shall have regulatory powers and shall make appointments to civil and military posts.

He may delegate certain of his powers to the ministers.

He shall replace, should the occasion arise, the President of the Republic as chairman of the councils and committees provided for under Article 15.

He may, in exceptional instances, replace him as chairman of a meeting of the Council of Ministers by virtue of an explicit delegation and for a specific agenda.

Article 22

The acts of the Premier shall be countersigned, when circumstances so require, by the ministers responsible for their execution.

Article 23

The office of member of the Government shall be incompatible with the exercise of any Parliamentary mandate, with the holding of any office at the national level in business, professional or labor organizations, and with any public employment or professional activity.

An organic law shall determine the conditions under which the holders of such mandates, functions or employments shall be replaced.

The replacement of members of Parliament shall take place in accordance with the provisions of Article 25.

TITLE IV: THE PARLIAMENT
Article 24

The Parliament shall comprise the National Assembly and the Senate.

The deputies to the National Assembly shall be elected by direct suffrage.

The Senate shall be elected by indirect suffrage. It shall ensure the representation of the territorial units of the Republic. Frenchmen living outside France shall be represented in the Senate.

Article 25

An organic law shall determine the term for which each assembly is elected, the number of its members, their emoluments, the conditions of eligibility and ineligibility and the offices incompatible with membership in the assembles.

It shall likewise determine the conditions under which, in the case of a vacancy in either assembly, persons shall be elected to replace the deputy or senator whose seat has been vacated until the holding of new complete or partial elections to the assembly concerned.

Article 26

No member of Parliament may be prosecuted, sought, arrested, detained or tried as a result of the opinions or votes expressed by him in the exercise of his functions.

No member of Parliament may, during Parliamentary sessions, be prosecuted or arrested for criminal or minor offenses without the authorization of the assembly of which he is a member except in the case of *flagrante delicto*.

When Parliament is not in session, no member of Parliament may be arrested without the authorization of the Secretariat of the assembly of which he is a member, except in the case of *flagrante delicto*, of authorized prosecution or of final conviction.

The detention or prosecution of a member of Parliament shall be suspended if the assembly of which he is a member so demands.

Article 27

All binding instructions [upon members of Parliament] shall be null and void.

The right to vote of the members of Parliament shall be personal.

An organic law may, under exceptional circumstances, authorize the delegation of a vote. In this case, no member may be delegated more than one vote.

Article 28

Parliament shall convene by right in two ordinary sessions a year. The first session shall begin on October 2nd and last eighty days.

The second session shall begin on April 2nd and may not last longer than ninety days.

If October 2nd or April 2nd is a public holiday, the opening of the session shall take place on the first weekday following.[3]

Article 29

Parliament shall convene in extraordinary session at the request of the Premier, or of the majority of the members comprising the National Assembly, to consider a specific agenda.

When an extraordinary session is held at the request of the members of the National Assembly, the closure decree shall take effect as soon as the Parliament has exhausted the agenda for which it was called, and at the latest twelve days from the date of its meeting.

Only the Premier may ask for a new session before the end of the month following the closure decree.

Article 30

Apart from cases in which Parliament meets by right, extraordinary sessions shall be opened and closed by decree of the President of the Republic.

Article 31

The members of the Government shall have access to the two assemblies. They shall be heard when they so request.

They may call for the assistance of commissioners of the government.

Article 32

The President of the National Assembly shall be elected for the duration of the legislature. The President of the Senate shall be elected after each partial re-election [of the Senate].

Article 33

The meetings of the two assemblies shall be public. An *in extenso* report of the debates shall be published in the *Journal Officiel.*

Each assembly may sit in secret committee at the request of the Premier or of one tenth of its members.

---

[3] As adopted by parliamentary amendment in 1963. The old Article 28 read as follows:

Parliament shall convene, by right, in two ordinary sessions a year.

The first session shall begin on the first Tuesday of October and shall end on the third Friday of December.

The second session shall open on the last Tuesday of April; it may not last longer than three months.

TITLE V: ON RELATIONS BETWEEN PARLIAMENT AND THE GOVERNMENT

Article 34

All laws shall be passed by Parliament.

Laws shall establish the rules concerning:

—civil rights and the fundamental guarantees granted to the citizens for the exercise of their public liberties; the obligations imposed by the national defense upon the persons and property of citizens;

—nationality, status and legal capacity of persons, marriage contracts, inheritance and gifts;

—determination of crimes and misdemeanors as well as the penalties imposed therefore; criminal procedure; amnesty; the creation of new juridical systems and the status of magistrates;

—the basis, the rate and the methods of collecting taxes of all types; the issuance of currency.

Laws shall likewise determine the rules concerning:

—the electoral system of the Parliamentary assemblies and the local assemblies;

—the establishment of categories of public institutions;

—the fundamental guarantees granted to civil and military personnel employed by the State;

—the nationalization of enterprises and the transfer of the property of enterprises from the public to the private sector.

Law shall determine the fundamental principles of:

—the general organization of national defense;

—the free administration of local communities, the extent of their jurisdiction and their resources;

—education;

—property rights, civil and commercial obligations;

—legislation pertaining to employment, unions and social security.

The financial laws shall determine the financial resources and obligations of the State under the conditions and with the reservations to be provided for by an organic law.

—Laws pertaining to national planning shall determine the objectives of the economic and social action of the State.

The provisions of the present article may be developed in detail and amplified by an organic law.

Article 35

Parliament shall authorize the declaration of war.

Article 36

Martial law shall be decreed in a meeting of the Council of Ministers.
Its prorogation beyond twelve days may be authorized only by Parliament.

Article 37

Matters other than those that fall within the domain of law shall be of a regulatory character.

Legislative texts concerning these matters may be modified by decrees issued after consultation with the Council of State. Those legislative texts which may be passed after the present Constitution has become operative shall be modified by decree, only if the Constitutional Council has stated that they have a regulatory character as defined in the preceding paragraph.

Article 38

The Government may, in order to carry out its program, ask Parliament to authorize it, for a limited period, to take through ordinances measures that are normally within the domain of law.

The ordinances shall be enacted in meetings of the Council of Ministers after consultation with the Council of State. They shall come into force upon their publication, but shall become null and void if the bill for their ratification is not submitted to Parliament before the date set by the enabling act.

At the expiration of the time limit referred to in the first paragraph of the present article, the ordinances may be modified only by law in those matters which are within the legislative domain.

Article 39

The Premier and the members of Parliament alike shall have the right to initiate legislation.

Government bills shall be discussed in the Council of Ministers after consultation with the Council of State and shall be filed with the Secretariat of one of the two assemblies. Finance bills shall be submitted first to the National Assembly.

Article 40

Bills and amendments introduced by members of Parliament shall not be considered when their adoption would have as a consequence either a diminution of public financial resources, or the creation or increase of public expenditures.

Article 41

If it appears in the course of the legislative procedure that a Private Member bill or an amendment is not within the domain of law or is contrary to a delegation [of authority] granted by virtue of Article 38, the Government may declare its inadmissibility.

In case of disagreement between the Government and the President of the assembly concerned, the Constitutional Council, upon the request of either party, shall rule within a time limit of eight days.

Article 42

The discussion of Government bills shall pertain, in the first assembly to which they have been referred, to the text presented by the Government.

An assembly, given a text passed by the other assembly, shall deliberate on the text that is transmitted to it.

Article 43

Government and Private Members bills shall, at the request of the Government or of the assembly concerned, be sent for study to committees especially designated for this purpose.

Government and Private Members bills for which such a request has not been made shall be sent to one of the permanent committees, the number of which shall be limited to six in each assembly.

Article 44

Members of Parliament and of the Government shall have the right of amendment.

After the opening of the debate, the Government may oppose the examination of any amendment which has not previously been submitted to committee.

If the Government so requests, the assembly concerned shall decide, by a single vote, on all or part of the text under discussion, retaining only the amendments proposed or accepted by the Government.

Article 45

Every Government or Private Members bill shall be examined successively in the two assemblies of Parliament with a view to the adoption of an identical text.

When, as a result of disagreement between the two assemblies, it has become impossible to adopt a Government or Private Members bill after two readings by each assembly, or, if the Government has declared the matter urgent, after a single reading by each of them, the Premier shall have the right to have a joint committee meet, composed of an equal number from both assemblies and instructed to offer for consideration a text on the matters still under discussion.

The text prepared by the joint committee may be submitted by the Government for approval of the two assemblies. No amendment shall be admissible except by agreement with the Government.

If the joint committee fails to approve a common text, or if this text is not adopted under the conditions set forth in the preceding paragraph, the Government may, after a new reading by the National Assembly and by the Senate, ask the National Assembly to rule definitively. In this case, the National Assembly may reconsider either the text prepared by the joint committee or the last text adopted [by the National Assembly], modified, when circumstances so require, by one or several of the amendments adopted by the Senate.

Article 46

The laws that the Constitution characterizes as organic shall be passed and amended under the following conditions:

A Government or Private Members bill shall be submitted to the deliberation and to the vote of the first assembly to which it is submitted only at the expiration of a period of fifteen days following its introduction.

The procedure of Article 45 shall be applicable. Nevertheless, lacking an agreement between the two assemblies, the text may be adopted by the National Assembly on final reading only by an absolute majority of its members.

The organic laws relative to the Senate must be passed in the same manner by the two assemblies.

Organic laws may be promulgated only after a declaration by the Constitutional Council on their constitutionality.

Article 47

Parliament shall pass finance bills under the conditions to be stipulated by an organic law.

Should the National Assembly fail to reach a decision on first reading within a time limit of forty days after a bill has been filed, the Government shall refer it to the Senate, which must rule within a time limit of fifteen days. The procedure set forth in Article 45 shall then be followed.

Should Parliament fail to reach a decision within a time limit of seventy days, the provisions of the bill may be enforced by ordinance.

Should the finance bill establishing the resources and expenditures of a fiscal year not be filed in time for it to be promulgated before the beginning of that fiscal year, the Government shall immediately request Parliament for the authorization to collect the taxes and shall make available by decree the funds needed to meet the Government commitments already voted.

The time limits stipulated in the present article shall be suspended when Parliament is not in session.

The Court of Accounts shall assist Parliament and the Government in supervising the implementation of the finance laws.

Article 48

The discussion of the bills filed or agreed upon by the Government shall have priority on the agenda of the assemblies in the order set by the Government.

One meeting a week shall be reserved, by priority, for questions asked by members of Parliament and for answers by the Government.

Article 49

The Premier, after deliberation by the Council of Ministers, may pledge the responsibility of the Government to the National Assembly with regard to the program of the Government, or with regard to a declaration of general policy, as the case may be.

The National Assembly may question the responsibility of the Government by the vote of a motion of censure. Such a motion shall be admissible only if it is signed by at least one tenth of the members of the National Assembly. The vote may only take place forty-eight hours after the motion has been filed; the only votes counted shall be those favorable to the motion of censure, which may be adopted only by a majority of the members comprising the Assembly. Should the motion of censure be rejected, its signatories may not introduce another motion in the course of the same session, except in the case provided for in the paragraph below.

The Premier may, after deliberation by the Council of Ministers, pledge the Government's responsibility to the National Assembly on the vote of a text. In this case, the text shall be considered as adopted, unless a motion of censure, filed in the succeeding twenty-four hours, is voted under the conditions laid down in the previous paragraph.

The Premier shall be entitled to ask the Senate for approval of a general policy declaration.

Article 50

When the National Assembly adopts a motion of censure, or when it disapproves the program or a declaration of general policy of the Government, the Premier must submit the resignation of the Government to the President of the Republic.

Article 51

The closure of ordinary or extraordinary sessions shall by right be delayed, should the occasion rise, in order to permit the application of the provisions of Article 49.

TITLE VI: ON TREATIES AND INTERNATIONAL AGREEMENTS

Article 52

The President of the Republic shall negotiate and ratify treaties.

. He shall be informed of all negotiations leading to the conclusion of an international agreement not subject to ratification.

Article 53

Peace treaties, commercial treaties, treaties or agreements relative to international organizations, those that imply a commitment for the finances of the State, those that modify provisions of a legislative nature, those relative to the status of persons, those that call for the cession, exchange or addition of territory may be ratified or approved only by a law.

They shall go into effect only after having been ratified or approved.

No cession, no exchange, no addition of territory shall be valid without the consent of the populations concerned.

Article 54

If the Constitutional Council, the matter having been referred to it by the President of the Republic, by the Premier, or by the President of one or the other assembly, shall declare that an international commitment contains a clause contrary to the Constitution, the authorization to ratify or approve this commitment may be given only after amendment of the Constitution.

Article 55

Treaties or agreements duly ratified or approved shall, upon their publication, have an authority superior to that of laws, subject, for each agreement or treaty, to its application by the other party.

TITLE VII: THE CONSTITUTIONAL COUNCIL

Article 56

The Constitutional Council shall consist of nine members, whose term of office shall last nine years and shall not be renewable. One third of the membership of the Constitutional Council shall be renewed every three years. Three of its members shall be appointed by the President of the Republic, three by the President of the National Assembly, three by the President of the Senate.

In addition to the nine members provided for above, former Presidents of the Republic shall be members ex officio for life of the Constitutional Council.

The President shall be appointed by the President of the Republic. He shall have the casting vote in case of a tie.

Article 57

The office of member of the Constitutional Council shall be incompatible with that of minister or member of Parliament. Other incompatibilities shall be determined by an organic law.

Article 58

The Constitutional Council shall ensure the regularity of the election of the President of the Republic.

It shall examine complaints and shall announce the results of the vote.

Article 59

The Constitutional Council shall rule, in the case of disagreement, on the regularity of the elections of deputies and senators.

Article 60

The Constitutional Council shall ensure the regularity of referendum procedures and shall announce the results thereof.

Article 61

Organic laws, before their promulgation, and standing orders of the Parliamentary assemblies, before they come into application, must be submitted to the Constitutional Council, which shall rule on their constitutionality.

To the same end, laws may be submitted to the Constitutional Council, before their promulgation, by the President of the Republic, the Premier or the President of one or the other assembly.

In the cases provided for by the two preceding paragraphs, the Constitutional Council must make its ruling within a time limit of one month. Nevertheless, at the request of the Government, in case of emergency, this period shall be reduced to eight days.

In these same cases, referral to the Constitutional Council shall suspend the time limit for promulgation.

Article 62

A provision declared unconstitutional may not be promulgated or implemented.

The decisions of the Constitutional Council may not be appealed to any jurisdiction whatsoever. They must be recognized by the governmental authorities and by all administrative and judicial authorities.

Article 63

An organic law shall determine the rules of organization and functioning of the Constitutional Council, the procedure to be followed before it, and in particular the periods of time allowed for having disputes before it.

TITLE VIII: ON JUDICIAL AUTHORITY

Article 64

The President of the Republic shall be the guarantor of the independence of the judicial authority.

He shall be assisted by the High Council of the Judiciary.

An organic law shall determine the status of magistrates.

Magistrates may not be removed from office.

Article 65

The High Council of the Judiciary shall be presided over by the President of the Republic. The Minister of Justice shall be its Vice President ex officio. He may preside in place of the President of the Republic.

The High Council shall, in addition, include nine members appointed by the President of the Republic in conformity with the conditions to be determined by an organic law.

The High Council of the Judiciary shall present nominations for judges of the Court of Cassation and for First Presidents of Courts of

Appeal. It shall give its opinion, under the conditions to be determined by an organic law, on proposals of the Minister of Justice relative to the nomination of the other judges. It shall be consulted on questions of pardon under conditions to be determined by an organic law.

The High Council of the Judiciary shall act as a disciplinary council for judges. In such cases, it shall be presided over by the First President of the Court of Cassation.

Article 66

No one may be arbitrarily detained.

The judicial authority, guardian of individual liberty, shall ensure respect for this principle under the conditions stipulated by law.

TITLE IX: THE HIGH COURT OF JUSTICE

Article 67

A High Court of Justice shall be instituted.

It shall be composed of members [of Parliament] elected, in equal number, by the National Assembly and the Senate after each general or partial election to these assemblies. It shall elect its President from among its members.

An organic law shall determine the composition of the High Court, its rules, and also the procedure to be followed before it.

Article 68

The President of the Republic shall not be held accountable for actions performed in the exercise of his office except in the case of high treason. He may be indicted only by the two assemblies ruling by identical vote in open balloting and by an absolute majority of the members of said assemblies. He shall be tried by the High Court of Justice.

The members of the Government shall be criminally liable for actions performed in the exercise of their office and deemed to be crimes or misdemeanors at the time they were committed. The procedure defined above shall be applied to them, as well as to their accomplices, in case of a conspiracy against the security of the State. In the cases provided for by the present paragraph, the High Court shall be bound by the definition of crimes and misdemeanors, as well as by the determination of penalties, as they are established by the criminal laws in force when the acts are committed.

TITLE X: THE ECONOMIC AND SOCIAL COUNCIL

Article 69

The Economic and Social Council, whenever the Government calls upon it, shall give its opinion on the Government bills, ordinances and decrees, as well as on the Private Members bills submitted to it.

A member of the Economic and Social Council may be designated by the latter to present, before the Parliamentary assemblies, the opinion of the Council on the Government or Private Members bills that have been submitted to it.

Article 70

The Economic and Social Council may likewise be consulted by the Government on any problem of an economic or social character of interest to the Republic or to the Community. Any plan or any bill dealing with a plan of an economic or social character shall be submitted to it for its advice.

Article 71

The composition of the Economic and Social Council and its rules of procedure shall be determined by an organic law.

TITLE XI: ON TERRITORIAL UNITS

Article 72

The territorial units of the Republic are the communes, the departments, the Overseas Territories. Other territorial units may be created by law.

These units shall be free to govern themselves through elected councils and under the conditions stipulated by law.

In the departments and the territories, the Delegate of the Government shall be responsible for the national interests, for administrative supervision, and for seeing that the laws are respected.

Article 73

Measures of adjustment required by the particular situation of the Overseas Departments may be taken with regard to their legislative system and administrative organization.

Article 74

The Overseas Territories of the Republic shall have a special organization, which takes into account their own interests within the general interests of the Republic. This organization shall be defined and modified by law after consultation with the Territorial Assembly concerned.

Article 75

Citizens of the Republic who do not have ordinary civil status, the only status referred to in Article 34, may keep their personal status as long as they have not renounced it.

Article 76

The Overseas Territories may retain their status within the Republic.

If they express the desire to do so by a decision of their Territorial Assemblies taken within the time limit set in the first paragraph of Article 91, they shall become Overseas Departments of the Republic or member States of the Community, either in groups or as single units.

TITLE XII: ON THE COMMUNITY

Article 77

In the Community instituted by the present Constitution, the States shall enjoy autonomy; they shall administer themselves and manage their own affairs democratically and freely.

There shall be only one citizenship in the Community.

All citizens shall be equal before the law, whatever their origin, their race and their religion. They shall have the same duties.

Article 78

The Community's jurisdiction shall extend over foreign policy, defense, currency, common economic and financial policy, as well as over policy on strategic raw materials.

It shall include, in addition, except in the case of specific agreements, the supervision of the tribunals, higher education, the general organization of external transportation and transportation within the Community, as well as of telecommunications.

Special agreements may create other common jurisdictions or regulate any transfer of jurisdiction from the Community to one of its members.

Article 79

The member States shall benefit from the provisons of Article 77 as soon as they have exercised the choice provided for in Article 76.

Until the measures required for implementation of the present title go into force, matters within the common jurisdiction shall be regulated by the Republic.

Article 80

The President of the Republic shall preside over and represent the Community.

The institutional organs of the Community shall be an Executive Council, a Senate and a Court of Arbitration.

Article 81

The member States of the Community shall participate in the election of the President according to the conditions stipulated in Article 6.

The President of the Republic, in his capacity as President of the Community, shall be represented in each State of the Community.

Article 82

The Executive Council of the Community shall be presided over by the President of the Community. It shall consist of the Premier of the Republic, the heads of Government of each of the member States of the Community, and the ministers responsible for the common affairs of the Community.

The Executive Council shall organize the cooperation of members of the Community at Government and administrative levels.

The organization and procedure of the Executive Council shall be determined by an organic law.

Article 83

The Senate of the Community shall be composed of delegates whom the Parliament of the Republic and the legislative assemblies of the other members of the Community shall choose from among their own membership. The number of delegates of each State shall be determined according to its population and the responsibilities it assumes in the Community.

The Senate of the Community shall hold two sessions a year, which shall be opened and closed by the President of the Community and may not last longer than one month each.

The Senate of the Community, when called upon by the President of the Community, shall deliberate on the common economic and financial policy before laws on these matters are voted upon by the Parliament of the Republic and, should circumstances so require, by the legislative assemblies of the other members of the Community.

The Senate of the Community shall examine the acts and treaties or international agreements, which are specified in Articles 35 and 53, and which commit the Community.

The Senate of the Community shall take executive decisions in the domains in which it has received delegation of power from the legislative assemblies of the members of the Community. These decisions shall be promulgated in the same form as the law in the territory of each of the States concerned.

An organic law shall determine the composition of the Senate and its rules of procedure.

Article 84

A Court of Arbitration of the Community shall rule on litigations occurring among members of the Community.

Its composition and its jurisdiction shall be predetermined by an organic law.

Article 85

By derogation from the procedure provided for in Article 89, the provisions of the present title that concern the functioning of the common institutions shall be amendable by identical laws passed by the Parliament of the Republic and by the Senate of the Community.

The provisions of the present title may also be amended by agreements concluded between all the States of the Community; the new provisions shall be put into force under the conditions required by the Constitution of each State.[4]

Article 86

A change of status of a member State of the Community may be requested, either by the Republic, or by a resolution of the legislative assembly of the State concerned confirmed by a local referendum, the organization and supervision of which shall be ensured by the institutions of the Community. The procedures governing this change shall be determined by an agreement approved by the Parliament of the Republic and the legislative assembly concerned.

Under the same conditions, a member State of the Community may become independent. It shall thereby cease to belong to the Community.

A member State of the Community may also, by means of agreements, become independent without thereby ceasing to belong to the Community.

[4] Added by parliamentary amendment of May 18, 1960.

An independent State not a member of the Community may, by means of agreements, join the Community without ceasing to be independent.

The position of these States within the Community shall be determined by agreements concluded to this end, in particular the agreements mentioned in the preceding paragraphs as well as, should the occasion arise, the agreements provided for in the second paragraph of Article 85.[5]

Article 87

The special agreements made for the implementation of the present title shall be approved by the Parliament of the Republic and the legislative assembly concerned.

TITLE XIII: ON AGREEMENTS OF ASSOCIATION

Article 88

The Republic or the Community may make agreements with States that wish to associate themselves with the Community in order to develop their own civilizations.

TITLE XIV: ON AMENDMENT

Article 89

The initiative for amending the Constitution shall belong both to the President of the Republic on the proposal of the Premier and to the members of Parliament.

The Government or Private Members bill for amendment must be passed by the two assemblies in identical terms. The amendment shall become definitive after approval by a referendum.

However, the proposed amendment shall not be submitted to a referendum when the President of the Republic decides to submit it to Parliament convened in Congress; in this case, the proposed amendment shall be deemed to be approved only if it is accepted by a three-fifths majority of the votes cast. The Secretariat of the Congress shall be that of the National Assembly.

No amendment procedure may be undertaken or followed when the integrity of the territory is in jeopardy.

The republican form of government shall not be subject to amendment.

[5] Added by parliamentary amendment of May 18, 1960.

Suggestions for Further Reading

There are now a number of texts dealing with the institutions and life of the Fifth Republic, but no "classic" has as yet been written, either in French or English, which compares with J. E. Bodley's *France*, 2 vols., London, 1898, which analyzes the first part of the Third Republic, and with P. M. Williams's *Crisis and Compromise*, London, 1964, which covers in great detail the political life of the Fourth. As we saw that changes which occurred during the present regime often originated from problems which arose under the previous system, P. M. Williams's text should be consulted and indeed studied by all those who want to acquire a better understanding of French political life. Among the shorter works devoted to the Fifth Republic, the most valuable are perhaps *De Gaulle's Republic*, by P. M. Williams and M. Harrison, London, 1960, which discusses the origins and the early period of the regime; *The De Gaulle Republic*, by R. C. Macridis and B. E. Brown, Homewood, Ill., 1960; and the *Fifth French Republic*, by D. Pickles, London, 1960. E. S. Furniss's *France, Troubled Ally, De Gaulle's Heritage and Prospects*, New York, 1960, is primarily concerned with foreign affairs, but deals also in detail with the institutions of the new regime. Readers should also consult some of the French texts on the subject, the most important being perhaps *La Cinquième République*, by M. Duverger, Paris, 1960; *La nouvelle constitution et le régime politique de la France*, by J. Chatelet, Paris, 1959; and the three-volume study of the *Institutions politiques de la France* published by *La Documentation Française*, Paris, 1959.

Many studies provide readers with background information on French political and social life: some of these are more specifically devoted to the French intellectual tradition, while others look at the problem of the slow decadence and rapid rejuvenation France experienced in the course of the twentieth century. The most authoritative English historical study of the Third Republic is that of D. W. Brogan, *The Development of Modern France*, London, 1940; the period of Vichy is analyzed in Robert Aron's *Histoire de Vichy*, Paris, 1954; and the Fourth Republic's life is described in J. Fauvet's *La Quatrième République*, Paris, 1959. The most brilliant study of French political traditions and ideologies is probably that of D. Thompson, *Democracy in France*, London, 1958. Of considerable interest are also the collections of short pieces contained in *Modern France*, edited by E. M. Earle, Princeton, 1951, and P. E. Charvet's *France*, New York, 1953. Traditional attitudes and modern recovery are examined perceptively in *France Against Herself*, by H. Lüthy, New York, 1955, and in *The New France*, by E. R. Tannenbaum, Chicago, 1961. Finally, it is hardly necessary to observe that a reading of De Gaulle's *Memoirs* is essential to an understanding of what remains after all his Republic, while one of the best accounts of the life and actions of the great French leader can be found in A. Werth, *De Gaulle*, London, 1965.

One can mention only a few of the numerous works on elections and parties, a general account of which can also be found in most of the texts listed earlier and, in particular, P. M. Williams's *Crisis and Compromise*. The best and most comprehensive account of electoral systems is to be found in P. W. Campbell's *French Electoral Systems and Elections Since 1789*, London, 1958. Studies of voting patterns started very early in France, mostly on a geographical basis, the classic in the field being A. Siegfried's *Tableau politique de la France de l'Ouest*, Paris, 1913: this has been followed by many detailed monographs of elections in the Provinces. Since 1956, the *Fondation nationale des sciences politiques* has published a study of each national election and referendum, that of 1962 being by far the most comprehensive and the most ambitious (F. Goguel *et al.*, *Le referendum d'octobre et les élections de novembre 1962*, Paris, 1965). Electoral behavior was first examined on the basis of surveys in *Partis politiques et classes sociales en France*, edited by M. Duverger, Paris, 1955, and, more recently and most perceptively, by P. Fougeyrollas in *La conscience politique dans la France contemporaine*, Paris, 1963.

The best account of the life of parties in general can be found in F. Goguel, *La politique des partis sous la Troisième République*, Paris, 1946, and in F. Goguel and A. Grosser, *La vie politique en France*, Paris, 1964. There are individual party studies, among which should be mentioned that of the Communist Party by J. Fauvet, *Histoire du parti communiste français*, 2 vols., Paris, 1965; of the Socialist Party by D. Ligou, *Histoire du socialisme en France*, Paris, 1962; of the Radical Party by F. De Tarr, *The French Radical Party from Herriot to Mendès-France*, London, 1961; and of the UNR by J. Charlot, *L'UNR*, Paris, 1967. The behavior of deputies and of French politicians in general is analyzed, in a critical and acid fashion, by N. Leites in *On the Game of Politics in France*, Stanford, 1959, and more dispassionately in a number of essays covering the Third and Fourth Republics, the most recent being R. Priouret's *La République des députés*, Paris, 1959.

A general study of French administration can be found in F. Ridley and J. Blondel, *Public Administration in France*, London,

1964. There are also many monographs of a more detailed character on various aspects of administration, such as R. Grégoire's *French Civil Service*, Brussels, 1964; B. Chapman's *Introduction to French Local Government*, London, 1953, and P. Bauchet's *Economic Planning: The French Experience*, London, 1963. Groups and their relationship with the Government have been analyzed by J. Meynaud in *Les groupes de pression en France*, Paris, 1958; the particular position of business is brilliantly studied by H. Ehrmann in *Organized Business in France*, Princeton, 1957.

Governmental policy before and since 1958 is naturally the subject of countless articles and books as are the trends and possible evolution of the new regime. The best short account can perhaps be found in the section the *Revue Française de science politique* devotes to the analysis of current political events in each of its issues. Special mention should be made of the following, however, as they either describe a problem or take a stand on a question of crucial contemporary relevance: A. Grosser's *Politique extérieure de la Quatrième République*, Paris, 1961, has now been followed by the *Politique extérieure de la Cinquième République*, Paris, 1965; the new "face" of the social groups is vividly described by M. Gervais *et al.* in *Une France sans paysans*, Paris, 1965, and in P. Naville, *La nouvelle classe ouvrière*, Paris, 1964; and the objections to the current system of planification are summarized in J. Ensemble's *Le contre-plan*, Paris, 1964. In their different ways, these books give an account of the changing character of French society and of the curious way in which the politics of tomorrow are slowly emerging from the complex mixture of old and new that still typifies the politics of today.

INDEX

Abbas, Ferhat, 171
Accords Matignon, 145
Adenauer, Konrad, 183, 189
administration:
  centralization of, 23–26, 31, 116–118, 129, 137–138
  communication between community and, 121–122
  dedication of personnel of, 118
  "detached" personnel of, 120
  of Fifth Republic, 117–118
  of First Empire, 116–117
  grand corps of, 119–121, 127
  policy initiation by, 31–32, 122
  territorial units of, 116
  of Third Republic, 117
  training of personnel of, 118–120
administrative courts (*see also* Council of State; judiciary)
  advisory function of, 127, 128
  appeal court of, 127
  and civil rights, 129–130
  evolution of, 116, 119, 127
  and executive decisions, 129
  jurisdiction of, 127
  Ombudsman characteristics of, 128
  procedural character of, 128–129
  separation of functions of, 128
Africa:
  and assimilation, 162
  colonization of, 161–162
  and Community, 165–169
  and competing colonial powers, 160
  and Constitutional reform, 167–168
  and 1956 French Union reform, 165
  and struggles of confederation, 169

agriculture (*see also* peasantry), 149–151
Algeria:
  Assembly of, 170
  and assimilation, 162, 170
  Charter of, 170–171
  colonization of, 162, 170
  and De Gaulle's return, 161
  and Evian settlement, 172–173
  French population of, 170
  granted independence, 39, 172
  Moslem population of, 170
  and 1945 rebellion, 171
  and 1946 constitution, 171
  and Liberation Front, 171
Algerian War, 160–161, 171–172
Alsace Lorraine, 162
amendment:
  Constitution on, 216
  as instrument of Gaullists, 29
  1962, for presidential election, 28, 45, 47
  overall constitutional change preferred to, 29
  use of referendum for, 36, 44–45
ancien régime, 3, 5, 7, 8
  and administrative centralization, 24, 31, 116, 137
  influence of, on sectionalism, 15
  and judiciary, 123
anti-Americanism, 138, 186
anti-authoritarianism, 13–14, 19, 21–26
anticlericalism, 21–23, 107
antirepublicanism, 2, 3, 8, 21–23, 57
anti-Semitism, 8, 21–22
apparentements, 61
aristocratic classes, 3, 12
arrêtés, 64–65
arrondissement, 116, 131
Atomic Energy Community, 182